NEW YORK

THE UNKNOWN CITY

NEW YORK

THE UNKNOWN CITY

Brad Dunn
and
Daniel Hood

ARSENAL PULP PRESS

VANCOUVER

NEW YORK: THE UNKNOWN CITY
Copyright © 2004 by Brad Dunn & Daniel Hood

ARSENAL PULP PRESS
103 - 1014 Homer Street
Vancouver, B.C.
Canada V6B 2W9
arsenalpulp.com

The publisher gratefully acknowledges the support of the Government of Canada through the
Book Publishing Industry Development Program for its publishing activities.

Design by Electra Design Group
Production assistance by Judy Yeung
Cover photography by Mike Waring

Printed and bound in Canada

Library and Archives Canada
Cataloguing in Publication

Dunn, Brad, 1973-
        New York : the unknown city / Brad Dunn and Daniel Hood.

Includes index.
ISBN 1-55152-161-X

        1. New York (N.Y.)—Guidebooks. I. Hood, Daniel II. Title.

F128.18.D85 2004   917.47'10444   C2004-902944-4

c o n t e n t s

acknowledgments

This book is dedicated to Brad's wife, Amy, and his daughter, Anna, and to Dan's nephews and nieces – Oliver, Nicholas, Gabriela, and Madeleine.

Thanks to:
Matt Berlin, Susan Brennan, Julia Carcich, Dr. Robert Della Rocca, Ranger Doug, Alex Dunn, Chris Dunn, Seth Fineberg, Neill Furio, Sharon Goldfarb, Alex Hood the Elder, Alex Hood the Younger, Kate Hood, Martha Hood, Ted Hood, Chuck Hunt of the New York State Restaurant Association, John P.L. Kelly, Melissa Klein, Pete Libasci, Jennifer Maguire, Noreen Mallory, Tracey Miller-Segarra, Brian Moss, Roger Russell, Detective Brian Sessa, Dan Skelton, Sarah Townley, Shari Turitz, Rob Whitaker, Mike Vukobratovich, and all the people at the Dive Bar, the unofficial headquarters of *New York: The Unknown City*.

Special thanks to:
Sarah Hood, for her sage advice, and for getting us into this in the first place; and the good folks at Arsenal Pulp Press, for crossing the border.

We claim all errors and mistakes, even if they're not our fault. As this city is a fickle, changeable place, some of the places we've mentioned may disappear in the interval between writing and printing; if you should discover one of these – or better yet, if you've found a New York secret you think we ought to know about – please let us know by e-mailing danhood@earthlink.net.

i n t r o d u c t i o n

"There is no question there is an unseen world; the question is, how far is it from midtown, and how late is it open." — Woody Allen

New York's pre-eminent nebbishy filmmaker asked the question, and we set out to find the answer. In fact, no one-liner could have provided a better premise for this book: search out the deepest, darkest secrets of the greatest city on the planet, root out its ghosts, scandals, and forgotten treasures, and shine a light on its myriad unknown worlds.

During our search, we discovered sealed-off stairways and secret underground passages. We learned where you can go to sign up for an orgy with strangers, and why a young Marlon Brando was an unruly roommate. We found out the best time of year to look for dead bodies floating in the East River, and why Rudy Giuliani wasn't the first cross-dressing politician the city has seen.

We found out about a 36-foot-tall, 60-ton concrete Picasso statue that no one ever notices, and where you can buy a full-sized stuffed zebra. We learned that it is still illegal to shoot at a rabbit from a moving trolley, and that both Leon Trotsky and Fidel Castro ate breakfast at the same café while plotting the overthrow of their governments. We discovered that if you throw a penny off the Empire State Building it will never hit the ground, and that the best Elvis sandwich (peanut butter, banana, honey, and bacon) is served in the Village. We found out where you can see Charlton Heston's chariot from *Ben-Hur*, and where you can be served dinner by a dominatrix who will chain you up and whip you if the tip is right.

Though we focused, perhaps inevitably, on Manhattan, the book contains the most fascinating stories and unusual facts of all five boroughs — tales that few New Yorkers know about, let alone visitors. If you don't believe us, test your knowledge of the unknown city: What famous author spent a winter homeless in City Hall Park? Why are acorns a recurring motif throughout Grand Central? Where was FDR's secret underground tunnel? What famous designer created the Yankees logo? What four street names appear in all five boroughs?

If you don't know the answers, read on. These pages are full of secret passageways, forgotten disasters, unknown artwork, and mysterious murders. A city of 8 million people tends to produce an awful lot of bizarre stories and unusual incidents over the centuries. Here's a look at some of the ones that have slipped between the cracks and fallen off into the unknown.

And, not to let Woody Allen down, in most cases we provide cross-streets and phone numbers, so you can call and find out how late these unseen worlds are open.

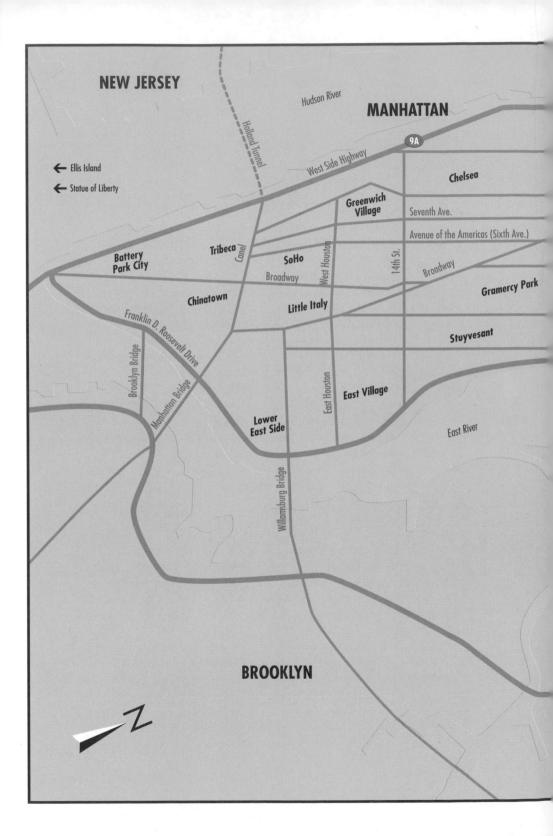

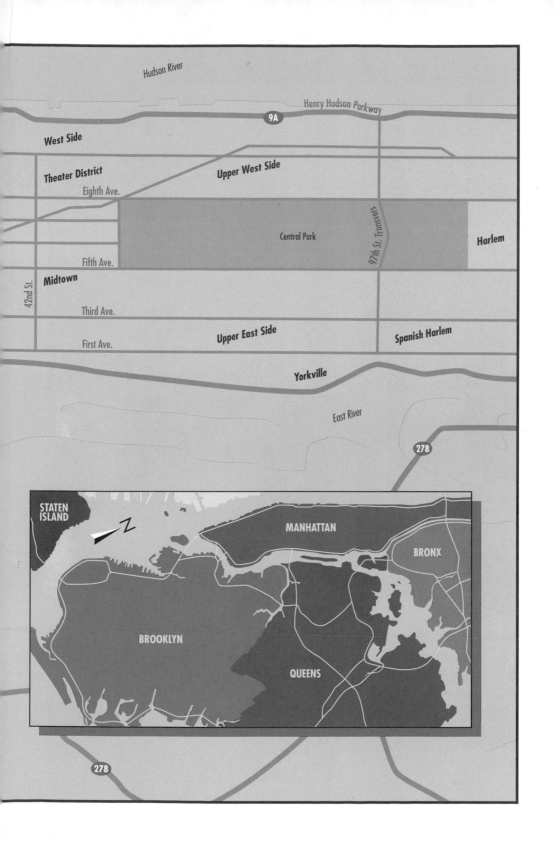

ONE WAY

Landmarks? We got your landmarks right here. Since 1965, New York's Landmarks Preservation Commission has named over 22,000 of them, which amounts to around 1.5 *every day*. And they're still going — landmarked properties amount to only 2 percent of the city's area, leaving lots of potential landmarks unprotected.

The U.N. – a.k.a. Blood Alley

Ironic that the headquarters of world democracy stands atop the most blood-drenched soil in New York City. Though critics of the **United Nations** have made much of the fact that it was built on the site of the city's oldest and largest slaughterhouse, few know of the incredible real estate deal that enabled the transformation of an 18-acre killing field into a nerve center of global diplomacy.

When the United Nations was created in 1944, several American cities vied to be the organization's host city: New York, Philadelphia, and San Francisco, to name a few. Many politicians, including the first U.N. Secretary-General, Trygve Lie, favored Manhattan, but no land could be found for development. By late 1946, the fledgling diplomatic body could wait no longer: it announced that the city had five days to find a site, or it would set up shop in Philadelphia.

The city scrambled, but the only suitable land that could be found was an area on the East Side, long known as "Blood Alley" for its cattle pens and slaughterhouses dating back to 1795. The land was owned by William Zeckendorf, a developer who had dreamed of turning the killing grounds into an ultra-modern housing complex called "X-City," but lacked the capital.

With just 12 hours until the deadline, Nelson Rockefeller stepped in. He ordered one of his aides to track down Zeckendorf and offer him $8.5 million if he signed over the land on the spot. The aide found the developer slightly drunk at his anniversary party. Zeckendorf happily accepted the deal, and signed all the necessary papers hours before the U.N. would have packed up for Philadelphia.

In hindsight, Rockefeller's $8.5 million was about as cheap as the fabled $24 that Peter Minuit paid the Native Americans for Manhattan. The United Nations brings millions of dollars to New York City, and adds "Diplomatic" to the city's title of Fashion, Media, Business, and Culture Capital of the World.

Photo: Daniel Hood

A quick glance at the Manhattan skyline shows a cluster of skyscrapers downtown at the foot of the island, and another in midtown, starting in the low 30s and reaching up into 60s, with a low stretch in between. The reason for the gap? Skyscrapers need to be rooted in the bedrock that underlies all of New York at varying depths; in midtown that's often just a few feet below the surface, and downtown it can be as little as 30 feet down, while in skyscraper-free places like the Lower East Side, the Village, Gramercy Park and Chelsea, it's often hundreds of feet below.

MISSION TO AMERICA

New York is the only American city that can boast an American Embassy — the United States Mission — located across the street from the United Nations.

Photo: Daniel Hood

Photo: Daniel Hood

Like its inhabitants, Manhattan has been getting fatter all along: since the first Dutch settlers, the island has grown by at least 10 percent on a steady diet of garbage, construction debris, and landfill.

Downtown, Pearl and Water Streets used to mark the eastern shoreline, while Greenwich Street touched the Hudson; all are now at least a block or more from water. Battery Park City stands on about a million cubic yards of landfill from the excavation of the tub that used to hold the World Trade Center. At one time you could see the Hudson from Hudson Street, while the East River Drive (to give the FDR Drive its original name) was built on landfill and piers that effectively block access to the river for much of the length of Manhattan.

Not all of this spread is local – East River Park, at East 12th Street and the river, is built on special "imported" landfill. Ships carrying Marshall Plan aid to the Old World after World War II often used dirt for ballast on the return trip (since Europe had nothing else worth taking away at the time), and when they reached New York, they simply dumped it here.

Manhattan isn't the only New York island to put on a few acres. Ellis Island was three smaller islets that were glued together with landfill, and Randall's and Ward's Island used to be separate until Robert Moses fused them together in the 1930s.

MANHATTAN-IN-THE-BRONX

Our favorite example of expansion has to be **Marble Hill**, the little slice of Manhattan that got away. Once a neighborhood at the far northern end of Manhattan, it was separated from the island in 1895, when the Army Corps of Engineers blasted the Harlem River Ship Canal to its south to accommodate the city's growing shipping business, making Marble Hill an island with only a shallow creek between it and the Bronx. Twenty years later, engineers filled in the creek, and Marble Hill became the only section of Manhattan on the mainland.

Where New York Gets Trashed

For more than 5,000 years, the Great Wall of China has stood as the largest man-made object on the planet. But in 1991, the title was stolen by New York City, when its **Fresh Kills Landfill** – the 3,000-acre pile of garbage on Staten Island – swelled to unprecedented dimensions.

In fact, both heavyweights on either sides of the globe are rumored to be the only man-made structures that can be seen from space with the naked eye. But where China took more than two centuries to set the record, New York, where everything is faster, took only 43 years to break it.

"Kil" is an old Dutch word for waterway, and Fresh Kills was named for its beautiful, open marshlands. Beautiful until 1948, that is. That's when city planner Robert Moses designated the area a dump so that he could build the Verrazano-Narrows Bridge, connecting Staten Island to Brooklyn. Soon the landfill was receiving up to 29,000 tons of solid waste a day, and eventually stood 500 feet tall, making it the highest point of land of the East Coast.

By the mid-1960s, New Yorkers were already concerned about the swelling behemoth in their backyard. Running for mayor in 1965, William F. Buckley proposed closing the dump, spraying it with man-made snow, and opening a ski area. Legends abound over what's buried there: many believe the body of Jimmy Hoffa, which was never found, lies in the refuse. One confirmed corpse, however, was that of a deceased elephant.

In 1995, the Environmental Protection Agency estimated that Fresh Kills was generating almost 2 percent of the world's methane – a major greenhouse gas. Today that gas is being extracted, bottled, and sold for heating fuel. Regardless, the EPA ordered the dump closed; it received its last load of trash in March 2001.

The final chapter in the unusual history of humanity's largest structure came when it was used to sort through the 1.25 million tons of wreckage from the World Trade Center.

Photo: Daniel Hood

THE SPHERE THAT PERSEVERED

Mayor Michael Bloomberg described it best when he said, "The **Sphere** in many ways symbolizes New York. It stood in the World Trade Center as a symbol for peace. On September 11, it was damaged, not destroyed."

He was speaking at the rededication ceremony of the 45,000-pound, steel-and-bronze sculpture that once stood as the centerpiece of a colossal fountain in the plaza between the Twin Towers. Designed by Fritz Koenig of Germany and dedicated in 1971 as a monument to world peace, the great globe was ripped open and partially crushed by falling debris during the 9/11 terrorist attacks.

Recovery workers discovered the Sphere largely intact, and reassembled it at nearby Battery Park. Today it stands there as a temporary memorial, until a permanent monument is constructed.

Photo: Judy Yeung

RAT DECO

Rats embody many of the qualities New Yorkers pride themselves on, like toughness, resilience, and the ability to survive in tight spaces. If they weren't filthy, pestilential little beasts, we'd probably celebrate them — but in 1927, at least one architect managed to do just that, incorporating rats into the design of the **Graybar Building**, at 420 Lexington, next to Grand Central. You can see the Art Deco rats on the struts that hold up the canopy over the Graybar entrance to the terminal — it looks like they're trying to climb a hawser into a ship — while the medallions over the entrance a little to the north (now an Equinox gym), where the struts used to reach the side of the building, are composed of a circle of rats' heads.

Photo: Brad Dunn

She may be one of New York's most recognizable landmarks, but if sculptor Frederic-Auguste Bartholdi had had his way, the **Statue of Liberty** wouldn't be here at all.

Though the idea for the statue was first broached at a dinner party in France in 1865, the fundraising campaign to build it took some years to get off the ground. In the meantime, Bartholdi, who had been at the historic dinner, traveled to Egypt, where he was so impressed by the monumental plans for the Suez Canal that he worked up a proposal for an equally monumental statue to stand at the canal's head. It would be a woman bearing a light and a resemblance to an Egyptian peasant, with broken chains in hand and the title, "Egypt Bringing Light to Asia." The young sculptor presented his grandiose plan to Egypt's government, but they weren't interested (though in 1871 they would commission *Aida* for the canal's opening).

Stuck with the plans, Bartholdi returned to France, and later hooked up with the committee responsible for designing the statue. Though he went to his grave denying any connection, there's no doubt he dusted off his Egyptian plans when it came time to design Lady Liberty in the 1870s — the resemblance between "Egypt Bringing Light to Asia" and "Liberty Enlightening the World" (as the Statue is properly known) is too pronounced to deny.

It may be a confused version of the statue's Egyptian backstory that has led to an Internet-borne conspiracy theory that holds that Lady Liberty was supposed to be a black woman holding broken chains (to represent the end of slavery during the Civil War), but a cabal of racist whites nixed the idea, forcing Bartholdi to use a white woman as a model and drop the chains (almost literally — in the final product, the chains are at her feet, in a spot that's hard to see given the height of the pedestal).

Now, we wouldn't put anything past the racist whites of the 1870s and 1880s, but though the driving force behind the gift, French scholar and historian Edouard de Laboulaye, was a staunch abolitionist, there's no evidence he ever intended the statue to be anything but a memorial to American democracy. And there's no evidence that Bartholdi ever intended the American Liberty to be black – though his Suez proposal had "African" features, none of his earliest models for the American version did. (Some of those models are at the **Museum of the City of New York**, *1225 Fifth Ave., at 103rd St., 212-534-1672, mcny.org*)

Besides, as any schoolkid knows, he used his mother as a model for the statue's face. What they don't tell schoolkids, though, is that Mom got tired sitting, and Bartholdi's mistress (and later wife) modeled for the statue's chest and arms.

Millions of immigrants, and not a few tourists, have glimpsed the great, green Lady of Liberty on their first approach of New York. But the famous statue also has inspired two not-so-famous knockoffs that hold up their torches of freedom atop lesser pedestals in Manhattan.

The first, and larger, replica stands on top of the building at 43 West 64th Street on the Upper West Side. Since this area is full of restaurants and movie theaters, check it out next time you catch a show. The best view is from the steps leading up to Lincoln Center Plaza at Columbus and 63rd Street. Go up the steps and look northeast toward 64th Street. This Lady Liberty is atop the same building that houses O'Neal's restaurant.

Another knockoff stands downtown at 219 West Broadway. Instead of copper, she's made of iron, so her familiar green patina owes its hue to paint, not weathering. She weighs almost exactly one ton – instead of thousands – but she's got all the detail where it counts: the crown, the tablet, the broken shackles at her feet. Of course, instead of holding up a beacon for liberty, this statue used to light the entrance to El Teddy's, a Mexican restaurant that closed down in 2003.

Photo: Daniel Hood

DÉJÀ VIEW

So, you're wandering through the heart of midtown, and you catch a glimpse of a unique curved skyscraper, and you think, "Hey, didn't I just see that building?"

You're not wrong – you've probably just seen the "glass ski slope" of the **Solow Building** *(9 W. 57th St., bet. Fifth and Sixth Aves.)* and its twin, the **W.R. Grace Building** *(41 W. 42nd St., at Sixth Ave.).* Groundbreaking architect Gordon Bunshaft, of Lever House fame, originally designed what would become the Grace Building for notoriously difficult developer Sheldon Solow. Solow hated it, and demanded revisions; Bunshaft complied, with 9 West 57th the result, but he sold the original plans to the developers of the Grace Building. Both buildings were completed in 1974 – and both immediately became objects of widespread loathing in the architectural community.

Faulted Ceiling

No doubt **Grand Central Terminal** is one of the most breathtaking – and most traversed – structures in Manhattan. But this Beaux Arts beauty has one big blemish that few know about: the magnificent ceiling mural in the Main Concourse, which depicts the night sky using 2,500 light bulbs, has all the constellations backwards.

The mirror-image mistake occurred in 1913, just before Grand Central had its grand opening after a decade of construction. French portrait artist Paul Helleu designed the mural, but artisan Charles Basssing actually installed it. When it was noted that Orion and his celestial comrades were pointing the wrong way, Helleu claimed it was done deliberately to provide a "God's-eye-view" of the six winter and spring constellations. He pointed out that medieval manuscripts often mapped the constellations in reverse as well, as if God were looking at Earth through them. Still, many at the time thought he was simply covering up the blunder.

Though some say Helleu deliberately designed it backwards and others that Basssing accidentally reversed the plans, few who stop today to admire the stunning mural realize they're gazing up at a not-so-parallel universe.

There's a lot more to Grand Central than meets the eye. A sampling:

• All those monumental blocks of stone that wall the main concourse? They're not blocks at all – they're thin layers of what's called "cast stone," a highly refined cement that's plastered on to make it look like cut stone. All the load-bearing is done by steel infrastructure beneath the plaster.

• You've probably heard of the Whispering Gallery – the large arched space outside of the Oyster Bar where, if you face one corner and whisper, a person facing the opposite corner can hear you perfectly clearly. The best part, though, is that it's unintentional, a fluke of physics that the architects didn't plan.

TRUMPED

A similar story of architectural recycling is told about Donald Trump – except this time, the disgruntled architect placed the twin right across the street. Take a look at the **Trump Plaza** on the west side of Third Avenue between 61st and 62nd Streets. Then look at the **Savoy**, on the east side of the avenue between 61st and 60th Streets. Different finishing touches, yes – but the underlying design is exactly the same.

• Pay attention to the decorative details, particularly in the windows, above the platform entrances on the lower level, and in the chandeliers. Everywhere you look, you'll spot a recurring theme of oaks, oak leaves, and acorns. It's a reference to "Great oaks from little acorns grow," the motto of the Vanderbilts, who built Grand Central. The motto was chosen for them by a hired consultant.

• In the northwest corner of the main concourse ceiling, notice the small pitch-black rectangle standing out against the beautifully restored green of the star chart. It's not a shadow, nor a PA speaker – it's a small patch they didn't restore, so that people could tell how bad the ceiling had gotten.

"Tombtastic!"

Photo: Brad Dunn

It's no secret who's buried in **Grant's Tomb** – though some are surprised to find that his wife Julia is in there with him – the real secret is the place itself, which is thoroughly undervisited.

War is (All) Over

If you really want to do Memorial Day right, New York offers more monuments and memorials to the defenders of democracy than anywhere else. No major conflict, foreign or domestic, is without a tribute in this town. In one day, if you have the stamina, you can visit shrines for everything from the Revolutionary War to the Vietnam War, with something for Gulf War I and probably II in the works. Here's one possible course:

Revolutionary War:
Independence Flagstaff
(*Union Square*)

War of 1812:
Grave of Capt. James Lawrence, Trinity Church (*Broadway and Wall St.*)

That may be because the Tomb was, until the mid-1990s, a graffiti-spattered eyesore and a favorite squat of the local homeless, with dime bags littering the plaza and the beaks blown off the ornamental eagles. In 1991, a Columbia student named Frank Scaturro started volunteering at the site and, appalled by the neglect, began a campaign to have the mausoleum restored. Pressure from Scaturro, various New York congressmen, *The New York Times*, and Illinois (which promised to take care of native son Grant if his adopted resting place wouldn't) led the National Park Service to take steps to protect the place, and the feds to approve a $1.8 million facelift and cleaning, which was completed in time for the Tomb's centennial in 1997.

Nowadays, it's clean, safe, nicely maintained, in a gorgeous spot on Riverside Drive at West 122nd Street – and still undervisited. That's too bad, because those who do find the place and the man himself deeply affecting, if the guestbook is anything to go by; it contains some of the most glowing reviews we've ever seen, including the title above and lots of inscriptions along the lines of, "I (HEART) USG!" and "U.S. Grant Is Sexy!"

As far as we know, tombophile Scaturro hasn't complained about the last review, but he did object to the "lascivious choreography" and scantily-clad backup singers at hip-hop sex kitten Beyonce Knowles' July 4th performance at the monument in 2003. Hey – that's just Beyonce being Beyonce. What Scaturro should concentrate on is removing the mosaic benches that ring the monument. This "art intervention," added by Chilean artist Pedro Silva and the Cityarts Workshop in 1973, might look funky in another location, but surrounding the neoclassical Tomb it just looks bizarre. (Plus, as benches they're remarkably uncomfortable.)

Mexican War:
Gen. William Jenkins Worth Monument *(Broadway and Fifth Ave.)*

U.S. Civil War:
Adm. David Farragut Monument *(Madison Square Park)*

Spanish-American War:
Maine Memorial *(Central Park at Columbus Circle)*

World War I:
Seventh Regiment Memorial *(Fifth Ave. at 68th St.)*

World War II:
East Coast Memorial *(Battery Park)*

Korean War:
Korean War Memorial *(Battery Park)*

Vietnam War:
Vietnam Veterans Memorial *(55 Water St.)*

Photo: Daniel Hood

The inscription to a stunning monument in front of a State Supreme Courthouse in Midtown reads, "Indifference to Injustice Is the Gate of Hell." Giant flames carved in marble rise up and arch directly toward the courthouse, threatening to devour the institution if they were real.

Few people notice the cautionary column at the **State Appellate Division Courthouse** at Madison Avenue and 25th Street, and fewer still take in its meaning. But right at eye level of the sculpture by artist Harriet Feigenbaum is a relief map of the death camp at Auschwitz, complete with the actual locations of the Torture Chamber, Execution Wall, Gas Chamber and Crematorium 1, and the Commandant's House.

The work is significant not only for its solemn reminder of the horrible cruelties the Axis powers inflicted on millions of people during World War II, but also for the indirect message it sends to the Allies. The map etched in the six-sided column is based on a photograph taken by an Allied bomber on August 25, 1944. Many art critics have speculated that by choosing this image, Feigenbaum is suggesting that the Allies must have known about the death camp long before admitting to it, and took no action.

Monuments You Might Have Missed

General Daniel Butterfield
Butterfield wrote (adapted, really) the classic bugle call "Taps" while serving as a general in the New York militia during the Civil War. The statue was commissioned by his widow, who so plagued sculptor John Gutzon Borglum with revisions that he signed the top of Butterfield's stone head, since that was the only part that hadn't been changed. Borglum later went on to bigger things — he carved Mount Rushmore. *Southeast corner, Sakura Park, W. 122nd St. and Claremont Ave.*

Strauss Square and Memorial
Isidor Strauss was a crockery and glassware salesman who made good — so good that he was able to buy Macy's in 1894, and was elected to Congress; his wife Ida was well-known in society and charitable circles. It wasn't for their lives that they got a square with a fountain and a statue, but for their deaths: they were on the *Titanic* in 1912, and when Isidor refused to enter a lifeboat before the women

Photo: Daniel Hood

Here's another one for the list of shamefully neglected and little-known New York landmarks: the **Hall of Fame for Great Americans**. Set high on a hilltop overlooking both the East River and the Palisades, in a colonnade designed by Stanford White, this is the *original* Hall of Fame, the place that created the very idea of Halls of Fame. Don't hold that against it. When New York University president Henry Mitchell MacCracken first envisioned the place in the 1890s as the centerpiece of a plan to create an "uptown" campus in the Bronx, he had no idea how the idea would be cheapened by a horde of imitators. And when it was dedicated in 1901, being a Hall of Famer was as good, if not better, than being a Nobel laureate.

But hard times fell on the place mid-century, and it was neglected until 1973, when NYU retrenched back around Washington Square and ceded the campus to Bronx Community College. Money was found to restore the 98 bronze busts and clean up the worst of the deterioration, but the Hall hasn't made the sort of comeback that, say, Ellis Island has. Part of the problem may be the location – University Avenue and West 181st Street isn't on most itineraries – and part may be the selection of honorees, some of whom aren't as famous as they were back in 1901 (Matthew Fontaine Maury, anyone? William Crawford Gorgas? Charlotte Saunders Cushman?).

Still, the setting is grand, the busts are considered one of the great collections of bronzes in the country, and there are no crowds. *(718-289-5161)*

and children, Ida decided to stay with him, reportedly saying, "Where you go, I go." 40,000 people attended their memorial service, and Macy's employees funded the statue; there's also a plaque in their honor at the 34th Street store. *Strauss Square, Broadway and 106th St.*

Eleanor Roosevelt

A 1996 statue of the New York-born better half of FDR, who, among her more famous endeavors, helped wrest control of the city's Democratic Party from Tammany Hall, and insisted that toilet seats in public housing here have lids. Builders had wanted to omit them to save money, but Eleanor recognized it as an insult to the dignity of the tenants. *Riverside Park, Riverside Drive at W. 73rd St.*

Clean and Sober

Photo: Daniel Hood

With plenty of establishments committed to New York's drinking life, few people know that the city also has a handful of monuments devoted to the teetotaling lifestyle.

Among the most notable is the 120-year-old **James Fountain** on the west side of Union Square between 15th and 16th Streets. Created by Karl Adolph Donndorf in 1881, the fountain stood as a tribute to the temperance movement and was installed to provide New Yorkers with easy access to fresh, clean water – and to keep them from quenching their thirst in the barroom.

Clean water alone was enough to tempt many residents to stop by for a drink. In the 19th century, New York's water system was far less reliable than it is today. Alcohol was often the beverage of choice simply because it contained none of the illness-inducing bacteria that clouded the tap water channeled from upstate.

Promoters of sobriety went great distances to persuade people to put down the bottle. The fountain is at the foot of an elaborate sculpture called Charity. A similar tribute to teetotaling can also be found in Tompkins Square Park.

Henry Hudson

The pedestal came first, in 1909, when the city first planned the Henry Hudson Bridge to connect Manhattan and the Bronx, and thought a statue of the man himself would look nice at the northern terminus. But money and siting problems stalled both bridge and statue, and by the time Mayor LaGuardia got the statue made in 1939, the bridge had moved but the pedestal hadn't, so Henry ended up with a park all to himself, and one of the greatest Hudson River views in the city.
Henry Hudson Memorial Park, Independence Ave. at West 227th St., the Bronx

The Firemen's Memorial

A monument to the city's bravest, erected in 1913 in honor of Deputy Chief Charles Kruger, who, ironically enough, drowned in the basement of a Canal Street building that was on fire.
Riverside Drive and 100th St.

The Irish Hunger Memorial

A little slice of Irish countryside recreated downtown in memory of the victims of the Potato Famine that drove so many immigrants to New York. The abandoned stone cottage dates from 1820.
Vesey St. and North End Ave., Battery Park City

PENNIES FROM HEAVEN

Drop a penny from 1,250 feet up (the height of the **Empire State Building**), and it may well develop enough momentum to crush a car or drive a hole right through a person's head. Drop a penny from the Empire State Building itself, though, and nothing of the kind happens — the shape of the building creates strong wind currents and updrafts that drive dropped coins back against the walls, where they then fall onto the roof of one of the setbacks. Most pennies from the 86th-floor observatory, for instance, end up on an 80th-story setback. The crews who work the building lights collect the loose change.

Photo: Courtesy Empire State Building

Photo: Daniel Hood

In 1929, two buildings were in a race for the title of tallest building in the city — the **Chrysler Building**, at Lexington Avenue and 42nd Street, and the **Bank of Manhattan Trust Building**, at 40 Wall Street. For months, their respective architects (who used to be partners) filed and refiled their plans, adding stories and spires and masts to try to outdo one another, until finally William Van Alen stopped redesigning the Chrysler, and let his downtown rival, H. Craig Severance, top out as the tallest. Secretly, though, Van Alen had built a 185-foot spire inside the top floors of his building, and once 40 Wall was complete, he hoisted it out and took the title.

It turned out to be a race for second place, as the Empire State Building would beat them both in less than a year. Worse was in store for 40 Wall, though: while the Chrysler would go on to be beloved, its downtown rival would be struck by a military plane in 1946, and later, after several bankruptcies, it ended up being sold to Donald Trump.

Prison Window

Photo: Brad Dunn

One of the small ironies of American history goes unnoticed by thousands of pedestrians every day in lower Manhattan. In almost the exact same spot where American patriots were imprisoned by the British during the Revolutionary War, today stands the headquarters of the largest American police force.

The **Sugar House Prison Window** lies about 100 yards from One Police Plaza, the heart of the New York City Police Department. Yet few people notice the 1763 artifact because it's practically camouflaged: the rusty, barred window is embedded in an unlikely brick wall behind the Municipal Building on Centre Street. If you take the subway to the Brooklyn Bridge Station, however, it's worth a quick detour to see this unusual, unknown, and mildly controversial relic.

The monument's bronze plaque says the window originally was part of a five-story sugar house – one of those impressive 18th-century structures where sugar was refined for everything from molasses to rum. During the Revolutionary War, the plaque contends, the house was converted into a prison by the British. But Victor Lederer, a New York City historian, disagrees.

Though a few sugar houses in lower Manhattan were known to have been used as prisons, he says that the window on display does not belong to one of them. Instead, during a swell of patriotism that followed the Civil War, journalists and politicians confused the old sugar house for a one-time jail and heralded it as a symbol of democracy's triumph. Lederer claims this emotional, inaccurate view of history is what saved the barred window from destruction.

Did imprisoned Revolutionary War soldiers peer out of the ancient window that now stands near NYPD headquarters? Take a look for yourself. Either way, you won't see too many more 240-year-old windows – even in New York.

Light It Up

Since the blimp mooring station at the top never worked out, the Empire State Building has served two useful purposes: as a broadcasting tower, and as a colorful, if sometimes cryptic, reminder of what day it is. The lighting scheme of the building's top is often straightforward – red, white, and blue for national holidays; red and green for the Christmas season; green for St. Patrick's Day – but since management accepts requests, some less-than-obvious color combinations have popped up.

Black, green, and gold:
Jamaican Independence

Black, yellow, and red:
German Reunification Day

Blue and red:
Equal Parents Day/Children's Rights

Blue, red, and yellow:
World Cup Archery Championship

Blue and white:
Greek Independence Day;
Colon Cancer Awareness; United Nations Day

Blue, white, and blue:
Israel Independence Day; First Night of Chanukah

Blue, white, and red:
Bastille Day

Blue, yellow, and black:
Bahamian Independence

Green, red, and white:
Wales/St. David's Day

Green and white:
Pakistan Independence Day

Green, white, and orange:
India Independence Day

Green, yellow, and blue:
Brazil Independence

Pink, pink, and white:
Race for the Cure

Pink and white:
Breast Cancer Awareness

Purple, teal, and white:
National Osteoporosis Society

Purple and white:
Alzheimer's Awareness

Red and blue:
Haitian Culture Awareness

Red, blue, and yellow:
Colombia Heritage and Independence

Red, red, and white:
Qatar Independence; Swisspeaks
Festival for Switzerland

Red and white:
Pulaski Day; Red Cross

really "pre-war"

Age has never been accorded any status in New York architecture; for much of its history, the city has torn down old buildings with gleeful abandon. That said, there are a few places where the past shows through.

The Conference House

A 17th-century stone farmhouse that hosted peace negotiations between Ben Franklin, John Adams, and Admiral Lord Howe in 1776; they re-enact the event every year.
7455 Hylan Blvd., Staten Island; 718-984-0415; conferencehouse.org

Dyckman Farmhouse

The oldest surviving Dutch farmhouse in the city, built in 1784.
4881 Broadway, at 204th St.; 212-304-9422

The Morris-Jumel Mansion

Built in 1765, the grand old mansion was once headquarters for George Washington, and is said to be haunted by Eliza Jumel, widow of Aaron Burr.
65 Jumel Terrace, at 160th St.; 212-923-8008

The Hamilton Grange

Photo: Daniel Hood

Built as a summer retreat for Alexander Hamilton and his family in 1802 (Harlem Heights was all countryside then), the Grange has been moved around a couple of times, and now sits near the end of a block of brownstones. To put it in its proper "rural" context, the National Park Service has plans to move it to nearby St. Nicholas Park – but they've had those plans for over 40 years, so don't hold your breath. In the meantime, go and let the inimitable Ranger Doug fill you in on how important Hamilton was to New York and the country.

287 Convent Ave., bet. 141st and 142nd Sts.; 212-283-5154

The Merchant's House Museum

The only completely preserved 19th-century family home in New York – because the spinster who was born there in 1840 never made an improvement through to her death in 1936. (She is said to have been the inspiration for Henry James' *Washington Square.*)
29 E. 4th St., bet. Lafayette St. and Bowery; 212-777-1089

Photo: Daniel Hood

The Mt. Vernon Hotel Museum and Garden

Once owned by John Adam's niece, Abigail Adams Smith, the Hotel was built in 1799 as a stables, and

later became a popular inn for downtowners looking for a day in the country – sort of the Hamptons of its day. *(421 E. 61st St., bet. York and First Aves.; 212-838-6878; mvhm.org)*

Photo: Daniel Hood

Red, white, and red:
Peru Independence; Switzerland admitted to the UN

Red, yellow, and green:
Portuguese Independence

If the top is unlit, it could be in recognition of the Day Without Art/Night Without Lights AIDS Awareness Campaign, or simply because they turn off the lights during the fall and spring peak migration seasons, as they tend to attract confused birds.

If you've got a cause or ethnic group you'd like to see highlighted, call 212-736-3100, or visit the ESB's Web site at *empirestatebuilding.com* for details. They won't do anything for personal events (like birthdays or anniveraries), and they shy away from commercial ones – though Snapple, the "official beverage of New York," managed to get it lit yellow once, and it was supposedly lit blue for the debut of the blue M&M.

The Fight for Height

The received wisdom says the attack of the World Trade Center has put New York out of the tall building business. That seems a little premature; the city has a long history of perpetually outdoing itself in reaching for the skies. A chronicle of the ever-shifting tallest buildings in town:

1664: The first claimant to tallest building – a two-story windmill.

1846: Trinity Church *(280 feet, with spire; 74 Trinity Place)*

Photo: Daniel Hood

1875: Fifth Avenue Presbyterian Church *(286 feet, with spire; Fifth Ave. and 55th St.)*

Crystal Ball of Fire

One of the city's most extraordinary buildings was the **Crystal Palace**, built for the country's first World Fair in 1853. It also served as kindling for one of the city's most spectacular fires five years later.

Based on London's Crystal Palace, the stunning structure erected on what is now Bryant Park in midtown Manhattan was an incredible architectural feat made almost entirely of glass and cast iron – only the floors and doors were made of wood. It housed the Exhibition of the Industry of All Nations, and signaled New York's official entry as one of the great modern cities of the world.

More than one million people visited the magnificent Palace, though its greenhouse tendencies made it a more comfortable venue in winter than summer. Architects had shaped the palace like a Greek cross, and highlighted it with a huge glass dome in the center. They boasted that its elements made it 100-percent fireproof, which was no sooner out of their mouths than it proved a fallacy: glass may not burn, but it melts pretty quickly.

In 1858, a fire broke out in a storage room, and the entire Crystal Palace burned down in less than 15 minutes. The wooden floors fueled the flames long enough to melt the glass and crumble the cast iron supports.

LANDMARKS & DESTINATIONS **29**

Pier Pressure

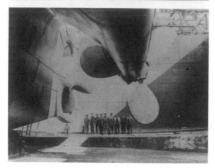

Two of the 20th century's most infamous sunken ships are fatefully linked to the same spot on the west side of Manhattan. Call it coincidence or curse, but both the *Titanic* and the *Lusitania* had a scheduled rendezvous with Pier 54. One of them never made it; the other never returned.

Today, Pier 54 is rusting heap of metal and warped pilings just south of Chelsea Piers, off the West Side Highway below 14th Street. But if you look closely at the ancient arch that used to welcome passengers onto the pier, you'll see the extremely faded words "White Star." The emblem represented White Star Lines, the company that maintained some of the largest, most luxurious ships in the world, one of which was the *Titanic*.

Of course, it's common knowledge that the ship that "only God could sink" sank on April 14, 1912, in the middle of the North Atlantic. But less commonly known is that the then-largest ship in the world was due to reach Pier 54 in New York on April 17. Instead, on April 18, only the 705 survivors made it.

Likewise, the tragic history of the RMS *Lusitania* involves the same piece of real estate. Just three years after the *Titanic* failed to arrive, the *Lusitania* set sail from Pier 54 en route to Liverpool, England. On May 1, 1915, however, a German U-boat torpedoed the passenger ship, causing it to sink in 18 minutes and killing about 1,200 passengers.

1877: Western Union Building *(230 feet; 195 Broadway; replaced by the AT&T Building in 1912)*

1890: World Building *(309 feet; Park Row and Frankfort St.; demolished 1965)*

1894: Manhattan Life Building *(348 feet; 64-68 Broadway; demolished 1930)*

1899: Park Row Building *(391 feet; 15 Park Row)*

1908: Singer Building *(612 feet; 149 Broadway; demolished 1968)*

1909: Metropolitan Life Insurance Tower *(700 feet; 1 Madison Ave.)*

1913: The Woolworth Building *(792 feet; 233 Broadway)*

1930: The Manhattan Company Building *(925 feet; 40 Wall St.)*

1930: The Chrysler Building *(1,030 feet; 405 Lexington Ave.)*

1931: The Empire State Building *(1,250 feet; 350 Fifth Ave.)*

1972: The World Trade Center *(1,362/1,368 feet; bet. Vesey and Liberty Sts.; destroyed 2001)*

2001: The ESB again.

200? (proposed): 1,776-foot-tall "Freedom Tower" *(Ground Zero)*

Some famous spots are still with us – just not in the locations where they first gained fame. Some peripatetic landmarks:

OUGHT TO BE IN PICTURES

Over the centuries, countless buildings in New York have been torn down to give way to newer projects. While some are of the magnitude of the old Penn Station, most are simple row houses, brownstones, and old office buildings. Many of these bygone structures live on only in the memories of those who lived or worked there, without so much as a single photograph to prove they ever existed.

In the 1980s, the City Council decided to change all that. The group passed a bill stating that photographic records must be made of any building in Manhattan slated for demolition. The photos are then stored in the city archives, allowing future generations to see exactly how the city evolved block by block. The bill's sponsor, Councilman Harry Stein, said his only regret was that no one thought of the idea 150 years ago, when the camera was invented.

Photo: Daniel Hood

Madison Square Garden

The most widely traveled building in the world, Madison Square Garden actually started on Madison Square – at 51 Madison Avenue and 26th Street – but it didn't have that name at first; it was P.T. Barnum's Hippodrome, and only became MSG I in 1875, when ownership passed to William Vanderbilt. The much grander MSG II was built on the same site in 1889 by architect Stanford White, who was murdered in the rooftop garden he designed. MSG II came down in 1925, because the New York Life Insurance Co., which owned the underlying land, decided it wanted to use it for its new headquarters (it's still there). MSG III opened less than a year later, on Eighth Avenue between 49th and 50th (now the site of World Wide Plaza). Finally, the destruction of the old Penn Station paved the way for MSG IV to move downtown in 1968 to its final location atop the new Penn Station, on Seventh Avenue between 31st and 33rd Streets.

The Metropolitan Opera House

Photo: Metropolitan Opera

Even the oldest old money was new at some point, and in the 1870s, the newly-minted fortunes of Vanderbilt, Rockefeller, Morgan, and Harriman were too fresh to get them into the old-line establishments, particularly the Academy of Music at 14th Street and Irving Place, where the old money of the time (now long squandered) went to listen to opera. Flush with cash, the nouveau riches decided to build their own opera house, and so the Metropolitan Opera House was born in 1880, in a location way, way uptown – between 39th Street and 40th Street on the west side of Broadway. The first house burnt down in 1892, and was replaced with a baroque splendor fit for rapidly aging money. It was there that the Met made its name, introducing Enrico Caruso to America, inaugurating their famous broadcasts, and generally helping make the parvenus look more respectable.

Despite its beauty, the place did have problems – it lacked backstage space (scenery was stored outside in nearby alleys and lots), and there was no air conditioning, so when Robert Moses bulldozed the

Photo: Metropolitan Opera

Once they were the talk of the town: meeting places and public spaces that shaped the city. But now some of New York's most famous names are only present in history books, period novels, and commemorative plaques.

Federal Hall

It served as City Hall from 1699, was remodelled by Pierre Charles L'Enfant (who was later to design Washington, D.C.) in 1788, and became the seat of government of the new United States in 1789, when George Washington took his first oath of office there. You'd think you would want to keep something like that around – but not New York's unsentimental city fathers. They sold it for a bundle in 1812, to a developer who promptly tore it down. The Federal Hall National Memorial at 26 Wall Street is on

Photo: Daniel Hood

San Juan Hill neighborhood around 66th Street in the 1960s, the Met allowed itself to be lured north to the questionable aesthetics of Lincoln Center, and debuted in its new hall in 1966. The old opera house (or rather, the second old opera house), with its beautifully crafted interior, was demolished in 1967, joining Penn Station on the list of reproaches to New York's architectural conscience.

Waldorf, Meet Astoria

The Waldorf and the Astoria weren't always as close as they are now – they were originally separate hotels, built by different members of the Astor family in 1893 and 1897, respectively. Since they were in the same block, though, common sense and family connections suggested a combination, so a hall was built to link them and a legend of hotel elegance was born. That common block, though, was not the stretch of Park Avenue between 49th and 50th where the current Waldorf-Astoria sits: It was almost 20 blocks south and two blocks west, where the first joint construction thrived until it was torn down in 1929 – to make room for the Empire State Building.

the right site, but the building is a customs house built in 1842 that was later turned into a gold depository for the Treasury.

Ebbets Field

Home of the Brooklyn Dodgers from 1913 until their heartbreaking departure for L.A. in 1957, Ebbets Field replaced slums and a garbage dump in Flatbush, and saw both the first televised baseball game (Dodgers vs. Reds, Aug. 26, 1939), and Jackie Robinson's debut as the first black player in the majors (April 15, 1947). It was torn down in 1960; a collection of high-rises called the Ebbets Field Apartments stands there now. Many in Brooklyn still haven't recovered.

Photo: Daniel Hood

A Multi-Purpose Castle

Photo: Daniel Hood

From its start as an island fortress to its current use as an inland ticket booth, **Castle Clinton** in Battery Park may be the city's most versatile building. Constructed offshore in 1807 to supplement the battery of guns in the nearby park, it was ceded to the city in 1822, renamed Castle Garden, and used as a hall for civic events and meetings. As landfill gradually surrounded it, it became a popular site for dances, banquets, balls, theater, and shows, including P.T. Barnum's wildly hyped introduction of Jenny Lind, "the Swedish Nightingale," to the U.S. in 1850. A few years later, in 1855, the castle was turned into the city's main immigration processing center, processing over 7 million people before Ellis Island opened in 1896. Improbably enough, the castle became the New York Aquarium, which was a favorite of downtown office workers until 1941, when Robert Moses needed space for his Brooklyn-Battery Tunnel. The Aquarium went to Coney Island, and the castle was reduced to a shell of its former self. Named a national monument in 1946, it's now used to sell tickets for trips to Ellis Island and the Statue of Liberty.

The Polo Grounds

The famous site of the "Shot Heard Round the World" in the 1951 pennant race between the New York Giants and the Brooklyn Dodgers was actually the fourth and last Polo Grounds. The first was just north of Central Park from 1883 to 1889, on a spot where the horsey set used to actually play polo. When the city took the land, baseball moved north to two different sites below Coogan's Bluff, between 155th and 159th Streets, and the last Polo Grounds stadium opened in 1911, on 159th between Eighth Avenue and the Harlem River. It hosted both the Yankees and the Giants until the Yankees got a home across the river in 1922; the Giants stayed until 1957, when they left for Frisco; and the infant Mets lived there in 1962 and 1963, while Shea was being built. Empty, it was knocked down in 1964 (by the same wrecking ball that took out Ebbets Field), and the site is now home to the Polo Grounds Towers, a public housing development.

The Croton Distributing Reservoir

Built between 1837 and 1842, this three-story fort of a water tank was the last major link in a huge system that delivered Manhattan's first running water from Westchester County to the north. Popular with fashionable strollers (and those who didn't like cholera from tainted wells), it was torn down in 1911 to make room for the main branch of the New York Public Library at 42nd Street and Fifth Avenue.

The Tombs

Built in 1837 over the filled-in Collect Pond, on the block between Franklin, Centre, Leonard and Lafayette Streets, this was the city's most notorious prison, where countless vicious criminals (and Melville's Bartleby) ended their days. Its nickname came from its design, which was based on an Egyptian mausoleum. It was torn down in 1897 to make way for another prison that inherited the name; the block has since been given over to court, municipal, and private buildings, but the name has been unofficially applied to whatever building serves as Manhattan's main house of detention, currently the Bernard B. Kerik Complex at 125 White Street.

Photo: Daniel Hood

Tammany Hall

The Democratic machine that dominated the city for almost two centuries started as the Tammany Society in 1789, and didn't get a hall until it acquired the back room of a tavern at Nassau and Spruce Streets, in 1798. Soon the

Photo: Daniel Hood

Those who frequently take the FDR Drive along the East River may have noticed the grand, roofless building decaying alone at the foot of Roosevelt Island. It's particularly noticeable at night, when the empty shell is lit up in the creepiest way possible – which is appropriate, given the building's less-than-pleasant past. It was built as a smallpox hospital in 1856, back in the day when Roosevelt Island was called Blackwell's, and the best thing they could think of to do with the contagious was to get them the hell out of the city. Built by prisoners from the Blackwell's Island Penitentiary (which later moved to Riker's Island), the building was used as a quarantine spot until the turn of the century, and then as a nursing school until the 1950s, when it was abandoned. Apart from serving as the site of the climactic battle in the *Spider-Man* flick (and a small cameo in an eminently forgettable Michael J. Fox movie), the building remains unloved and unused to this day, even though it was designed by James Renwick, who is more famous for St. Patrick's Cathedral and Grace Church.

Zipping along the Harlem River Drive or the Major Deegan Expressway, you can spot a tall, Rapunzel-style tower rising above a forested crag towards the northern end of Manhattan. It could be a lighthouse, or a fire-spotting tower, or even a rich man's folly — but it's not. It's the **Highbridge Water Tower** *(W. 173rd Street, in Highbridge Park)*, an old piece of city infrastructure that used to equalize the pressure of the water in the Croton Aqueduct, which ran into Manhattan from the Bronx across the nearby High Bridge (the island's oldest connection to the mainland, built in the 1830s). Once vandalized by arsonists, it's since been restored.

On the western side of Manhattan, our mystery landmark is the set of three connected arches visible from the Henry Hudson Parkway just south of the exit for Fort Tryon Park. They look a little bit like a medieval cloister, but they're not part of the nearby Cloisters — they're actually all that's left of the embankment for the driveway to **Tryon Hall**, the estate of a Chicago capitalist named C.K.G. Billings. In the early 1900s, the palatial estate occupied much of the high ground thereabouts, but Billings moved downtown to Park Avenue and sold the land to the Rockefellers in 1917. The mansion burned down in 1925, and in the 1930s, the Rockefellers donated the land to the city for the park and the museum, which are some of New York's nicer amenities. Just think, though — if the driveway looked that good, how cool must the mansion have been?

organization itself became known as Tammany Hall, and the society called its headquarters the Wigwam. In 1812, they moved a short distance to a $55,000 purpose-built Wigwam at Nassau and Frankfort (a spot now under the Brooklyn Bridge ramp), and in 1867 they took up much grander digs on 14th Street between Third Avenue and Irving Place. That location was torn down in 1929, to make way for the Con Ed building, while the Hall built its final Wigwam for $1 million at the southeast corner of 17th and Park, overlooking Union Square. By then, though, its influence was on the wane, tainted by corruption and scandal, and over the next 20 years Tammany would slowly fade away. The last Wigwam is the only one still standing — it currently houses the New York Film Academy.

The Third Avenue El

With the Second, Sixth, and Ninth Avenue Els already gone, the tearing down of the Third Avenue line in 1955 marked the passing of an era.

Architectural Gems

Lever House

Built in 1952, this is the building that introduced the all-glass skyscraper to the city.
390 Park Ave., bet. 52nd and 53rd Sts.

The Seagram Building

Mies van der Rohe designed this first of the big-glass-box-with-plaza buildings.
375 Park Ave., bet. 52nd and 53rd Sts.

Bayard-Condict Building

The father of the skyscraper, Louis Sullivan, did most of his work in Chicago, but he left one elaborately carved beauty here.
65-69 Bleecker St., at the head of Crosby St.

Photo: Daniel Hood

Photo: Daniel Hood

It's incredible, but true: the only globe larger than the **Unisphere** is the Earth itself.

The 140-foot-tall steel sphere that sits in Flushing Meadows, Queens, is the largest globe ever constructed. Built for the 1964-1965 World's Fair by the U.S. Steel Corporation, the Unisphere has become a symbol of the borough – and the city – as millions of visitors catch a glimpse of it before landing at nearby LaGuardia or driving along any of the major arteries in Queens.

Dedicated to "Peace Through Understanding," the Unisphere weighs about 900,000 pounds, and since the mass of continents is above the equator, the steel plates that represent them make the sphere extremely top heavy – so much so that the engineers had to balance the gargantuan globe down to the inch to ensure it wouldn't tumble.

Celebrated when it was first unveiled, today the Unisphere has become a beloved icon for Queens residents, as well as Mets fans and tennis enthusiasts thanks to the proximity of Arthur Ashe and Shea stadiums.

Few locations on Earth, let alone the United States, can boast as many society-altering inventions as **Westbeth**, the large factory once home to Bell Laboratories. From recorded sound to digital computers, many of the 20th century's greatest advancements in science were made in Chelsea.

Established in 1907, only eight years after Thomas Edison invented the incandescent light, Westbeth attracted the best minds working for the American Telephone & Telegraph Co. and the Western Electric Co. Located at the corner of West Street and Bethune Street (hence the name), the giant, open space housed an enormous range of technical projects and experimentation, which led to an unprecedented synergy between experts who had never before worked together.

Though electricity itself was still new to New York City, tinkerers at Westbeth invented cable switchboards and other critical telephone paraphernalia. In 1912, the high-vacuum tube was given birth here, as well as the amplifier, which allowed phone wires to carry sound across the continent. The condenser microphone was next, which led to the first electronic audio recordings and paved the way for sound in motion pictures. While working on a radio-based altimeter for airplanes in 1919, one scientist discovered and developed radar.

During World War II, Westbeth hosted some of the biggest breakthroughs in atomic research under the Manhattan Project. After the war, the lab's fertility produced everything from phonograph records, hi-fidelity sound, and television (followed years later by color television). Perhaps the most creative invention came in 1937. Mathematician George Stibitz arrived for work at Westbeth carrying an odd homemade device: a breadboard with bulbs, batteries, old tobacco tins, and discarded telephone relays. It was the first successfully operating electrical digital computer using binary number notation.

The heyday of invention at Westbeth ended in the 1960s, when Bell Labs put the factory up for sale. Today, the innovations continue, though in a more poetic sense: the space was turned into a artist's colony. If you want to move in and tap the atmosphere of more than 300 artists, just submit an application proving your artistic vision. Then wait for nine to 10 years for your name to come up on the waiting list.

Woolworth Building lobby
The building's great, but the lobby inspired the name "the Cathedral of Commerce." Look for owner Frank Woolworth in the murals, counting his fives and dimes.
233 Broadway, at Barclay St.

Williamsburgh Savings Bank
Brooklyn's tallest building, and a beaut — its clock was once the largest in the world.
1 Hanson Place, at Flatbush Ave., Brooklyn

Cast Iron Historic District
In the 1850s and 1860s, New Yorker James Bogardus started making cast iron façades that allowed buildings to be taller and have more windows, creating the sort of look familiar from *Ghost* and countless car commercials.
Between Canal and West Houston, and Sixth Ave. and Lafayette St.

Condé Nast Building
This new addition to the Crossroads of the World is the "greenest" building going, setting high standards for eco-friendly design.
4 Times Square, Broadway at 43rd St.

Photo: Brad Dunn

American Radiator Building

This black-and-gold beauty (below) was the first major design of Raymond Hood, who later went on to do the first McGraw-Hill Building and the old Daily News buildings, at opposite ends of 42nd Street, and played a big part in Rockefeller Center. *40 W. 40th St., bet. Fifth and Sixth Aves.*

Photo: Brad Dunn

University Plaza

Not a gem, actually — a surprisingly ugly couple of concrete dormitories, despite the parklike setting and the Picasso sculpture. We'd have thought I.M. Pei could do better. *West Houston St., bet. LaGuardia Place and Mercer St.*

On Nov. 13, 1903, an 83-year-old man named Andrew Haswell Green was shot to death outside his Park Avenue home by a jealous furnace tender, who had mistaken Green for the man who stole his girlfriend. It was probably the first time in his life Green wasn't recognized – but it sure wasn't the last.

In the century since, Green has been largely ignored, but in his lifetime, some argue, he did more for New York than almost any other person in its history. Check out this resumé: while on the Central Park Board of Commissioners, he championed visionary designers Olmsted and Vaux against the meddling of other commissioners, and saw to it that the park as built stayed true to their beautiful design (he also pushed successfully to have the park extended by four full blocks). In the early 1870s, he brought the city back from the brink of financial ruin after the corrupt excesses of the Tweed Ring, even to the point of paying some municipal salaries himself. He was also instrumental in the establishment of Morningside Park, the Metropolitan Museum of Art, the American Museum of Natural History, the Central Park Zoo, and the New York Public Library.

His crowning glory, though, is nothing less than the creation of the city we know today. After arguing for the consolidation of Manhattan, the Bronx, Queens, Brooklyn, and Staten Island since 1868, in 1895 he became president of the committee that drafted the legislation that created this vast metropolis, and earned himself the title of "Father of Greater New York."

The title – and little else. His achievement is memorialized in a sculpture in the Surrogates' Court/Hall of Records *(31 Chambers St., bet. Centre and Elk Sts.)* and the man himself gets a single bench (a bench!) in Central Park *(106th St., near East Drive).*

great buildings that happen to have museums in them

American Museum of Natural History

With the hanging blue whale restored to the Hall of Ocean Life and the Rose Center/Hayden Planetarium fresh from a spectacular revamp, this is still the most fun in the city. Be grateful for the majestic front entrance with its statue of Teddy Roosevelt – the architect originally wanted to place the entrance in a cave in Central Park, with a tunnel under Central Park West.
Central Park West and 79th St.; 212-769-5100

Photo: Daniel Hood

Photo: Daniel Hood

DON'T TREAD ON IT

No matter how small your studio is, it's still not the smallest piece of property in the city – that's probably the tiny mosaic triangle in the sidewalk just outside Village Cigars, at the southwest corner of Seventh Avenue South and Christopher Street, which reads: "Property of the Hess Estate which has never been dedicated for public purposes." Seventh Avenue used to go no further south than 12th Street, blocked by the tangle of Greenwich Village, but in 1914 the city condemned a 100-foot-wide, 10-block-long swathe of buildings to accommodate the extension of the IRT subway. David Hess, who owned one of the condemned buildings, kept hold of his little patch of sidewalk in symbolic protest. It measures less than two feet on all three sides – about 500 square inches.

Audubon Terrace Museum Group

This large complex holds the American Academy and Institute of Arts and Letters, the American Numismatic Society (though it plans to move), and the Hispanic Society (whose collection includes El Greco, Goya, and Velazquez), and once was home to the American Geographical Society and the National Museum of the American Indian. But the real reason to go is the complex itself, an impressive group of Spanish Renaissance buildings around a plaza, built by a philanthropist in the early 20th century on land once owned by John James Audubon.
3745-3755 Broadway, bet. 155th and 156th Sts.; 212-234-3130

Lower East Side Tenement Museum

An original tenement building from the 1863, with apartments restored to represent various eras' immigrant experience. Much cooler than it might sound.
Ticket office: 90 Orchard St., at Broome St.; 212-431-0233

National Museum of the American Indian

An offshoot of the Smithsonian, in the grand old Alexander Hamilton U.S. Customs Building.
One Bowling Green, bet. State and Whitehall Sts.; 212-514-3700

Museum of Jewish Heritage

"A Living Memorial to the Holocaust," this new institution celebrates Jewish life and culture before, during, and after World War II.
36 Battery Place; 646-437-4200

ACTIVITY UNDERFOOT

It's the city's biggest and longest-running construction project ever, and you can't see it, tour it, or buy postcards of it. That's because **Tunnel No. 3** lies somewhere between 400 and 800 feet below the surface. A major expansion of New York's ancient water supply, the 10- to 24-foot wide tunnel will bring water from the Kensico Reservoir in Westchester down through the Bronx and Manhattan, and eventually to Queens, Brooklyn, and Staten Island. Conceived in the 1950s and begun in 1970, it's not expected to be finished until 2020, at a cost of around $6 billion.

Transportation

Cram eight million people into a fairly compressed space, and you'd better have a way for them to move around. New York does it (albeit not always smoothly) by going up, down, and around, on land, sea, and air — accounting for 40 percent of the mass transit in the U.S. in the process.

The *First* First Subway

People will tell you that New York's **first subway** was completed in 1904 and ran from City Hall to Harlem in 15 minutes — but don't believe them. That's just the city's first *successful* subway; another one was built over 30 years earlier, ran just 312 feet, and only lasted a few years.

In 1868, Alfred Ely Beach, publisher of the *New York Sun* and *Scientific American* and a prolific inventor, decided that the solution to the city's chronic traffic congestion (and all those horse apples) was an underground train. But two things stood in the way: first, the smoke and fumes produced by locomotives, which Beach proposed to do away with by using a pneumatic system similar to those used to send letters along tubes; second, and more important, was Boss William Tweed.

Tweed was the all-powerful chief of Tammany Hall, the city's Democratic machine, and he intended to make a huge amount of graft off a rival plan for an elevated train system. So Beach had to be sneaky. He applied for a permit to dig a small pneumatic tube for delivering mail and packages, which was quickly granted. Then he rented the basement of a store on the corner of Broadway and Warren Street and started digging — at night, using wagons with muffled wheels to haul away the much larger volume of earth. In just 58 nights he completed his tunnel, which ran from Warren to Murray, and opened to the public in February 1870. The smooth, air-powered ride of the pneumatic subway, and the opulent station and single car, were immediate hits; 400,000 people paid a nickel a piece in the first year of operation for a test ride.

But Tweed was not amused, and when Beach applied to extend his line, the Boss made sure permission was denied. By the time Tweed had fallen from power in 1873, the country was in a financial panic, and Beach couldn't raise the money to pursue the project. He died in 1896, and his subway lay abandoned until 1912, when its tunnel was uncovered and incorporated into the BMT line, and all trace of the city's first subway line disappeared.

Born in a Hole in the Ground

There are 469 subway stations in New York City, 722 miles of track, and 4,379 subway cars. If you think getting around underground is laborious, you don't know the half of it: on average, 80 women go into labor in subways every year.

Photo: Daniel Hood

IRT, BMT, IND: old-timers like to refer to the city's subway lines by these confusing and unhelpful initialisms. The simplest way to decipher them is to remember that IRT trains all have numbers, while BMT/IND trains all have letters. So if some geezer tells you to take the East Side IRT, you know he means the 4/5/6, while the Eighth Avenue IND is the A/C/E.

It all comes from the time when New York had three separate subway lines. The first, the Interborough Rapid Transit, opened in 1904, followed shortly by the Brooklyn-Manhattan Transit; both were private companies. The Independent Subway System, which started service in 1932, actually wasn't independent: it was created and run by the city as an alternative to the others. All three ran into money troubles in the 1930s, so the city bought out the IRT and BMT and consolidated them into the current single system in 1940. Since the IND had been built to the same specifications as the BMT, the two now run the same types of trains (and are designated with letters), while the IRT's narrower tunnels require different rolling stock.

Hylan's Grudge

All through his tenure as mayor in the 1920s, John Hylan bashed the city's private subway companies, the IRT and the BMT — refusing to let them raise the nickel fare, denying them the right to expand, and, finally, building the IND line to compete with them directly. There was good public policy to justify it all, of course, but there may have been another reason for his vendetta: while working his way through law school in 1897, Hylan was fired from his job as a motorman on an elevated train run by the Brooklyn Rapid Transit Co. — whose direct descendant was the BMT.

ROAD MAP

There's a sidewalk in SoHo that's good for getting around in more ways than one.

At 110 Greene Street between Spring and Prince Streets, you'll find a network of stainless steel bars zigzagging across the sidewalk. A first glance might suggest an ancient computer network or some kind of urban crop circles. But the title of the piece reveals its purpose: "Subway Map Floating on a New York Sidewalk."

Though it's not nearly as accessible — or accurate — as the subway map in your pocket, this stretch of pavement contains the most artistic, unusual guide to the city's underground maze. The 87-foot-long, 12-foot-wide installation was created in 1986 by Belgian artist Francoise Schein. The three major subways lines — the IRT, BMT, and IND — are depicted with half-inch-wide bars embedded in concrete, with circles indicating stops (the nearby SoHo stations even get small lights). Schein spent about $30,000 to create the informative sidewalk, and it was named the best art project of 1986 by the City Art Commission.

Despite the installation's originality, transit purists take note of its numerous flaws: the map is upside-down (north on the map points south), there are numerous stations missing (57th Street at Sixth Avenue, for one), and connections to other boroughs are not even hinted at. As for the latter criticism, Schein addressed it reasonably at the time. "I couldn't fit Brooklyn or Queens on the sidewalk."

When it comes to transportation disasters, New Yorkers have a historical memory that's just about two events deep: the most recent one, and the one that came just before, which seems to be remembered mostly for purposes of comparison. That may explain why no one talks about the **Malbone Street Crash**, by far the subway system's worst disaster ever.

On Nov. 1, 1918, in the midst of a motormen's strike, the Brooklyn Rapid Transit put a barely trained operator named Anthony Lewis on the Brighton Line train to Coney Island. Having fallen behind schedule due to a missed turn, Lewis tried to make up the time by speeding along so fast that he missed a stop, and then barreled into a sharply curved tunnel under Malbone Street, near Prospect Park. Trains were supposed to take the curve at six miles an hour; Lewis was doing 30. The train derailed, with the old wooden cars plowing into one another and splintering to pieces. When rescuers were finally able to clear the tightly packed wreckage, 97 people were dead and hundreds more injured. Unscathed but in a daze, Lewis wandered home, where he was later arrested. City officials, though, led by Mayor Hylan, were more interested in taking on the subway's management.

Bankrupt, the BRT disappeared in the legal fallout, to eventually re-emerge in 1923 as the Brooklyn-Manhattan Transit. Malbone Street got a new name, too: for most of its length, it's now Empire Boulevard, with only a single block still called Malbone.

The Ghost Under City Hall

There are two City Hall subway stations: the one you can use, and the one you can't. The first, the Brooklyn Bridge/City Hall stop on the 4/5/6, is a perfectly good, utilitarian station that does its job, but the second is an abandoned gem from the system's earliest days.

When the **Interborough Rapid Transit** line was first completed in 1904, the City Hall station was both a terminal and a showpiece, with chandeliers, skylights, glass tilework, and beautiful archways. It was meant to impress, and it did — at least until 1945, when the platform proved too short and sharply curved for longer modern trains, and the number of passengers using it had dwindled. So it was closed, turned into the greatest and most elegant of ghost stations, with the loop of tracks used only to turn southbound 6 trains around.

It used to be that you could get a look at the faded grandeur of the station simply by staying on a 6 train and hoping the conductors didn't notice you, or by taking one of the occasional tours run by the New York Transit Museum. Unfortunately, the station is directly under City Hall, and in these post-9/11 days, the conductors are much more vigilant and the tours have been cancelled.

The Transit Museum

Rather than wall up the old Court Street station in Brooklyn in the late 1970s, the MTA pulled a couple of old trains in there and charged a token to come see them. Now it's a full-fledged museum packed with subway cars, buses, and trolleys from all periods, as well as displays and exhibits on transit history. As elsewhere in the system, the fare has gone up, but it's definitely the most interesting subway station in the city. *Boerum Place and Schermerhorn St., Brooklyn Heights; 718-694-1600*

Other Ghost Stations

The original IRT had stations that could accommodate only five cars; when longer trains came into service, some whole stations were abandoned (though not the South Ferry stop on the 1/9, which is why you have to be in the first five cars to get out there).

Worth Street
On the 4/5/6 line, local sides. *North of Brooklyn Bridge/City Hall Station*

18th Street
On the 4/5/6, local sides. *North of 14th Street/Union Square Station*

91st Street
On the 1/2/3/9, local sides. *Bet. 86th and 96th Street Stations*

Stairway to Haven

Photo: Brad Dunn

There are even life-long New Yorkers who travel through **Times Square** every day who have never noticed it. And if they do, chances are they have no idea what it means.

On the north end of the platform where you catch the shuttle to Grand Central, offset from one of the busiest parts of the Times Square subway station, is a locked door with an ancient sign over it reading, "Knickerbocker." The door hasn't been used publicly in decades, but behind it lies a staircase that used to lead weary commuters directly to a world-class bar.

The gin mill was located in the Knickerbocker Hotel at 1466 Broadway, and the passage gave straphangers a fast link from train tunnel to top-of-the-line watering hole – no streets or sidewalks necessary. Today, the Knickerbocker is an apartment building, and below the closed-up staircase is a manhole leading to subway power and communications systems. And if you want to find the closest bar to the Times Square station, you'll have to navigate through swarms of tourists and across some of the most crowded sidewalks in the city.

Other stations were abandoned because of declines in ridership, unnecessary duplication, or simply because the city's plans changed.

19th Street
On the PATH train.
North of 14th Street station

86th Street
On the Metro-North line out of Grand Central.
86th Street and Park Ave.

42nd Street/Port Authority
On the A/C/E, which still stops here on one level – but not on the second level, which used to run race trains and special excursions, but is now closed off.
Below current 42nd St. platforms

The Hollow Brownstone

When subway and tunnel infrastructure sticks its head aboveground, it's usually obvious, like, say, the ventilator towers for the Holland and Lincoln Tunnels (they're the big square buildings standing just offshore in the Hudson at Canal Street and West 38th Street). But you can't stick a big honking ventilation shaft in the middle of a nice neighborhood, so when they needed to air out the subway tunnels that run deep below leafy Brooklyn Heights, they bought one of those classy brownstones on Joralemon Street, hollowed it out, and ran the shaft inside the façade. For a time, the moan of air rushing through had neighbors worried the place was haunted, but now that they know the deal, they're just grateful for their property values.

FDR's Secret Tunnel

Rumor has it that when President Franklin D. Roosevelt came to town, he used a secret tunnel in the depths of **Grand Central Terminal** to travel directly to his suite at the Waldorf-Astoria Hotel – possibly as a shortcut, possibly as a way to avoid the public while he was still disguising his polio. True or not, the tunnel's existence is a piece of city lore that goes all the way back to the ground-breaking of the hotel, as revealed in a *New York Times* article from Sept. 9, 1929: "The new Waldorf-Astoria Hotel … will have a private railway siding underneath the building. … Guests with private rail cars may have them routed directly to the hotel … and may leave their cars at a special elevator which will take them directly to their suites or to the lobby."

Let's look at the facts: the site of the Waldorf was once occupied by a city power station, with a network of tunnels and crawlspaces beneath it. When developers dismantled the station, they may have left the underground passageways in place.

Renowned subway historian Joseph Brennan claims that there was a secret tunnel with an elevator and staircase, but that it provided access to 49th Street directly across from the Waldorf – not into the hotel itself. Either way, the underground structure must be relatively large. According to legend, Andy Warhol used the same secret underground platform to host a party in 1965.

Underground Art

We get some of the new art the MTA commissions to decorate various subway stations. "Platform Diving," for instance, a series of mosaics of sea creatures frolicking through water-filled subway platforms at Houston Street on the 1/9, is clever and fun. Some of the installations baffle us, though, like the vast display at the Union Square Station of the 4/5/6/N/R/L, and Tom Otterness's dozens of intriguing little moneybag-people statues scattered around the 14th Street Station of the A/C/E. Fortunately, the MTA has put together an online guide called Art en Route that describes them all, and explains some of the harder ones. Check it out at *mta.nyc.ny.us/mta/aft.*

THE ONCE AND FUTURE SUBWAY

Much has been made recently of plans for a **Second Avenue subway** to relieve crowding on the East Side of Manhattan. Proposals range from a "stubway" connecting 125th Street with 63rd Street, to a full-size line running from the Bronx down Second and then Chrystie Street to the bottom of the island. Skeptics point out that plans for this line have popped up in the past – from as early as 1919 – but nothing has ever come of them.

Atlantic Avenue's Secret

Antiques abound on Brooklyn's Atlantic Avenue – and the most interesting one isn't in the shops aboveground; it's deep beneath the street. In 1844, the Long Island Railroad dug a tunnel there between Hicks and Court Streets to transport passengers out to the North Fork of the island. It was a monumental achievement – 21 feet wide, 17 high, and around 2,000 long – but it wasn't in use long, since the LIRR was soon forced to use another route, and the tunnel was closed up and buried in 1861. None other than poet Walt Whitman wrote its elegy, in a collection of essays called *Brooklyniana*.

After that it was mostly forgotten, until 1979, when a young Brooklynite named Bob Diamond heard a brief mention of the lost tunnel, and started combing through old newspapers and city transportation records. He finally got hold of an old set of plans, figured out a likely way in, and, with the permission of the city, went down a manhole at Atlantic and Court Street, dug an entry, and pulled a Howard Carter on the Atlantic Avenue Tunnel.

There were no gold sarcophagi, just Whitman's "passage of Acheron-like solemnity and darkness," but it's an undeniably cool spot, which has since been the preserve of both spelunking tourists and art happenings. Diamond himself has run annual tours through his Brooklyn Historic Railway Association *(brooklynrail.com)* – but that leads us to another story.

In addition to re-opening the tunnel, Diamond hoped to bring trolleys back to Brooklyn. Through the BHRA, he raised money and got the city's permission to start laying light rail tracks in Red Hook. He had several blocks laid in the waterfront area, and grand plans to extend the line all the way to downtown Brooklyn, but by 2003 funding problems had brought work to a stop, and the city decided that the unfinished tracks were a hazard. They promptly tore them up, crushing the dreams of those who hoped to see trolleys in New York again after more than 70 years. Whitman, we suspect, would have disapproved.

In fact, something has: there are three small sections of tunnel, built in the late '60s and early '70s, lying abandoned deep in the bedrock. The largest runs from 110th to 119th Streets; the other two from 99th to 105th Streets, and from Chrystie to Bowery. (Another, from 9th down to 2nd Streets, is said to have been dug and filled back in.) Work on them stopped when the city faced bankruptcy in 1975, but they're still there, just waiting for trains and riders.

Photo: Daniel Hood

ROBERT MOSES

MASTERBUILDER
FRIEND OF FORDHAM

In most cities, when they talk about the things that have competely reshaped the urban landscape, they talk about devastating fires, massive earthquakes, and hugely destructive wars. In New York, they talk about **Robert Moses**.

Though he was never elected to public office, Moses amassed enormous power from a series of appointed positions at both the state and local level (at one point he held as many as 12 different titles, including chief of the Triborough Bridge and Tunnel Authority and City Parks Commissioner). With that power, from the 1930s through the 1950s, Moses pretty much rebuilt the city to his liking – and what he liked were cars.

His parkways, expressways, bridges, and tunnels are everywhere, and they're meant for cars and more cars: the parkway overpasses are too low for buses, and the bridges were deliberately built without provision for trains or subways. Other forms of transportation weren't all that lost out to Moses' love affair with the car, since he had no compunction about destroying thriving, if lower-class, neighborhoods to push his roads through. It's been estimated that around 250,000 people were displaced from their homes for his construction projects.

By the 1960s, many New Yorkers were sick of his high-handed ways. He lost battles to oust Shakespeare in the Park and a popular playground from Central Park (he wanted to replace the latter with a parking lot), and then another over a plan to drive a huge elevated expressway across Manhattan through Greenwich Village. Governors and mayors started easing him out of

"NEW, DEADLY SCOURGE"

A headline in the May 30, 1896 *New York Times* blared: "Monstrous Horseless Carriage New, Deadly Scourge of Streets." Yes, it turns out that New York City, a place that boasts many firsts, can lay claim to the **world's first car accident**.

On that fateful spring day, Miss Evelyn Thomas was pedaling her bike on Broadway near West 74th Street, when Henry Wells, an out-of-towner, lost control of his Duryea Motor Wagon and swerved into history. Automobile struck bicycle, and Miss Thomas was thrown off, knocked unconscious, and later treated for a fractured femur. Police kept Wells in custody overnight until it was clear that his victim would survive.

his many positions of power, and by the early 1970s he retired, a much-reviled man. For many, he is the embodiment of evil in urban planning; at best, he is considered monumentally wrongheaded.

Much of that wrongheadedness may be explained by one simple fact: the man who completely reshaped New York in favor of the car – and who once said, "Cities are created by and for traffic" – never learned how to drive.

Photo: Courtesy MTA

Some of What Moses Built:
Triborough Bridge
Throgs Neck Bridge
Bronx-Whitestone Bridge
Verrazano Narrows Bridge
Henry Hudson Bridge
Brooklyn-Battery Tunnel
Queens Midtown Tunnel
Brooklyn-Queens Expressway
Staten Island Expressway
Cross-Bronx Expressway
Grand Central Parkway
Belt Parkway
Laurelton Parkway
Taconic Parkway
Henry Hudson Parkway
Riverside Park
Jones Beach
Orchard Beach
Lincoln Center
1964 World's Fair
658 playgrounds
16 public housing projects (28,000 apartments)

Mixed Signals

Photo: Daniel Hood

"Traffic signals in New York are just rough guidelines," David Letterman once joked. True, but if you want to see really rough guidelines, go back to the 1920s when **traffic signals** were timed differently at every intersection. Talk about road rage.

In fact, New York was the first city in the world to invent a way to synchronize traffic signals — and it spent more than a decade learning how to do it. The transition from horse to horseless went like lightning in Manhattan; by 1918, there were almost a million automobiles jammed in the city. The status quo traffic system — a cop waving drivers across an intersection — produced nothing but bumper-to-bumper insanity. Finally, the city came up with a solution.

At the 50 busiest intersections, engineers installed small traffic towers where officers could control the signals mechanically. Then, they built one tall tower on each avenue. When the traffic signal changed in the tall tower, the officers in the smaller towers saw it and followed suit. For the first time, an entire avenue turned green or red at once.

The system was first tried on July 10, 1924, and it synchronized all the signals on Broadway from Rector Street to West 85th Street. It worked phenomenally: never before could a car go five or six blocks without stopping.

Five years later, a rudimentary electronic apparatus replaced the officers in the tall towers, followed later by those in the shorter towers. By the early 1930s, the city's traffic system was controlled entirely out of the Police Department's 14th Precinct. It was a remarkable accomplishment: before there were computers, New York City could control more than 4,000 signals at 2,000 intersections from one room.

Which still, as Letterman points out, says nothing about whether those signals are obeyed.

GEOGRAPHICALLY SPEAKING

Sure, New York City is the center of the world, but where is the center of the center of the world? It all depends on how you look at it.

For transportation purposes, all distances to the city are measured from City Hall, which, if you drive in from the north, puts you in Manhattan about 12 miles sooner than you might have expected. This measuring system actually began before City Hall, as we know it today, was built. To measure how far they traveled, and how much to charge customers, postal carriers of the late

Wrong on Red

Right turns at red lights are banned throughout all five boroughs – or so they tell you. In fact, you're not allowed to make a right on red *unless there's a sign*. Problem is, of course, that there are very few of these permissive signs – less than ten, we're told – and they're at places like the 21st Street exit off the 59th Street Bridge in Queens, or at one of the intersections approaching the Manhattan Bridge. For most of the city, if it's red, you can't move.

Only two cities in North America inflict this royal pain on drivers – New York and Montreal. What makes it even more annoying is that the whole notion of making a right on red was created here, in 1918, and only banned in 1937. We suspect the ban may have been an attempt to discourage the hordes of Jersey-types who flooded the city after the opening of the Holland Tunnel in 1927, the George Washington Bridge in 1931, and the first tube of the Lincoln Tunnel in 1937, but can offer no proof.

1700s tallied their journeys from steps of the old City Hall, which stood at Nassau and Wall Streets. The only route out of town was Broadway, and they placed stone markers at one-mile intervals (hence the term milestone) all the way up to the Harlem River, which was about the 14th milestone.

The geographic center of the island, however, lies somewhere near 57th Street and Sixth Avenue. But, after all, New York is much more than Manhattan. If you really want to get to the center of it all, you have to go to Long Island City, Queens.

Hicks from the Sticks

Streets are usually named after people, not vice versa. But a little road in Brooklyn gave the English language a new word: hick. In the early 1800s, the Hicks Family's farm occupied a stretch of land in what is now Brooklyn Heights. Once a week, farmhands loaded a boat with fresh produce, crossed the East River, and sold what they could near the Fulton Street markets. Because they were from what was then a rural area, the farm workers were seen as country bumpkins by their more-sophisticated clientele in Manhattan. Gradually, the term "hick" came to life. And though the Hicks' farm has long since been replaced by row houses and brownstones, its name lives on as much on the signs of its namesake street, as in the English dictionary.

Four Names, Five Boroughs

What do King, Clinton, Park, and Broadway have in common? They're the only street names in New York City that appear in every borough.

It's a Dirty Job

Photo: Brad Dunn

If the city's police officers are known as New York's Finest and its firefighters New York's Bravest, then who are New York's Strongest? One hint: they earned their nickname for the 13,000 tons – not the odors – they pick up every day. They are the members of the city's **Department of Sanitation.** And they have a street named after them to prove it.

For decades, the only city agency honored with a street name was the Police Department, with its Avenue of the Finest. But in July of 1996, Mayor Rudy Giuliani officially renamed the stretch of Worth Street between Broadway and Centre Street the "Avenue of the Strongest," a distinction paying homage to the incredible feat that the city's 9,500 sanitation workers had achieved earlier that year.

The blizzard of '96 buried New York City in almost eight feet of snow. To keep ahead of the storm, almost every sanitation worker put in 12-hour shifts for 14 straight days. First, they plowed streets and hauled off truckloads of the heavy snowfall. Then they collected a record amount of garbage: 120,000 tons – the equivalent weight of a nuclear-powered aircraft carrier.

The renaming of a public street is a momentous event. Not even New York's Boldest (also known as the Department of Corrections) have had that honor, yet.

Lost Namesake

In the early 1980s, an arboreal dynasty seemed to be near its end on a charming little street in the Village: there was only one cherry tree still standing on a street once known as **Cherry Lane.**

And like the iceberg that doomed the *Titanic*, it was an errant delivery truck that dealt a cruel hand of fate to the lone blossom. Cut down in its prime by an ill-fated traffic mishap, the last of the lane's namesakes was hauled off to Fresh Kills.

Also Known As ...

Ask a cabbie to take you to Edgar Allan Poe Street, and you'll get a bewildered stare through the rear-view mirror. Tell him instead to go to James Cagney Place, and he might turn around and laugh at you. Change it to Tito Puente Way, and he'll throw you out of the car.

But these are real streets, or at least the official nicknames of real streets. A city of eight million people tends to produce a bevy of notable personalities over the years. Many of them leave behind honorary namesakes. Here's a short list of street aliases in Manhattan:

Charlie Parker Place:
East Village

Photo: Amy Della Rocca

Jack Dempsey Corner:
Broadway and 48th St.

The tragic setback, however, was not the first for the little road. Cherry Lane was actually renamed Commerce Street in the early 1800s, when a glut of downtown businesses moved north to the nascent, but quickly expanding, Greenwich Village. If you stroll down Commerce Street today, you'll see a little plaque at its intersection with Bedford Street that describes the lane's colorful history.

Just as the word commerce replaced cherry on street signs, so too did storefronts slowly outstrip the fragrant blossoms. In fact, when Edna St. Vincent Mallay helped found the Cherry Lane Theater in 1924, the cherry trees had all but vanished — making it difficult for theatergoers to find the playhouse to this day.

Instead of giving up and just renaming their playhouse the Commerce Street Theater, the owners, along with local residents, have pushed to return the lane to its historical roots — literally. In 2003, they got enough signatures on a petition not only to prompt the City Council to rename the street Cherry Lane, but also to get permission from the Parks Department to plant new cherry trees in 2004. As the street prepares to restore its history and launch a new reign of pink- and white-blossomed cherry trees, only one thing haunts planners: ill-fated delivery trucks.

Leonard Bernstein Place:
Broadway and 65th St.

Martin Luther King Jr. Boulevard:
All of 125th St.

Edgar Allan Poe Street:
W. 84th St.

Duke Ellington Boulevard:
W. 106th St.

Yitzhak Rabin Way:
Second Ave. bet. 42nd and 43rd Sts.

James Cagney Place:
E. 91st St.

Norman Vincent Peale Way:
W. 29th St. bet. Broadway and Fifth Ave.

Rodgers & Hammerstein Row:
44th St. bet. Broadway and Eighth Ave.

Tito Puente Way:
E. 110th St.

Malcolm X Boulevard:
Lenox Ave.

Sack Sixth Avenue

In 1945, **Sixth Avenue** had a sleazy reputation, and New York had a mayor every bit as bent on de-sleazing the city as future clean-up guy Rudy Giuliani. And though Mayor Fiorello LaGuardia had every reason to rename the island's central artery, New Yorkers had every reason to resist it.

"Avenue of the Americas" was foisted on the city not only to pay homage to the newly formed Organization of American States, but also to cast a new image on the mean street. From the get-go, however, the public relations gambit had problems. Avenue of the Americas is not only about seven syllables longer than most New Yorkers can be bothered with, it is also numberless — stripping away every convenience Manhattan's grid offers the first-time visitor.

Predictably, residents tried to hold on to Sixth Avenue. In turn, City Hall redoubled its commitment to the name in the early 1950s: it installed new lampposts all along the avenue, each with a medallion of a country from North, South, or Central America.

Businesses gave in first, and the words "Avenue of the Americas" began to supplant "Sixth Avenue" on business cards up and down the strip. Though both names are used interchangeably today, Mayor LaGuardia ultimately saw the error of his ways. Years after renaming the road, he said, "When I make a mistake, it's a beaut."

When Porsche Comes to Shove

Alternate-side parking is a real drag. But what can you do? Apparently, if you're **Jerry Seinfeld**, you just buy an old row house, gut it, and turn it into a private, multi-level parking garage.

That's exactly what the super-rich comedian did to house part of his collection of 13 Porsche sports cars. A rabid car enthusiast, Seinfeld found the ideal location for his personal garage – West 83rd Street between Columbus and Amsterdam Avenues – and now keeps up to seven Porsches there at a time. The spot is just three blocks from his $4.35 million duplex at the Beresford, so Jerry doesn't even get a chill walking from car mansion to penthouse pad.

According to city records, Seinfeld bought the two-story house for $880,000 and threw in another $500,000 to transform it into what the *New York Observer* called the Porsche-Haus. His little carpark was refurbished with terrazzo floors, wood paneling, and a huge skylight. On the third floor, the former sitcom star installed a carpeted, 844-square-foot office with curved ceiling, as well as a small kitchen and bathroom with shower.

The building also has a high-capacity elevator that can shuttle cars to the second floor, where whichever are his least-used sports cars will no doubt accumulate. Either way, Seinfeld's collection of Speedsters, Boxsters, and Carreras finally have a place they can call home.

BIG YELLOW TAXIS

They weren't always – in fact, New York came late to the game. Before World War I, Chicago entrepreneur John Hertz was in the business of building taxicabs (it was only much later that his name became synonymous with rental cars), and he conducted a "scientific" study that determined that yellow was the most visible color. By 1915, he was franchising **yellow cabs** across the country, but they didn't catch on here for quite some time, and cabs could be any color they liked (Tom Buchanan's mistress in *The Great Gatsby* insists on waiting for one that's lavender). It was only in the 1950s that medallioned cabs started being painted yellow to distinguish them from the new flood of gypsy cabs, and it wasn't until 1967 that the city required that all 12,000-odd medallioned cabs be painted yellow.

Photo: Daniel Hood

WHY YOU CAN'T GET ONE

There's never a cab when you need one — unless you need one in 1931. Back then, over 20,000 prowled the streets, and competition was so fierce that the Haas Act was passed in 1937 to try and regulate the pandemonium. Among other things, it introduced the medallion system, which reduced the number of cabs on the streets to around 12,000 and improved both service and the wages of cabbies. Unfortunately, it also pretty much set the number of taxis in stone; while the city has nearly doubled in population, the number of medallions available has only crept up to 12,187.

Taxi Tips

Being a cab driver isn't an easy job, but neither is being a passenger. A taxi primer:

When the numbers on top are lit, the cab is free. When nothing is lit, the cab is occupied (we can't tell you the number of lifelong New Yorkers we've seen cursing and stamping their feet because an unlit — and thus occupied — cab passed them by). If it's all lit, the driver is off duty (that's why it says "Off Duty"), but you can still hail the cab; it's up to the driver if he wants to take you where you're going.

If you have any kind of luggage, hold it behind you or leave it out of sight on the curb. Cab drivers frequently "don't see" passengers with bags, because they're afraid you want to go to an airport. Cab drivers hate going to the airports.

If there are no cabs on your street, try heading a block over to a street headed in the opposite direction. Paying the extra 50 cents or so that it'll cost to turn around beats gnashing your teeth for half an hour.

If you're forgetful, take your receipt. It has the medallion number of the cab, which makes tracking down left-behind items easier. Just ask Yo-Yo Ma, who once forgot his cello in a cab. Of course, if he couldn't remember a cello, there wasn't much chance he would remember to get a receipt. The cabbie noticed the giant instrument case, and returned it.

Not Quite the Bat Signal

Photo: Daniel Hood

Driving a cab in New York is one of the most dangerous professions in the world, and given the numbers of cabbies who are mugged or killed every year, it only makes sense that they have some way to signal if a passenger has turned dangerous: it's called the trouble light, and it's that little yellow disk on the trunk lid that looks like a bicycle reflector. If a cabbie's being mugged, he can hit a button that lights it up, telling the police that he needs help — and you to find another cab.

Walking over Water

The standing joke used to be that if Jesus really did walk on a body of water, it was probably the East River, but that much-maligned body (actually a tidal strait, not a river) has now been cleaned up significantly, so foot traffic has to make do with crossing one of four bridges.

Photo: Daniel Hood

As the first bridge built between Manhattan and Brooklyn, the **Brooklyn Bridge** was a huge hit with walkers from the very start: over 160,000 people strolled across on the first Sunday after it opened in May of 1883. Not even an ugly incident a few days later – when a massed crowd panicked over rumors that the bridge was collapsing and trampled 12 people to death – could dent its popularity, and today the broad walkway is still the favored crossing for pedestrians, possibly because it connects two places they actually want to go to. Swarms of tourists and commuters cross every day, as do plenty of local office workers who make the walk there and back at lunch for exercise (or as an excuse for a bigger meal).

About 3,000 people cross the Brooklyn Bridge on foot or bicycle each day, while the walkways on the three other East River crossings – the **Manhattan**, **Williamsburg**, and **Queensborough Bridges**, all of which have excellent views – see only about 1,000, in large part because of their locations, but also because they're uncomfortably close to the traffic.

Photo: Daniel Hood

SAVE THE TOLL

Heading north out of Manhattan on the East Side? Don't bother with the Triborough Bridge and its massive toll. If you're on the FDR, continue on one exit past the Triborough and take the **Willis Avenue Bridge** (or just head up First Avenue all the way to the end), which can connect you to the Major Deegan Expressway and Bruckner Boulevard. Coming in from either of them, take the **Third Avenue Bridge**, which connects you to Second Avenue and the FDR toll-free.

Further north, the **Triborough Bridge** also has a pedestrian walkway across the Harlem River from the far eastern end of 125th Street to Randall's Island (again, connecting two places not that many people want to go). There is talk of opening the **High Bridge**, which is actually an aqueduct built in the 1840s, to pedestrians, but talk is cheap, and rehabilitating bridges isn't.

Finally, the Everest of river crossings has to be the **George Washington Bridge**, with its gorgeous views of the Hudson. There are a pedestrian walkway and bicycle path on the south side, and another pedestrian walkway on the north, all on the upper level (or "George," as some call it – the lower level being "Martha").

Death, Be Not Proud

When it was open to traffic in 1937, the record was official: the Lincoln Tunnel was the first major tunnel project in the country to be completed without a single fatality.

Credit went to the tremendous emphasis the Port Authority put on safety. As workers, or "sandhogs," tunneled deeper beneath the Hudson River, the agency limited them to one hour of work per day to prevent life-threatening cases of the bends – 30 minutes in the morning, 30 minutes in the afternoon, with at least five hours of rest in between.

Two crews set to work on either side of the river. The New York side started digging at West 38th Street; the New Jersey side started in Weehawken. Work began in 1930, and the crews finally connected in 1935. The first "hole through" occurred when a hydraulic engineer from the New Jersey crew was pushed by his feet through an opening to meet the New York crew.

The first tube (out of three) of the Lincoln Tunnel was opened on Dec. 22, 1937, at a cost of $75 million – just $10 million over budget.

The project was a tremendous success not only because no workers died, but also because it opened what would become one of the most important arteries into Manhattan. Today, the Lincoln Tunnel carries approximately 120,000 vehicles per day, making it the busiest vehicular tunnel in the world.

A New Penn Station

Photo: Daniel Hood

Much ink has been (and will continue to be) spilled over the wanton demolition in 1963 of the old **Penn Station** on Seventh Avenue between 31st and 34th Streets. Given that forgetting the past is a local tradition, the loss was clearly traumatic, and hundreds of thousands of people are reminded of it every day as they pass through or by the subterranean hideousness that currently disgraces the old name. Which explains the plans championed by the late, revered New York senator Daniel Patrick Moynihan to move Penn Station a long block west into a beautiful neo-classical building that at least approximates the station's old glory –

Photo: Daniel Hood

the James A. Farley Post Office on Eighth Avenue (right, which was designed by McKim, Mead and White, the same firm that designed the old station, and the scene of many a late-night-April 15 tax return meltdown).

As always, holding your breath is not advised: the plans have kicked around for years now, stalled at different points by the Post Office's fiscal woes and post-9/11 troubles. In the end, the only thing that seems sure is that the new station will be named after Moynihan – if it ever happens at all.

THE TRAIN TO THE TRAIN

Let's face it – New York seems to have lost its touch when it comes to trains. After years of trying to convince people to "take the train to the plane," the city finally gave up on the notion that people would schlepp their bags onto the A train for an hour-plus ride to a spot vaguely in the vicinity of JFK Airport, and decided to build a dedicated rail link. The **AirTrain**, which started operating in late 2003, runs a mere 8.1 miles, but it took over four years to build, ran $400 million over budget, and cost the life of a driver in an accident during a test run.

And for all that, it still doesn't fill the bill – while it does start right in JFK, it only runs to a station in Jamaica, Queens, where you have to switch to the Long Island Rail Road or the subway to get into Manhattan or the other boroughs. Which means that now, instead of taking the train to someplace sort of near the plane, you can take the train to the train to the plane.

Grid Tips and Tricks

Photo: Daniel Hood

Established in 1811, Manhattan's grid plan makes it relatively easy to get around above Houston Street on the east and 14th Street on the west (Greenwich Village was exempted because it already existed when the plan was devised). That's *relatively* easy — it's still a city, after all. So, some tips:

"Even east":

Generally speaking, even-numbered one-way streets run east.

Major cross-streets:

Each marks a one-time frontier in the northward expansion of the city, and is now a two-way street. Houston, 14th, 23rd, 34th, 42nd, 57th, 66th, 72nd, 86th, and 96th.

Sidewalks of New York

According to writer Russell Baker, "New York is the only city in the world where you can get run down on the sidewalk by a pedestrian." Hey, if Baker got run down, it was his fault — he was probably gawking at something. The city's sidewalks are arguably the most used transportation system in the world. You have to stay focused, and you have to keep moving.

Let's face it: there are 12,500 miles of sidewalk in this city, and, for starters, about 340,000 people use them as their sole means to get to work every day. Add to that the other eight million pairs of feet who live here, plus the millions of others that are just passing through, and you can see why things can get a little jammed. To handle all that human mass, New York sidewalks, by regulation, must be at least four inches thick.

As far as keeping sidewalks presentable, the city has a slew of laws that are enforced, at best, irregularly. No spitting. No littering. You must curb your dog. Overall, most neighborhoods keep on top of the trash. Do you know what really gums up the works?

No, those aren't splotches of tar or asphalt. They're the sometimes decades-old remnant of a Bazooka Joe, a Juicy Fruit, a Chicklet. They tend to mass around pedestrian hubs like flies around a candle. Gum spots are the bane of shopkeepers, whose job it is, not the Sanitation Department's, to remove them if desired.

All it takes is a 2,000-pounds-per-square-inch steam hose that's as loud as a jackhammer to blast the blemish to smithereens.

Which is probably what Russell Baker was gaping at when he got run over by someone trying to get to work.

Life in the Pig City

Of course, before there were cars, the streets of New York were packed with horses. But few people remember (and the city isn't likely to remind you) that before there were garbage trucks, the streets of Manhattan were packed with pigs.

The porcine prowlers were the best, and virtually only, sanitation system available in the first half of the 19th century, and New York became infamous for them. Though privately owned, the **street pigs** roamed the sidewalks and gutters surviving on the refuse of a rapidly expanding city. Wall Street, in particular, was constantly being polished by porkers, and a common complaint of early stock traders was not their presence, but their tear-inducing odor.

As the city prospered in the 1850s, it decided to clean up its image. Just as the Pied Piper led all the rats out of Hamelin, so did municipal workers push the pigs northward. By 1860, not a pig was seen below 86th Street, well past the official city limit at the time.

In their place, the city put garbage collectors on the payroll. Of course, the human refuse removers weren't as clean about waste disposal: they carted most of it to the Hudson or East River and watched it float out to the Bay.

Button to Nowhere

Photo: Daniel Hood

Known to just about every New Yorker, but only slowly realized by visitors, the **traffic-signal buttons** for pedestrians who wish to traverse crosswalks are about as useful as a three-dollar bill. If they're connected to wires at all, they might as well be wired directly to the sewer: the lights simply do not change on demand in this city. Still, those buttons are pressed probably thousands of times a day by out-of-towners eager to keep moving.

The reason pedestrians cannot summon a traffic halt is obvious: if they could, the island would be gridlocked in

The split:

Fifth Avenue divides the city — and all its street addresses — into east and west.

Northbound avenues:

First, Third, Madison, Sixth, Eighth, and Tenth.

Southbound avenues:

Second, Lexington, Broadway (below 59th St.), Fifth, Seventh, and Ninth.

Both ways:

Third (below 25th), Park, Broadway (above 59th), and Eleventh (above 43rd).

Where's Fourth?

There is a little stub of Fourth Avenue, running from 14th Street down to East 4th Street below Cooper Square. Above 14th, Park takes over where Fourth should be.

less than 30 seconds. There are far more people than cars; to cast aside the timed signals and give reign to the whim of walkers would be to unleash anarchy.

The real question is: why are those buttons there in the first place? According to the city's Department of Transportation, they exist because the law says they must. Moreover, they do have a purpose in an emergency: if the timed-signal system fails, the buttons become operational. If you don't want to wait for such an emergency, and yet still want to command traffic, ambulate over to Riverside Drive. Many of the crosswalks have buttons that actually prompt a light change.

Getting addresses:

Most phone books include a handy little calculation to figure out the cross-street of an address on an avenue. Simply take the address, drop the last digit, divide the remaining three-digit number by two, and add or subtract the special, avenue-specific number given with the instructions. It's not amazing that it works (it does, roughly); it's amazing that they expect anyone to go through all that. Unless you love math, just call and ask for the cross-street.

You're on your own:

Below Houston, history is your enemy, since the city had already made its haphazard way up that far by 1811. In far northern Manhattan, the rough terrain made the grid impractical, and the handy north-south avenues start to disappear or twist and turn around 125th Street.

Pedal of Honor

Traffic in Manhattan was basically gridlocked for most of the 1970s. Trains were packed. Sidewalks were jammed. Businesses couldn't get packages and documents to each other on time. Just when the city's transportation infrastructure needed a shot in the arm, a new class of postal carrier was born: the **bicycle messenger**.

Young, fit entrepreneurs darted through the traffic on ten-speeds with impossible packages strapped to their backs. They were paid by how many deliveries they could make, and so became renowned for their astonishing recklessness and sometimes dramatic collisions with cars and pedestrians. The young profession even produced a celebrity: Nelson Vails, whose speed left people in awe. After making deliveries, Vails would ride to Central Park and casually out-pedal the professional riders in training. As he gained notoriety, he was asked to try out for the Olympic Team, and in 1984 won a silver medal at the Los Angeles Games.

Vails even made a cameo in the movie about him and his kind, *Quicksilver*, which glorified the profession at its height. (Vails appeared as the messenger in the maroon beret.) By the late 1980s, as fax machines and overnight delivery services spread across the city, the pedaling entrepreneurs dwindled. Today, though bicycle messengers can still be seen artfully swerving around potholes and dodging midtown traffic, the profession has witnessed its best days gone by.

Now Arriving in Newark

As mayor from 1933 to 1945, **Fiorello LaGuardia** could be expected to recognize his own city, so when he booked a flight from Chicago to New York in 1934, and the airline tried to drop him at the commercial airport in Newark, N.J., he was understandably upset – so much so that he insisted the airline fulfill the itinerary on his ticket and deliver him to New York proper. At the time, though, there were no commercial airfields in the city, so they eventually flew him, alone, to Floyd Bennett Field, a military airfield in Brooklyn. Thoroughly annoyed, LaGuardia began a crusade to build a proper airport within city limits. Five years later, "Fiorello's Folly," built on vast amounts of landfill in North Beach, Queens, opened to air traffic, and soon proved his critics wrong by becoming the country's busiest airport, with over 200 flights a day (despite the fact that the runways almost immediately began to sink as the landfill was compressed beneath the pounding of landing gear). Originally called North Beach Airport, and informally nicknamed "La Chargia" because of the high rents the city charged concessionaires, it was quickly and almost unanimously rechristened after its creator, in recognition of his vision.

Going Down

Elevators are far and away the safest mode of transportation in the world; the nightmare image that sometimes haunts you of a frayed cable ready to snap and send you tumbling down an elevator shaft is a virtual impossibility thanks to a bevy of modern safety systems.

Still, few people know that New York City holds the not-so-flattering record of being the one place where an elevator car actually went into free-fall – the only such incident in the history of modern elevators. And it happened no place other than the Empire State Building.

When a B-25 plane crashed into the skyscraper in 1945, Betty Lou Oliver was serving her last day as an elevator operator. She was perched alone in the car at the 79th floor, sipping a cup of coffee, when the plane's wing sliced through the building above her and severed every cable attached to her car. She went into free-fall in an empty shaft more than 1,000 feet tall.

Back to the Water

Photo: Daniel Hood

Ferries once thronged the Hudson and the East River, until they were put out of business by bridges and tunnels (many built, ironically, to ease congestion on ferries), and by the 1970s ferries had almost completely disappeared from the harbor (the Staten Island Ferry and the Statue of Liberty Ferry being the main hold-outs).

But in the 1980s, as people rediscovered the waterfront and ridership on the PATH climbed, the Port Authority and others started warming up to the idea of commuter ferries, and by 1986 service had been established between Jersey and the West Side of Manhattan. Since then, the number of ferries has slowly but surely increased.

NY Waterway

The first and by far the largest, with service between Manhattan (stops at Pier 11 at Wall Street, the World Financial Center, and W. 38th St.) and New Jersey (stops from Weehawken down to Jersey City, as well as the Jersey Shore). You can flag down their buses at many regular city bus stops in midtown and downtown. They also do trips to Shea Stadium and Yankee Stadium on game nights.
800-533-3779; nywaterway.com

Liberty Park Water Taxi

Liberty State Park to the World Financial Center.
201-985-8000; llmarina.com

New York Water Taxi

All around Manhattan (E. 90th St., E. 34th St., Pier 11 at Wall Street, the World Financial Center, Chelsea Piers, and W. 44th St.), with stops in Queens (Hunter's Point) and Brooklyn (Fulton Ferry Landing and Brooklyn Army Terminal).
212-742-1969; nywatertaxi.com

New York Fast Ferry

Jersey Shore to Pier 11 and E. 34th St.
800-693-6933; nyff.com

SeaStreak

Jersey Shore to Pier 11 and E. 34th St.
732-872-2628; seastreak.com

Witnesses on the ground floor recalled hearing a woman's screams getting louder and louder as the car hurled down the shaft. When an explosion was heard in the sub-basement, rescuers rushed down to find the car completely demolished. They cleared the rubble and, to their astonishment, found Ms. Oliver still alive in the corner of the car. Amazingly, she had only suffered two broken legs and a spinal injury. She recovered fully within eight months.

Ironically, it was the elevator cable that actually saved her life. During her fall, the 1,000 feet of cable below her piled up beneath the car and absorbed the impact. So take note: if you're going to enter free-fall during your next elevator ride, it's better to start from a really high floor.

No MetroCards Accepted

Photo: Liberty Helicopters

Transit MetroCards will prove their worth when you can use them to charter a helicopter to get you to work. In the meantime, break out the serious plastic if you want a spin around Manhattan. **Liberty Helicopter Tours** *(212-967-6464; libertyhelicopters.com)* has a large number of set tour itineraries of different lengths starting at around $60 for five to seven minutes, with longer tours going for up to $275 for half an hour from the West 30th Street Heliport or the Pier Six Heliport near the Staten Island Ferry Terminal. **Helicopter Flight Services** *(212-355-0801; heliny.com)* has fewer itineraries with a similar price scale.

Both offer private charters, and this is where that unlimited MetroCard would come in handy: if you want to set the destination, you can't get off the ground for much less $1,000 an hour.

Sports & the Outdoors

The Yankees. The Mets. The Belmont Stakes. The Garden. The Marathon. No wonder *The Sporting News* has named New York the "Best Sporting City" in North America. While we're at it, we might throw in Central Park, Coney Island, two rivers rebounding from environmental devastation, a revitalized coastline, and some hellacious rock climbing. So get outside already!

Photo: Brad Dunn

Faster than the NBA

No other court in the land promises as much action, suspense, and jaw-dropping razzle-dazzle. Forget Madison Square Garden, the best basketball in New York City can be seen daily on a legendary patch of concrete in the Village.

The **West 4th Street Court**, affectionately known as "The Cage," hosts pickup games every day the weather permits, and audiences up to 10 people deep line the chain-link fence to witness some of the fiercest competition around. The legendary court at the corner of Sixth Avenue stages regular five-on-five play, as well as pulse-pounding two-on-two tourneys with some of the hottest young players and seasoned street-ball pros you'll ever see. Hang around long enough, and you might be catch an ex-NBA star trot out and teach the younger guys a lesson.

Fancy freestyle moves and half-court alley-oops are *de rigueur*. If you're tempted to lace up and try to get in on a pickup game, your skin had better be as tough as your lay-up: the taunting can be relentless; the on-court insults draw in as many passersby as the slam dunks.

Pickup games generally start at 1 p.m. on weekdays, with league play taking over the court at 6 p.m. On weekends, events ranging from children's basketball programs to prize tournaments get started around 10 a.m. And, unlike the NBA, it's free to watch — even from front row court-side.

Photo: Brad Dunn

Edible Central Park

Who said there's no such thing as a free lunch? Amid the thousands of species of flora in **Central Park**, any botany-savvy visitor can munch on numerous edible plants that grow in the urban wild. Look hard enough and you can find wild black cherries, carrots, plantains, water mint, mustard seeds, day lily shoots, and wild grape leaves.

If you don't want to bite into a poisonous mushroom, you should take a foraging tour with "Wildman" Steve Brill – the notorious naturalist who was arrested in Central Park in 1986 for eating a dandelion (the charges were dropped when his lawyer argued that Brill's foraging is delicate and sparing). Brill leads groups through city parks and shows them how to identify, pick and prepare wild plants for eating. The suggested $15 fee for his tour is voluntary. Log on to *wildmanstevebrill.com* to find out more.

You may not want to dig up your own dandelion salad, but here's a list of other plants with medicinal properties that could help you out in a pinch.

Tufted grass: makes tea to soothe a stomachache

Chicory roots: for fevers and diarrhea

Milkweed: for fevers and diarrhea

Beach roses: for rheumatic pain and dysentery

Dogwood tree twigs: substitute for quinine

Bark of witch hazel: astringent

LAMP CODE

With the myriad roads and winding pathways in **Central Park**, it's all but impossible to gauge exactly where you are after even the briefest of strolls. You enter at, say, West 79th Street, but after wandering just a half hour you could wind up as far north as the Tennis Courts, or as far east as the Met, with no idea where you are in the city's grid.

But the park is actually sprinkled with geographical clues – you just have to know where to look. Along the entire Loop – that circuitous, two-lane artery – as well as on several smaller roads, every lamppost is marked with a vertical string of characters that look like serial numbers. Take a closer look: the series always starts with an "E" or "W" and is followed by two or three numbers. This handy inscription tells you exactly which cross-street you're currently at, including whether you're closer to the east or west side of the Park.

Photo: Brad Dunn

Bard Yard

Photo: Brad Dunn

VENICE, ANYONE?

Forget Mulberry Street and Arthur Avenue. There's a little Italy right in Central Park.

Daughter of Venice is 37 feet of pure Italian elegance. Imported from Venice in 1862, the handcrafted gondola glides across the waters off the Loeb Boathouse under the power of an authentic Venetian gondolier. For more than 140 years, the sleek, black craft has transported innumerable romantic couples — or just curious groups of up to six — back to the canals of Venice. You'll pass the rustic foliage of the Ramble, the magnificent Bethesda fountain, and one of the most stunning cast-iron bridges in Central Park. It's a delightful voyage, best taken at sunset, that runs you $30 per half-hour cruise. Though a widely unknown luxury, the gondola does require reservations. Call 212-517-2233.

"I know a bank whereon the wild thyme blows, / Where oxlips and the nodding violet grows, / Quite over-canopied with luscious woodbine, / With sweet musk-roses, and with eglantine." These lines from *A Midsummer Night's Dream* contain six of the 180 different types of flora mentioned in Shakespeare's collected works. They also describe one of the most pastoral, peaceful, and widely unknown places in New York.

The **Shakespeare Garden** on the west side of Central Park between 79th and 80th Streets is four acres of botanical bliss and solitude. Inaugurated in April 1916 to mark the 300th anniversary of the Bard's death, the garden is home to more than 120 species of plants, trees, shrubs, perennials and herbs — every name of which at one time flowed from the poet's quill. Bronze plaques that recount these botanical passages are staked next to their living counterparts throughout the hilly retreat.

Just as his words are brought to life on stage at the nearby Delacorte Theater, so too are Shakespeare's gardening efforts: many of the plants here sprung from seeds from his actual garden, which still thrives in Stratford-on-Avon. The most notable of these reincarnations is the 40-foot-tall white mulberry tree, which casts an enchanting shadow over the garden's entrance. It came from a graft of a tree that King James I presented to Shakespeare, and which the poet himself planted in 1602.

Nature-lovers say late summer and autumn are when the garden is at its best. Herbal aromas abound from ferns, poppies, mallows, and black-eyed Susans, and a fairy-tale-like array of color blooms with the asters, broom sedges, and ornamental grasses.

Because the Shakespeare Garden is frequently empty, it is a terrific place to rest and reflect. Best of all, it's free.

Photo: Spencer T Tucker/NYC Dept of Parks & Recreation

Photo: Spencer T Tucker/NYC Dept of Parks & Recreation

What's better than settling down on the lawn under the stars with a glass of wine and listening to some of the most talented musicians alive? Try all that and the admission is free.

A program known to many New Yorkers, but rarely realized by visitors, **Central Park SummerStage** holds dozens of free concerts and performing arts festivals every summer. Established in 1986, the organization provides a stage to contemporary, traditional, and emerging artists, while at the same inviting audiences to enjoy their work for free. The outdoor venue is located just north of Poet's Walk, and admission is first-come, first-served.

Celebrating every performing art from dance and stand-up comedy to spoken word and rock and roll, SummerStage has drawn more than 5 million people over the last 18 seasons. 2003's most popular concerts featured performers including Aimee Mann, Sonic Youth, Ani DiFranco, Jimmy Cliff, Colin Quinn, Ben Folds, Wilco, The Indigo Girls, Patty Griffin, The White Stripes, and Elvis Costello and The Impostors.

The program also hosts a wide range of World Music concerts, jazz vocalists, and big band and cabaret performances. Of course, a free outdoor venue in the middle of Central Park is going to have some rules, but they're pretty obvious: No chairs, pets, bicycles, rollerblades, coolers, flash cameras, or video or audio recording equipment.

Also: if you will be sipping wine, make sure it's in a plastic glass.

SEMANTICS IN THE PARK

Size comes down to definitions: the *city's* largest park is **Pelham Bay Park** on the northeastern frontier of the Bronx, at 2,764 acres, including a couple of golf courses and the colonial Bartow-Pell Mansion and gardens *(718-430-1890)*. The largest park *in the city*, though, is the **Jamaica Bay Wildlife Refuge** in far southeastern Queens, at a whopping 9,151 acres. It's run by the National Park Service *(718-318-4340)*, and much of it is, admittedly, marshland — but that's the point, since it serves as a major stop on the path of migratory birds.

For the record, Central Park is a measly 840 acres.

Photo: Spencer T Tucker/NYC Dept of Parks & Recreation

Speed-Boat Racer

Photo: Amy Della Rocca

NO EUROPEANS ALLOWED

If the park at LaGuardia Place and Houston Street looks a little shaggy and overgrown, that's the point: it's supposed to represent the landscape of Manhattan before European settlers arrived. Conceived by eco-artist Alan Sonfist in the 1960s and created in 1978, the **Time Landscape** contains only pre-colonial plants and trees, with non-native species rigorously excluded. In fact, people are rigorously excluded too, since there are no paths and the landscape is completely fenced off.

Not owning a boat shouldn't stop you from racing one; just think smaller.

New Yorkers who frequent Central Park near East 74 Street know all about the model yachts that ply the calm waters in front of the Krebs Memorial Boat House. But few realize that the **Central Park Model Yacht Club**, which brings many remote-controlled captains to the scene, was one of the first model yacht clubs in the country – and in 1916 established the standards and classes in which the tiny vessels still compete today.

You can try your navigational handiwork from March to November. Yacht rentals, as well as a bevy of refreshments and snacks, are available at the Boat House. Once you've got your tacking and veering down pat, then you're ready for the big time. The city's Parks and Recreation Department sponsors races on most Saturdays between 10 a.m. and 2 p.m. Good luck and smooth sailing.

The city's oldest park still bears a reminder of an ironic twist of fate that occurred during the American Revolution. What had once stood as a tribute to Britain's king was transformed, literally, into ammunition for the rebellion.

Since at least the 1680s, residents had used **Bowling Green** as both parade ground and marketplace. With its pleasant view of the harbor and proximity to the southern terminus of Broadway, the space was a natural site for an official public park. So, in 1733, three British loyalists leased Bowling Green from the city for the hefty rent of one peppercorn per year. The only stipulation was they had to improve the park with grass, trees, and a wooden fence "for the Beauty and Ornament of the Said Street as well as for the Recreation & Delight of the Inhabitants of this City."

This they did, and Bowling Green became one the city's most-treasured outdoor jewels. By 1770, the still British-backed municipal government decided to install the first statue in a city park: King George III mounted on a steed. The gilded lead monument was erected in the

PRESERVING THE VIEW

In New York real estate, few things are as compelling as a river view, and George W. Perkins knew that better than most — he drove the creation of the Palisades Interstate Park just to preserve the view from his Riverdale estate in the Bronx. Now a city-owned park and cultural center, **Wave Hill** has the most beautiful Hudson views around, as well as landscaped gardens, a greenhouse, art exhibits, environmental education and kids programs, a café, and two mansions.

Photo: Daniel Hood

center of the park, and in 1771 a wrought-iron fence was built around it to protect the king's tribute.

Everything went swimmingly until the Declaration of the Independence came out. On July 9, 1776, a public reading of the manifesto at City Hall Park inflamed the crowd and prompted thousands to march down to Bowling Green and hack the statue of George III to pieces. Revolutionary soldiers then recast the lead fragments into musket balls, which were used a few months later in the Battle of Long Island (in present-day Prospect Park). It was rumored that the bullets from the king's statue killed at least 400 Redcoats.

The British were finally forced to leave New York on Nov. 25, 1783, which was dubbed Evacuation Day. The new city government expanded the parks downtown, put in more trees, planted gardens, and installed new statues. In Bowling Green, city administrators decided to leave the wrought-iron fence that once protected George III's monument as a reminder of the Revolution. The fence still stands today as one of the oldest New York landmarks.

Since it was established in 1844, the estate has hosted more than its share of the famous: Teddy Roosevelt spent part of his childhood there (and in 1900 helped Perkins push through Palisades Park), while Mark Twain, Charles Darwin, T.H. Huxley, and Arturo Toscanini all were either guests or renters. If you're feeling flush, you can rent it, too, for corporate conferences and private events like weddings. There is a small fee for regular admission, but it's well worth it for the uncrowded tranquility. 675 W. 252nd St., at Independence Ave., the Bronx; 718-549-3200; wavehill.org

Recharging the Battery

For decades the largest park in lower Manhattan was more pavement than plant life. But thanks to an $8 million state grant in 2003, the 23-acre **Battery Park** got a much-needed infusion of flora. The centerpiece of the vegetation renovation was the creation of the Gardens of Remembrance in the Battery, a wonderful sea of flowers that stretches 10,000 square feet. Designed by Dutch horticulturalist Piet Oudolf, the garden includes hostas, phlox, salvia, asters, and many other perennials that bloom in a crescendo of wild color in autumn. Phase Two of the project, which is still underway, calls for tearing up more than 30,000 square feet of asphalt and replacing it with smaller gardens and tables and chairs. Finally, the Battery Conservancy plans to build a carousel similar to the one in Central Park, as well as a 80-foot-long wading fountain where children can play.

New attention was paid to Battery Park after 9/11, when the globe statue that stood at the World Trade Center was installed in the park as a memorial. Hundreds of thousands of commuters pass through the area every day.

In a Pear Tree

Stop by Kiehl's pharmacy at the northeast corner of Third Avenue and 13th Street and you might notice an unusual tree jutting out of the sidewalk. If you happen to be a botanist, you will recognize it as a pear tree. If you happen to be a New York City historian, you'll recognize it as the embodiment of a 350-year-old legacy.

This corner is the alleged site of the **Stuyvesant Pear Tree**, which was considered the oldest tree in Manhattan until its grisly, untimely end. The story goes that New Amsterdam Governor Peter Stuyvesant brought the tree back from the Netherlands and planted it with his own hands on this spot in 1647. It was the crown jewel of his giant orchard in what is now the East Village.

As Manhattan's grid took shape, the spot became known as "Pear Tree Corner," and the tree far outlasted the man who planted it. In fact, it went on growing in that spot for two centuries. Local residents loved the pear tree, and fearing for its life amid the growing hustle and bustle, they enclosed it behind a tall iron fence. But sadly, not even iron could stave off fate: in 1857, two horse-drawn wagons collided head-on and plowed into the 210-year-old pear tree. It did not long survive the accident.

The store at Third Avenue and 13th Street, which in the 1850s was called the Pear Tree Pharmacy, later changed its name to Kiehl's, which still stands today. In 2003, Kiehl's asked the city to establish a new "Pear Tree Corner." Parks officials accepted and Kiehl's celebrated the rebirth of this historic spot by installing a timeline that runs across its three storefronts and highlights the interesting events that have taken place in the world since Stuyvesant's pear tree fell and the new one was planted.

Getting Some Perspective

The city can be a little claustrophobic, what with all those canyons, so sometimes you need a little distance – or just a spot for a good picture of the skyline.

The Brooklyn Promenade
Simply the best views of downtown Manhattan. Built directly over the Brooklyn-Queens Expressway in Brooklyn Heights, just south of the Brooklyn Bridge, it's a mighty relaxing (and potentially romantic) place, as well as a popular spot for watching Fourth of July and New Year's Eve fireworks on the East River.

Gantry Plaza State Park

Midtown Manhattan from the east (great for the Chrysler Building, the Empire State, and particularly the U.N.). The "Gantry," in case you're wondering, is from two railroad loading gantries that are part of the park.

49th Ave. and the East River, Long Island City, Queens

Photo: Daniel Hood

Pier A Park and Sinatra Park

Great views of downtown Manhattan from the west, from Hoboken, N.J.

Hamilton Park

This park in Weehawken, N.J., has great views of Manhattan from the west — and it commemorates the spot where Aaron Burr killed Alexander Hamilton in a duel in 1804. (Weehawken was a popular spot for that sort of thing, because duelling had been outlawed in New York.)

Don't Mind the Smell

Photo: Daniel Hood

It sounds like a win-win situation: Fend off the cries of environmental racism that arose from locating a sewage treatment plant right next to a poor, ethnic neighborhood like West Harlem by offering to put a park on top of it for local residents to use. (Wealthier, whiter folks had already nixed the original site for the plant, at the end of West 72nd Street.)

Urban design experts rejoiced. When the North River Wastewater Treatment Plant was completed in 1986, the city was finally able to stop pumping raw sewage into the Hudson, and when the $129 million **Riverbank State Park** on the plant's roof was completed in 1983, West Harlem's mostly poor, mostly black and Latino residents were presented with a 28-acre gem complete with a covered skating rink, an indoor pool, basketball and volleyball courts, a track, a carousel, and spectacular views of the Hudson River. The problem was, the park stank.

Design flaws in the plant, which stretches from 137th Street to 145th Street, caused great clouds of sewage funk to sweep in off the Hudson. Needless to say, West Harlemites were not pleased. Engineers sprang into action, and while the funk lingered through 1993 and 1994, they finally devised a $55 million plan to fix the smell — or at least most of it. Whiffs of chlorine and sewage still escape from the plant from time to time, and local environmental action groups are concerned about elevated levels of asthma in the area, but the park is by and large a success: over 4 million people a year use it (making it the second-busiest state park in New York State), the facilities really are great, and the views of the river are second to none. Just don't go on hot, windy days.

Saving the High Line

For a long time, the only people who liked the **High Line** were the pigeons infesting its underbelly and the fence-hopping urban archaeologists who braved steep fines and angry railroad guards to climb up onto the elevated railroad tracks that run from the train yards at 33rd Street down Tenth Avenue and Washington Street into the Meat-Packing District, ending at Gansevoort.

Built by Robert Moses in 1934 to elevate dangerous rail traffic off Tenth (where pedestrians were so regularly mown down by freight trains that the street was called "Death Avenue"), the High Line declined with the rise of trucking in the 1950s, and saw its last train in 1980. The structure was left standing, to the delight of trespassing explorers and the chagrin of local property owners, who hoped to cash in on the development rights to a High-Line-free Tenth Avenue, and of Mayor Giuliani, who fought to have the viaduct torn down right up to the end of his term in 2001.

That he failed was due, in no small part, to the efforts of writer Joshua David and artist Robert Hammond. Inspired – and a little obsessed – by the abandoned line and its freight of wildflowers, the two men founded the nonprofit group Friends of the High Line (highline.org) in 1999 to promote the idea of rehabilitating the double-bed tracks into a park in the sky. Despite Rudy's best efforts, the line endured, and FHL found supporters among artists, local businesses, residents, politicians, and a list of celebrities including Edward Norton, Martha Stewart, Kevin Bacon, Sandra Bernhard, Glenn Close, Todd Oldham, and writer Sebastian Junger (who happens to co-own a restaurant in the neighborhood).

Most crucial, though, may have been Mayor Bloomberg, who came out early in support of the idea. With backing from City Hall, FHL was able to hold a competition to develop proposals for the design of the park, and by 2003 had secured $15 million of the $40 million they estimate it will take to refurbish the High Line. But many a worthy scheme has gone off track in New York, so supporters are keeping their fingers crossed. In the meantime, FHL is careful to note, the High Line is off limits to all but railroad personnel....

Photo: Daniel Hood

CALLING ALL DARING YOUNG MEN

"Forget fear," says **Trapeze School New York**, but when you're a first-timer hanging by your knees from a bar above Hudson River Park, that seems an unlikely idea – as unlikely, in fact, as the idea that there should be a trapeze school on the far west side of Tribeca. But there it is: a set of towers and trapezes, complete with safety net, just off the West Side Highway between Vestry and Desbrosses Streets. Founded in 2001, TSNY teaches all levels of flying for all ages from six up, and offers group and corporate events. Best of all, they have a perfect safety record, so go ahead – forget fear. (trapezeschool.com)

Photo: Trapeze School New York

GIDDY UP

Hansom cab drivers and mounted police aren't the only ones allowed to leave steaming piles of horse manure everywhere they go. Now you can, too.

In fact, New York City lays claim to the oldest continuously operated stable in the United States: the **Claremont Riding Academy** on the Upper West Side. Just head up to Amsterdam Avenue and 89th Street, and follow your nose. There are more than 100 steeds champing at the bit to take you on a galloping tour of Central Park. Primarily a riding school, Claremont's 15 instructors specialize in dressage and hunt seat equitation, but also offer lessons in both saddle seat and side saddle riding. If you already know your way around the reins, you can sign up for one of the Academy's signature events: the Christmas Ride or the Summer Solstice Ride. But if you find the hourly rates too pricey, you could always take the same amount to Belmont and try to win enough for lessons.

Scaler's Delight

Though no doubt better known for its corporate climbing, New York City also has tons of routes to offer the **rock climber** – ace and amateur alike. There are cliffs along the Harlem River, large boulders near the Botanical Garden in the Bronx, and steep rock faces near Columbia University. Of course, if you consider all the man-made structures, there is an endless supply of "buildering" routes – notably the large rock walls throughout Fort Tryon and Riverside Parks. Many climbers practice their handiwork on the stone facades near the 79th Street Boat Basin and then throw back a beer or two at the outdoor pub.

But if you prefer your climbs natural, there's plenty of glaciated metamorphic rock in Central Park alone to lure the most veteran of spider-men and women. Be warned, however: some spots can be climbed legally, while others may get you thrown out of the park. If the prospect of getting caught on an illegal ascent adds some thrill, just make sure you're prepared to pay a fine. The requisite resource for getting started is "A Climber's Guide to Popular Manhattan Boulder Problems," published by *ClimbNYC.com*, and available free at their Web site.

If you want to meet fellow climbers and get initiated into this underground society, go immediately to Rat Rock, which is actually two large boulders that lie near the large children's playground in the extreme southwest corner of the Park. (Officially it's called

Umpire Rock, but climbers have renamed it for its furrier, bewhiskered tenants.)

In addition to offering the most popular climbs in the city, Rat Rock has some of the hardest bouldering problems you'll find. On a beautiful day, you may be put off by the crowds that gather here, but you're guaranteed to connect with local pros who can point you in new directions.

If you're feeling lucky, you can attempt what ClimbNYC calls the most difficult inner-urban free climbs in the world: The overhanging arch on the North Wall at Belvedere Castle. The group not only suggests that you climb it at night to avoid the authorities, they say it hasn't been climbed successfully since 1985. Try it at your own risk.

Midnight Run

Instead of running up a bar tab on New Year's Eve, more and more people are running up and down Central Park in a four-mile race that begins at the stroke of midnight.

The **New Year's Eve Midnight Run**, hosted by the New York Road Runners Club, is a great way to get an early jump on your New Year's resolutions. You get a good dose of exercise, you cut out the booze (the event is non-alcoholic), and, with admission at only $25, you save yourself a lot of cash that otherwise would have been spent in the barroom. As the event's popularity has increased over the years, runners have turned the race into a mini-Halloween parade by showing up in costumes that run the gamut from the Statue of Liberty to semi-naked, and usually shivering, Baby New Years.

The party gets started at 10 p.m., with live music and dancing at the Park Bandshell near the 72nd Street Transverse. At about 11:30 p.m., runners start massing near Tavern on the Green for the four-mile jaunt. Then, when the ball drops in nearby Times Square, the race begins. Along the way, you can refresh yourself with free paper cups of champagne (again, non-alcoholic). Though the race is not exactly official – nobody will tell you where you rank – you can check your time on the huge clock at the finish line.

Best of all, at the last few Midnight Runs, racers were given their first free breakfast of the year. Representatives from Jimmy Dean handed out eggs, sausages, and other protein-laden grub in the Tavern on the Green parking lot.

Photo: Spencer T Tucker/NYC Dept of Parks & Recreation

Skate Parks

Apart from all those tasty corporate plazas, all of Central Park, and, of course, the skate rat mecca around Alamo at Astor Place, the city offers some more structured locations for skateboarders and roller-bladers. Note that all city park locations require protective gear.

Forest Park Skate Park

A launch ramp, a grinding rail, a quarter pipe, a table top, a wedge, and a grinding ledge.
Forest Park, by Greenhouse basketball courts, Woodhaven Blvd. near Myrtle Ave., Queens

Photo: Spencer T Tucker/NYC Dept of Parks & Recreation

Hudson River Park Skate Park

A bowl, a street course, a mini half-pipe, and an amazing view of the Hudson.
Hudson River Park, bet. Pier 26 and Pier 32, near Vestry St.

Millennium Skate Park

A recent development — 14,000 sq. ft. of bowls, ramps, and rails for all varieties of skate rat.
Owl's Head Park, 68th St. and Colonial Rd., Bay Ridge, Brooklyn

Mullaly Skate Park

Considered the city's first, and recently rebuilt with help from Snapple, this park has a six-foot mini, a spine, a six-foot launch box, and an assortment of quarters.
E. 164th St., at Jerome and River Aves., the Bronx

Riverside Skate Park

Five ramps, including half pipes, quarter pipes, and rails.
Riverside Park, 108th St. and Riverside Drive, lower level

Photo: Spencer T Tucker/NYC Dept of Parks & Recreation

There's no question that New York's most gruelling race is the annual Marathon, organized by the **New York Road Runners Club**. What started in 1970 with a cadre of serious runners doing four or so laps around Central Park got a big bump during the Bicentennial celebrations of 1976, when the course was expanded to its current round of all five boroughs (though it spends as little time as possible in Staten Island and the Bronx). Nowadays, the race attracts 30,000 runners, 12,000 volunteers, and a couple of million spectators, and turns Central Park into the largest repository of blood-filled sneakers in the world.

But the Road Runners organize another race that we like even better — the Empire State Building Run-Up, which is exactly what it sounds like: a race from the lobby of the ESB up 1,576 steps to the 86th floor. The invitational event takes place in February, and the record time is held by five-time champ Paul Crake, a twenty-something Australian, who, at 9:33, is also the only runner to get to the top in under 10 minutes.

For those who don't want to end their races wheezing at high altitudes or vomiting by Tavern on the Green, the NYRR runs a whole slate of walking and running events, including a New Year's Eve Run (see opposite page). Plus, they offer changing rooms, facilities, toilets, and a running shop right near Central Park.
9 East 89th St., bet. Madison and 5th; nyrrc.org; 212-860-4455

Cricket in Times Square?

Photo: Spencer T Tucker/NYC Dept of Parks & Recreation

Not the insect from the classic children's book – the impenetrable English game **cricket** that is, by some measures, the city's fastest growing sport. Immigrants from Pakistan, India, and the Caribbean brought the game here in the 1980s, and you can watch them bowling googlies and defending wickets in their whites on most weekends in good weather in all five boroughs (the City Parks Department has a full list of pitches at nycparks.gov, though they insist on calling them "fields"). The New York/New Jersey area is home to seven adult leagues, a junior league, and almost a quarter of the U.S.'s 10,000 serious players.

The epicenter of the New York cricket world is Van Cortlandt Park in the Bronx, which has over a dozen pitches available, and there's a new 17-acre cricket center in Spring Creek Park near Jamaica Bay in Brooklyn, but to get suited up, you'll want to head to Queens, to **Singh's Sporting Goods** *(100-06 101 Ave., bet. 100th and 101st Sts., Ozone Park, Queens; 718-925-9058; singhsports.com)*, the unofficial headquarters of New York cricket, which sells all the bats and padding and other paraphernalia you'll need.

By the way, though the game seems like a newcomer, it has deep roots: the first recorded match took place in 1751, on the site of the Fulton Fish Market, and some cricket historians claim that the first-ever international match took place in 1844 on 31st Street, between the U.S. and Canada.

Photo: Spencer T Tucker/NYC Dept of Parks & Recreation

EXTREME MAKEOVER, CARNY EDITION

In New York, the fine line between nostalgia and misery, between camp and grunge, between sideshow fun and carny creepy runs right through **Coney Island**.

In the early 1900s, Coney Island's complex of amusement parks – Sea Lion Park, Steeplechase, Dreamland, Luna Park, and others – drew over 500,000 mostly working-class New Yorkers a day for 5-cent hotdogs, swimming, freak shows, and some of the most bruising, stomach-churning carnival rides ever. Attendance hit over a million a day by the time the subway reached Stilwell Avenue in 1919, but the Depression hit Coney hard, and it entered a long decline from which it is still struggling to recover.

Old-Timers

Photo: Daniel Hood

The **Wonder Wheel** at Deno's Wonderland still offers great views in all directions, the original **Nathan's Famous** still slings its classic dogs, you can still stroll the old boardwalk or go for a swim, and the barkers will gladly take your money for a ring toss.

For our money, the best Coney has to offer is Astroland's **Cyclone**, which roller-coaster enthusiasts consider one of the best in the world. Built in 1927, this creaking wooden monster still gives a ride that's like a kick in the teeth, and is more terrifying than most modern coasters precisely because it's so old – you keep waiting for it to collapse, and we find it hard to believe that some of those sharp turns and drops would pass muster with 21st-century safety inspectors. Five bucks for your first ride may be a little steep, but they knock a dollar off your next ride if you stay in the car.

Recent boosterism is beginning to clean the place up – the new Keyspan Park for minor league baseball and the MTA's ongoing $250 million renovation of the Stilwell Avenue-Coney Island Terminal being the two most prominent examples – but there's still a gritty, slightly dangerous feel to the place. It's like Times Square in mid-facelift, but with carnies instead of prostitutes, and some grand old survivors.

Photo: Daniel Hood

The Least Dangerous Game

Photo: Daniel Hood

If the only thing holding you back from a game of paintball is the part where you get shot at, Coney has the game for you: **"Shoot the Freak."** The freak in this game, which opened in 2002, is some poor actor in a helmet and football pads dodging around in a sunken pit filled with barely adequate cover, while sadistic bastards like you pump paintball after paintball down on his head. We can't guarantee that a game this perfect will last, so get there fast.

Freak Shows

If you'd rather watch freaks than shoot them, there's the **Coney Island Circus Sideshow** for illustrated men, fire eaters, and more, and the **Coney Island Museum** has exhibits on the history of the area, as well occasional movie screenings. If you want to be a freak, the group that runs those also has a **Sideshow School** that'll teach you how to swallow swords and charm snakes. *(All at 1208 Surf Ave., near W. 12th St., Coney Island; 718-372-5159; coneyislandusa.com)*

We will pass up the obvious segue, and simply say that if you mixed the homey neighborliness of a small-town Fourth of July celebration with the worst excesses of a Greenwich Village Halloween, you still wouldn't touch the weird fun of the annual **Mermaid Parade** on Surf Avenue in the last week of June (rain or shine). Since anyone in costume can participate, you'll see the cutest little kids in mermaid costumes, and then transvestites in nothing but fish-scale glitter. It's great. One thought, though: when it comes to revealing outfits on Brooklynites who've been inside on the couch all winter, sometimes more is more.

Logo Legends

Outsiders love to complain that the **Yankees** are nothing but money and arrogance – buying great players, wearing pinstripes like bankers, refusing to put player's names on their jerseys (it's up to you to know who they are). Fans will tell you otherwise, but the origin of one of the team's most enduring icons, the "interlocking" NY symbol, doesn't help their case: in 1909, when the Yankees were still known as the Highlanders, the team lifted the logo from, of all things, a medal of honor created in 1877 by designer Louis B. Tiffany to honor John McDowell, the first New York policeman to be shot in the line of duty.

Pool Halls

Where did Paul Newman go in *The Hustler* to make it big? That's right, New York: home to the best, oldest pool halls in the country. If you can't find a game of 9-ball here at 3 a.m. on a Sunday night, you won't find it any-where. Here's the short list of places to practice your masse (just don't tear the felt).

THE BEST

Amsterdam Billiard Club
Excellent dessert menu and beverage bar. Frequent cameos by Jerry Seinfeld, Eric Clapton, and other pool-shark celebs.
344 Amsterdam Ave., bet. 76th and 77th Sts., 212-496-8180; 210 E. 86th St., bet. Lexington and Third Aves., 212-570-4545

Chelsea Bar and Billiards
Large loft space with dozens of pool tables, including billiards and snooker. Open seven days a week, 24 hours a day
54 W. 21st St., bet. Fifth and Sixth Aves.; 212-989-0096

Corner Billiards
Cozy atmosphere with its own micro brewery. Popular with the NYU crowd.
85 Fourth Ave., at 11th St.; 212-995-1314

Mini-Mets and Baby Bombers

Photo: Brooklyn Cyclones

THE REST

Broadway Billiards

10 E. 21st St.; 212-388-1582

Boulevard Billiards & Games

2256 Seventh Ave.; 212-283-8707

Cafe Billiard Luz

2153 Amsterdam Ave.;
212-740-6920

Fat Cat Billiards

75 Christopher St.; 212-675-6056

Grand Billiard & Cafe

90 Eldridge St.; 212-431-9232

Haeum Chung

566 W. 181st St.; 212-928-8235

Mammoth Billiards

114 W. 26th St.; 212-675-2626

It's a good time to be a baseball fan in New York. Yankees-Mets matchups, which used to be reserved to an always-hoped-for Subways Series, are now a staple of inter-league play. And if you can't get tickets to those, you can watch their farm league teams, the **Brooklyn Cyclones** and the **Staten Island Yankees**, fight it out in a whole slew of regular season games in the McNamara Division of the New York/Penn League.

Both teams started out in 2001, in new stadiums that have done a lot for their neighborhoods. The Cyclones' **KeySpan Park** *(1904 Surf Ave., bet. W. 17th and W. 19th Sts.; 718-449-TIXS; brooklyncyclones.com)* is one of the cornerstones of the revitalization of Coney Island, while the fantastic views from the Baby Bombers' **Richmond County Bank Ballpark** *(75 Richmond Terrace, Staten Island; 718-698-9265; siyanks.com)* have created yet another reason to take the Staten Island Ferry. Best of all, the tickets are much cheaper than at Shea or Yankee Stadium — and they're available.

Photo: Spencer T Tucker/NYC Dept of Parks & Recreation

There are lots of really cool things to do in New York, and lots of free things, but there aren't a lot of really cool free things. Free kayaking in the Hudson is one of them.

Yes, *free*, and yes, the *Hudson*. Thank (or wonder about the sanity of) the **Downtown Boathouse**, a group of kayak-mad volunteers that makes its fleet of kayaks available *for free* during the warm months at three locations on the West Side. All you have to do is show up and sign a waiver, and pretty soon you're out in the river with a wet butt, digging the swell.

OK, it's a little more complicated than that, but not much. You have to know how to swim; you have to wear a life jacket; and it's wise to listen to the volunteer staff's safety tips and kayaking instructions. You're also required to stay within the designated embayment near the shore, but when you're sitting on a plastic sliver fighting the current, you'll start to realize how big those embayments are. (The group also runs longer expeditions – still free, mind you – up and down the river for more experienced kayakers.) You will get wet: either leave valuables at home, or bring a lock for the lockers they make available. Last, and most important, they do have limited hours and it can get pretty busy, so check the times and go early; since they started in 1995, the Boathouse has put over 12,000 people in the water, and they aim to do more.

Besides the walk-up kayaking, the Boathouse also holds evening classes and has a kayak polo program. Donations are accepted, but there's no pressure. Seriously. It's *free*.
Pier 26 at North Moore St.; Pier 64 at W. 24th St.; W. 70th St. in Riverside Park; 646-613-0375; downtownboathouse.org

Watercraft, Watercraft Everywhere

If you still can't wrap your mind around the whole free thing, the decade-long opening up of the city to its own waterfront has created a slew of places where you can rent all sorts of floatables.

Chelsea Piers
Kayak and sailboat rentals, tours, and lessons.
W. 23rd St., on the river;
212-336-6666

The Boat Livery
Motor- and rowboat rentals.
663 City Island Ave., City Island, the Bronx; 718-885-1843

Manhattan Kayak Co.
Rentals, tours, and instructions.
Pier 63, at W. 23rd St. (Chelsea Piers); 212-924-1788

Two Rivers Run Through It

Photo: Spencer T Tucker/NYC Dept of Parks & Recreation

The New York Sailing Center & Yacht Club

Sailing lessons and rentals.
560 Minneford Ave., City Island, the Bronx; 718-885-0335

Offshore Sailing School

Sailing lessons and rentals.
Chelsea Piers, at W. 23rd St.; Liberty Landing Marina, Jersey City, N.J.; 888-454-8002

Smitty's Boat Rental

Motorized skiffs on Jamaica Bay.
E. 9th and Lanark Rds., Broad Channel Island, Queens; 718-945-2642

Sure, the East River is a notorious spot for dumping bodies, and the Hudson River was all but sterilized by chemical pollution in the late 1980s. But today, thanks to an incredible marine rejuvenation, you can catch a healthy 20-pound sturgeon while fishing just blocks away from the tallest skyscrapers in the world.

Urban fishing has grown about as fast as the state's environmental regulations over the past decade. As the levels of PCBs go down, the waters around Manhattan have attracted stripers, blues, weakfish, and bass. In fact, in New York Harbor – where the Hudson and East Rivers unite – more than 200 species of marine life frolic below the network of ferry routes and shipping lanes. If you have equipment, you can go down anytime to almost any pier and drop in a line. The city, however, only allows you to keep one fish per person per day. But this is a rule that is, let's just say, extremely difficult to enforce.

The Harlem Meer in the northeast corner of Central Park is a great place to take your kids fishing in the city. The Central Park Conservancy provides poles, bait, and instruction for pulling big bass out of the 11-acre lake. If want to play it cheap, the park will even loan you bamboo poles for free. All fish, however, must be released.

Harlem Meer has its advantages over fishing the rivers – especially during what the Coast Guard calls "Floaters Week" in late April or early May. This uniquely New York phenomenon occurs when the rivers warm up and bacterial activity bloats the previous winter's murders and suicides. In macabre crescendo, body after body rises to the surface. Some anglers say the annual cadaver bloom actually marks the start of the season: they claim the stripers don't start biting until the bodies start floating.

Washington Square Boneyard

Photo: Daniel Hood

Below the fountain and majestic arch, below the jugglers, chess players, and folk singers, below one of Manhattan's most celebrated parks lie the remains of more than a thousand victims of yellow fever.

Washington Square Park, in the heart of Greenwich Village, was established atop a massive Potter's Field that received the casualties of two violent epidemics about 200 years ago. When the city first opened the public burial ground in 1797, during an outbreak of yellow fever, the area that would become the Village was still largely uninhabited. But by 1822, when the disease struck again, many people had settled in the area. This time the death count was even higher. By 1825, the burial ground hit its capacity and the city officially closed it.

It was the residents of that early Greenwich Village, many of them immigrants who had lost someone in the epidemic, who took the first step in transforming the potter's field into the vibrant park that it is today: instead of leaving it a place of death, they took all the dirt they had dug up to make streets, covered the burial ground again, and planted trees.

Bowling

You might not guess by looking at it, but New York just might be the bowling capital of the world. Check out this list of lanes and lawns.

AMF Chelsea Piers Lanes

40 lanes, with night bowling parties featuring black lights, Day-Glo pins, music, and fog machines.
Chelsea Piers, bet. Pier 59 and 60, at 23rd St and the Hudson River; 212-835-2695

Bowlmor Lanes

The Greenwich Village legend.
110 University Pl., bet. 12th and 13th Sts.; 212-255-8188

Leisure Time Bowling Center and Cocktail Lounge

Port Authority Bus Terminal, Eighth Ave. at 41st St.; 212-268-6909

The New York Lawn Bowling Club

Join the club for $35 a year, and all equipment and lessons are free.
Central Park, near W. 69th St. pedestrian entrance; 212-345-5573 or 212-724-1042

Golf Courses

No one's yet figured out how to run links through Central Park, but the City Parks & Recreation Department maintains a pretty large number of public courses in the outer boroughs, as well as driving ranges in all five (Manhattan's is on Randall's Island). They see a lot of play, and generally involve a long trip by subway or car, but the price is right — between $25 and $35 for 18 holes, depending on time of day and week. You can reserve tee times for some of them online at *nycgovparks.org*, under Things to Do.

BRONX

After a long battle with environmentalists and community groups, a Jack Nicklaus-designed course is now scheduled to open in 2005, on an old landfill in Ferry Point, near the Whitestone Bridge.

Van Cortlandt Park

The country's oldest public golf course, created in 1895.
Bailey Ave. and Van Cortlandt Park South; 718-543-4595

A Rose for Noses

Photo: Cranford Rose Garden,
Courtesy Brooklyn Botanic Garden

Given that flowers are as beloved for their smell as for their visual beauty, it's surprising that places like the Fragrance Garden at the **Brooklyn Botanic Garden** aren't more common: it's the first in the country designed specifically for the blind. The intimate garden is divided into different categories of smell, as well as a section full of differently textured plants that visitors are meant to touch, with Braille plaques identifying all the flora.

Innovative as the Fragrance Garden is, the rest of the BBG is pretty impressive too, particularly the elegant Japanese Hill-and-Pond Garden and the enormous Cranford Rose Garden.
1000 Washington Ave., near Eastern Pkwy., Brooklyn; 718-623-7200; bbg.org

Photo: Japanese Hill-and-Pond Garden,
Courtesy Brooklyn Botanic Garden

Shakespeare 1, Environment 0

Call it an act of misguided Bardolatry: in the 1880s, wealthy New York drug manufacturer **Eugene Schieffelin** decided that what America lacked was a sample of every songbird mentioned in Shakespeare's works, and set out to correct the situation by releasing immigrant birds in Central Park. His first attempts with thrushes, skylarks, and chaffinches didn't come to much, as the birds didn't adapt well to the New World.

In 1890, though, he hit ornithological paydirt when he released a large number of starlings in the park. Starlings get a one-line mention in *Henry IV Part I*; more importantly, they're tough, scrappy omnivores, and squatters *par excellence*. Within the year, a colony was roosting under the eaves of the American Museum of Natural History, causing all sorts of cleaning problems; within five years they blanketed Manhattan; and after that there was no stopping them.

From an original population of about 100, there are now over 200 million starlings in North America, pushing out native bird populations and irritating municipal authorities from Cincinnati to Vancouver. And Schieffelin, who only wanted to bring a little touch of Shakespeare to New York, is widely reviled in environmental circles as a one-man eco-disaster.

Go Galan!

Photo: Spencer T Tucker/NYC Dept of Parks & Recreation

Everyone knows that New York has tons of pigeons. What's less well known is that the city has a fair number of **hawks** – they like to nest atop the tall buildings lining Central Park West, in particular – and that hawks hate pigeons as much as the rest of us. It seemed appropriate to take advantage of this natural enmity, therefore, by running a trial program in Bryant Park on 42nd Street, where trained hawks were used to keep down the pigeon and rat population. Apparently, it worked very well, until a hawk named Galan mistook a parkgoer's pet chihuahua for prey, and tried to tear the dog apart. The chihuahua survived, but the program was hastily shelved. We suggest that Galan simply had a broader definition of rodent.

Mosholu
3700 Jerome Ave. and Bainbridge Ave.; 718-655-9164

Pelham/Split Rock
Shore Road, north of Bartow Circle; 718-885-1258

BROOKLYN

Dyker Beach
Seventh Ave. and 86th Street; 718-836-9722

Marine Park
2880 Flatbush Ave., near Belt Parkway; 718-338-7149

QUEENS
Queens also has two pitch & putt courses, one in Flushing Meadows Corona Park (718-271-8182) and one at Breezy Point in Jacob Riis Park (718-474-1623).

Forest Park
101 Forest Park Drive; 718-296-0999

Religious Branch

Photo: Amy Della Rocca

Clearview
202-12 Willets Point Blvd.;
718-229-2570

Douglaston
6320 Marathon Parkway;
718-428-1617

Kissena
164-15 Booth Memorial Ave.;
718-939-4594

STATEN ISLAND

LaTourette
1001 Richmond Hill Road;
718-351-1889

Silver Lake
915 Victory Blvd., near Forest Ave.;
718-447-5686

South Shore
200 Huguenot Ave.; 718-984-0101

Tompkins Square Park may be forever branded by the violent riots and heroin trade of the late 1980s, but few visitors to this East Village playground know that a peace-loving religion first entered the western world here – right under an elm tree that still thrives today.

In 1966, the spiritual leader Bhaktivedanta Swami Srila Prabhupada led his followers in a two-hour chant of the 16-word Hare Krishna mantra. They recited the sacred lines, danced, played cymbals, tambourines, and drums, and attracted the curiosity of hundreds of park visitors. Beat poet Allen Ginsburg, who lived around the corner, actually took part in the chant. It was the first time in history the ritual was performed outside India. Dancing in the shadow of a giant American Elm, the group decided the old tree was sacred. The East Village in the 1960s was ripe for a peaceful, optimistic religion, and beats, folkies, and hippies filled the fledgling movement with devoted members.

Prabhupada, who went on to found the International Society for Krishna Consciousness at a storefront on nearby Second Avenue, died in 1977. To commemorate his work, as well as the birth of Hare Krishna in the western hemisphere, Mayor Rudy Giuliani installed a plaque at the base of the ancient American elm in 2001.

Let's put it this way: only seven entire states have as many restaurants as there are in New York City alone. In fact, according to the New York Restaurant Association, there are over 23,000 "food service establishments" in the five boroughs. That's a whole lot of places to eat — though be warned: four out of five of them close or change hands within five years of opening. Still, with the average apartment kitchen measuring about the same as a shoebox, and so many choices, why wouldn't you want to eat out? Well....

For Your Health

One of the most fascinating, repulsive, wish-you-hadn't-known-about-it secrets of the city's dining world is actually not a restaurant at all. It's a Web site.

The **New York City Department of Health and Mental Hygiene** operates an amazing, free service on the Web: It posts current restaurant inspection results on every eatery in town. Once you start clicking through the reports at *nyc.gov/html/doh/html/rii/ index.html*, you might never stop.

As part of the city's stringent health code, inspectors go in and test for just about everything: rats, chemicals, spoiled food, unsanitary kitchens, you name it. Restaurants that don't pass get three months to clean up their act; if nothing changes, they're out of business.

But what a collection of comments these inspectors make. Standard entries include "Food from unapproved or unknown source, spoiled, adulterated, or home canned," "Hot food not held at or above 140°F," and "Evidence of roaches or live roaches present in facility." (Mice, rats, and flies are also frequently interjected in this entry.) The site not only lists the date of the last inspection and the inspector's comments, but also whether the restaurant passed the exam or if it flat-out failed. Once you've checked out your local regulars, it's hard to stop investigating.

One of our favorite bars in the city, which out of respect we won't name, had the comment: "Live animal present in food storage, preparation or service area. Citation may include and is not limited to cockroaches, flies, mice, rats, cats, and dogs." That doesn't sound good.

Here's a good one we found at another favorite spot: "Toxic chemical improperly labeled, stored or used so that contamination of food may occur." You have to love this one: "Harmful, noxious gas or vapor detected."

Despite all the surprise and disgust we felt learning about the darker sides of our local restaurants, we learned happily that of all the dinner-serving pubs on our all-time favorites list, only one had a completely clean bill of health, which we're happy to name: O'Lunney's Times Square Pub on West 46th Street between Sixth and Seventh Avenues.

Photo: Daniel Hood

Power Breakfasts

By lunchtime, all the power is gone: in these uncertain times, the movers and shakers are getting up very early.

Fifty Seven Fifty Seven
The Four Seasons Hotel's dining room. *57 E. 57th St., bet. Madison and Park Aves.; 212-758-5757*

Michael's Restaurant
Wall-to-wall media moguls, stars, and midtown players. *24 W. 55th St., bet. Fifth and Sixth Aves.; 212-767-0555*

14 Wall Street
Captains of finance start the day in J.P. Morgan's old penthouse. *14 Wall St., 31st floor, bet. Broadway and New St.; 212-233-2780*

540 Park Restaurant
The Regency Hotel makes an elegant claim to being the originator of the power breakfast. *540 Park Ave., at 61st St., in the Regency Hotel; 212-339-4050*

It really wouldn't be right to start a discussion of New York restaurants with anything other than **Delmonico's**. Appalled by the state of cuisine in the New World, the Swiss immigrant Delmonico Brothers started serving meals in their confectioner's shop in the late 1820s. Two things made the place special: the high quality of the food, and the fact that you could order what you wanted, not whatever the cook happened to have made. It was, in fact, New York's (and America's) first restaurant, with its first written menu – and it was a huge success. From its starting point at 23 William Street, the Delmonico empire spread north, eventually encompassing outposts all over downtown, as far north as 26th Street, and, perhaps most famously, in a giant palace of a place on 14th and Fifth.

Delmonico's was more than just popular – it was innovative. The restaurants' chefs set trends the entire country followed, inventing Oysters Rockefeller, naming and popularizing Baked Alaska (in 1867, after the U.S. bought the territory), and, we're told, creating Eggs Benedict (supposedly for regulars Mr. and Mrs. Benedict, who wanted something different).

But the restaurants' most interesting culinary invention didn't come from one of their chefs – it came from a customer. Sea trader Ben Wenberg was a favored regular at the 26th Street outpost in the 1870s.

Great Burgers

Burger Joint

Tucked away behind a curtain in the lobby of the Parker Meridien Hotel.
118 W. 57th St., bet. Sixth and Seventh Aves.; 212-708-7414

Corner Bistro

Worth braving the crowd.
331 W. 4th St., at Eighth Ave.; 212-242-9502

Island Burger

More kinds of burger than you can eat.
766 Ninth Ave., bet. 51st and 52nd Sts.; 212-307-7934

Jackson Hole

232 E. 64th St., bet. Second and Third Aves.; 212-371-7187

Schnack

The mini-burgers are genius.
122 Union St., at Van Brunt St., Brooklyn; 718-855-2879

Returning from a trip in 1876, he demanded some lobsters and a variety of other common ingredients, to which he added a secret ingredient he'd brought with him at the last minute. Patrons and staff alike agreed that the result was fantastic, and Wenberg was persuaded to name the secret ingredient – cayenne pepper – and allow the restaurant to serve Lobster à la Wenberg. Some while later, Ben offended the Delmonicos (no one knows quite how), and he and his dish were banned from the restaurant. Pressed to allow at least the lobster to return, the family scrambled some of the letters, and from then on presented diners with Lobster à la Newburg.

After nearly a century of prominence, the last Delmonico faded from the New York restaurant scene in the 1920s, and all their locations closed. The name was appropriated here and there, but never achieved the same prominence until 1998, when a new group opened up in one of the family's old palatial locations and revived the restaurant's rep as a financial district gathering place.
56 Beaver St., at South William St., 212-509-1144; Mon.-Fri. only

Food Fests

The two most important words in New York dining are **Restaurant Week**. Twice a year, in winter and summer, around 160 of the city's best restaurants set up three-course lunches and dinners that they sell for a fixed amount based on the year (i.e., in 2005, lunches will be $20.05, dinners $30.05). It's a brilliant way to get into places you couldn't ordinarily afford. For details and dates, check out *nycvisit.com*.

Also worth noting is the **Ninth Avenue International Food Festival**. Between 37th Street and 57th Street, Ninth Avenue may well contain the most ethnically diverse set of restaurants anywhere, so when they close the stretch to traffic for a weekend in late May, the eating doesn't get much better.

Times Square isn't as diverse, but the **Taste of Times Square** festival, in June, is worth a visit. For dessert, if you can wait that long, there's the **Chocolate Show** in November *(Metropolitan Pavillion, 125 W. 18th St., bet. Sixth and Seventh Aves.; chocolateshow.com)*, an industry event whose entry fee may be worth it for chocolate devotees.

The Cement Doughnut

If we love a thing here – and there can be no doubt that New Yorkers love **bagels** – then we also love to argue about it. We'll argue where the name came from (the German *bügel*, for stirrup or circle, or the Yiddish *beigl*, for "small arc"), where it originated (in Germany, as a decoration for post-hunt feasts; in Poland, as a gift for pregnant women; or in Austria, in honor of the stirrups of a Polish king who saved Vienna from the Turks), and, most important, where to find the best ones.

Everyone agrees, though, that the true New York bagel should be sizable (from four to six inches wide), with a fairly tough (some might say leathery) skin and a dense, chewy interior. It should not be puffy or air-filled or have grid marks on the bottom; these are all signs that the dough has not been properly boiled before baking. Boiling is crucial – simply spritzing the dough with water as it bakes is an unacceptable short cut – so naturally there are those who argue that there is something special in New York water that makes local bagels better, and a vocal minority claims that Brooklyn water is best. Scientists and bagelogians are divided on the question.

All of these debates have been festering since the 1880s, when Jewish immigrants brought the bagel here from Eastern Europe. For a long while it was almost exclusively a New York item (though outposts of bagelry existed in a few places, like Montreal and Philadelphia), and in 1907 a group of about 300 bagel makers tried to restrict the trade by forming the International Bagel Bakers Union in the city, with entry to one of the 36 union shops in the area limited to their apprenticed sons. The union has long since disbanded, done in by the two events in the 1960s – the invention of a bagel-making machine and the introduction of frozen bagels by Harry Lender – that would contribute to the bagel's growing nationwide popularity. Since 1984, bagel consumption has grown 169 percent, making it the fastest growing breakfast food by far.

Battling Bagel-Mavens

Photo: Daniel Hood

The bagel cognoscenti all have their favorites, and would rather fight than switch. We just like a good bagel, which all of these places have in spades.

Bergen Bagels
473 Bergen St., at Flatbush Ave., Brooklyn; 718-789-7600

Columbia Bagels
A major supplier of Zabar's.
2836 Broadway, at 110th St.; 212-222-3200

Ess-A-Bagel
359 First Ave., at 21st St.; 212-260-2252

H&H Bagels
Probably the best-known New York bagel – though some claim they're too sweet.
2239 Broadway, at 80th St.; 639 W. 46th St., at 12th Ave.; 800-NY-BAGEL

The First, Authentic, Genuine, Really, Truly Original Famous Ray's Pizza

Photo: Daniel Hood

Long before there was a Starbucks on every corner of Manhattan, there was Ray and his famous pizza. So famous, in fact, that an endless crop of shops have stolen his good name to sell slices. They get away with it by using a unique combination of adjectives on their marquees to convince you just how bona fide their pizza is – while at the same time dodging trademark entanglements.

Who is Ray? Which pizzeria is really the original one? These are timeless questions asked by fans of New York-style pizza for more than two generations. Despite decades of idle inquiry at the cash register, however, the answer remains as slippery as a pepperoni; the mystery as deep as a slice of Sicilian.

By many accounts, the **Original Ray's Pizza** on 6th Avenue at 11th Street is the real deal; all the others just shameless imitations. The store even touts its authenticity with a plaque that reads: "This is 'The One and Only Famous Ray's of Greenwich Village' store. We are not affiliated with any other store bearing a similar name." But, of course, anyone can put up a plaque.

Kossar's Bialys
They have bagels, but are famous for the bialy, the bagel's flatter, oniony cousin.
367 Grand St., bet. Essex and Norfolk Sts.; 212-473-4810

Murray's Bagels
500 Sixth Ave., bet. 12th and 13th Sts.; 212-462-2830

Tal Bagels
979 First Ave., bet. 53rd and 54th Sts.; 212-753-9080

Tasty Bagels
Makers of the "Big Wheel," a two-foot-wide bagel.
1705 86th St., at 17th Ave., Bensonhurst, Brooklyn; 718-236-1389

This is, The One and Only Famous Ray's of Greenwich Village store. We are not affiliated with any other store bearing a similar name. ...Thank You

Photo: Brad Dunn

To trace the true ancestry of this family of clones, you have to start with the facts.

What few people know is that the original Ray is Ralph Cuomo, a mobster who worked within the Lucchese crime family and is currently doing time at a federal prison in Minnesota. He opened his first pizza shop in 1959 – three years after he was caught in an armed robbery and allegedly pistol-whipped by police. His business flourished, and he gained a tremendous reputation for serving the best pie in town. But slices weren't the only items on the menu.

In the basement, just below the pizza ovens, Ray and his Lucchese cohorts ran a major heroin operation. The enterprise lasted until 1969, when police reportedly captured Ray with 50 pounds of heroin worth $25 million. After a lengthy trial, he pled guilty only to using the phones in his pizzeria to discuss drug sales. He was convicted of trafficking and sentenced to four years in prison.

If the original Ray was a heroin dealer involved in organized crime, then where was his first pizzeria? At 27 Prince Street, near Mott Street.

Photo: Brad Dunn

Pizza for the Masses

Most of us can't wait an hour to get a coal-oven pizza, or muster enough friends to eat a whole pie, which is why the vast majority of pizza parlors sell slices. They tend to have a thicker crust and more cheese (which is why blotting up the extra grease is considered perfectly polite). Here are some places to get a good standard slice.

Delizia 92
1762 Second Ave., at 92nd St.;
212-996-3720

Di Fara Pizzeria
1424 Ave. J, bet. E. 14th and E.
15th Sts., Brooklyn; 718-258-1367

Joe's Pizza
233 Bleecker St., at Carmine St.;
212-366-1182

Whatever they tell you, pizza wasn't invented here – that honor goes to Naples – but New Yorkers know a good thing when they eat it. Like many things Italian, the pie and the slice came here in the early 1900s, and thrived.

The first pizza parlor, **Lombardi's**, opened at 53 Spring Street in 1905, and is still dishing out beautiful pies of classic "New York" pizza, though at a different location a few blocks away (*32 Spring St., at Mott St.; 212-941-7994*), because the rumble of the subway below threatened their coal-fired oven.

That's important, since a coal-fired brick oven is still considered the sign of a top-tier pizza parlor, the kind people wait in line to get into. The pizza at these places tends to have a thinner, crispier crust, and it's only sold as full pies – no slices. Don't ask! Seriously; besides great pizza, these old New York parlors all boast plenty of attitude and little patience.

Photo: Daniel Hood

Locals will argue endlessly over which is best, but fine examples can be found at **Totonno's** (*1524 Neptune Ave., at 16th St., Coney Island; 718-372-8606; and in Manhattan at 1544 Second Ave., bet. 80th and 81st Sts.; 212-327-2800*), founded in 1924 and just as surly as ever; **John's** (*278 Bleecker St., bet. Morton and Jones Sts.; 212-243-1680; 408 E. 64 St., bet. First and York Aves.; 260 W. 44th St., bet. Seventh and Eighth Aves.*); the widely extended **Patsy's** (*2287 First Ave., bet. 117th and 118th Sts.; 212-534-9783; and at 1312 Second Ave., at 69th Street; 61 W. 74th St., bet. Columbus Ave. and Central Park West; 67 University Pl., bet. 10th and 11th Sts.; 318 W. 23rd St., bet. Eighth and Ninth Aves.; and 509 Third Ave., bet. 34th and 35th Sts.*); and the ever-crowded **Grimaldi's** with its great Brooklyn Bridge location (*19 Old Fulton St., Brooklyn; 718-858-4300; and a location in Hoboken, N.J.*).

Mike's Pizza

Considered one of the best in the Bronx.

380 E. 200 St., at Bainbridge Ave.; 718-365-5486

Pinch

For something a lot funkier, Pinch sells pizza not by the slice, but by the inch.

416 Park Ave. South, near 29th St.; 212-686-5222Sal & Carmine's Pizza 2671 Broadway, bet. 101st and 102nd Sts.; 212-663-7651

Two Boots

Since it grew out of the East Village, you can expect something a little funkier.

37 Ave. A, bet. Second and Third Sts.; 212-505-2276

A Pie by Any Other Name

It's not quite the city-wide battle over the Famous Ray's moniker, but New York's coal-oven elite had a bitter family feud of their own. It starts with original pizza man Gennaro Lombardi on Spring Street, who taught a young man named Patsy Lancieri the secret of the perfect pie. Lancieri struck out on his own with a coal-oven oasis on 118th Street, and in 1941 hired his 10-year-old nephew, Patsy Grimaldi. In time, Grimaldi wanted his independence too, so he opened a place in Brooklyn that he wanted to call Patsy's – which would have been fine, and all in the tradition of New York pizza apprenticeships, except that Uncle Patsy Lancieri had by that time sold out to a company that wanted to franchise the name. Threats and bitter litigation followed, until Patsy G. finally gave in and used his last name. He retired a few years ago, but dedicated **Grimaldi's** fans – and the restaurant's placemats – keep the memory of the fight alive, and fuel the fires of an anti-Manhattan grudge.

Golden Arches, Tinkling Ivories

Photo: Daniel Hood

Love 'em or hate 'em, you have to give **McDonald's** points for consistency: everywhere you go, from Australia to Zimbabwe, they're almost exactly the same. Which is why the franchise in the financial district is such a surprise: in a nod to late-1980s Masters-of-the-Universe excess, this McDonald's features chandeliers, a doorman during the lunch rush, and a tuxedoed pianist working the keys of a grand piano to soothe the savage breasts of all those over-excited floor traders and Eliot Spitzer-hating stock analysts.
*160 Broadway, bet. Cortland and Liberty Sts.;
212-385-2063*

Lunch Hour

When you're hunting for a job in New York, the number and quality of places to eat near a company's offices are almost as important as the salary being offered. The financial district and the northern part of midtown are notoriously weak in this regard, which may explain the corporate cafeterias and law firm dining rooms in those areas. Here are some places worth switching jobs for.

Bruce's Burger Drive-In
A counter-only joint, with tasty burgers and fries.
Pedestrian walkway east of K-Mart, bet. Seventh and Eighth Aves. and 33rd and 34th Sts.

Eisenberg's Sandwich Shop
An old-fashioned luncheonette.
*174 Fifth Ave., near 22nd St.;
212-675-5096*

Falafel House
Tiny and Middle Eastern.
1752 Second Ave., bet. 91st and 92nd Sts.; 212-987-6077

Fanelli's
A century-old corner cafe in SoHo.
*94 Prince St., at Mercer St.;
212-226-9412*

The Gray Dog's Coffee

Perennially packed Village coffee shop with canine-themed art and fantastic sandwiches.
33 Carmine Street, bet. Bedford and Bleecker; 212-462-0041

Hale & Hearty Soups

Great soups, without the Nazi.
22 E. 47th St., at Fifth Ave.; 49 W. 42 St., bet. Fifth and Sixth Aves.; 462 Seventh Ave., at 35th St.; 75 Ninth Ave., bet. 15th and 16th Sts.; 849 Lexington Ave., bet. 64th and 65th Sts.; 32 Court St., at Remsen St., Brooklyn

Lunchbox Food Co.

Next to a strip club, just off the West Side Highway, this stylish diner shouldn't work, but it does.
357 West St., bet. W. Houston and Clarkson; 646-230-9466

Shopsin's

Eccentric, friendly, and artsy Village diner with the biggest menu ever.
54 Carmine St., at Bedford St.; 212-924-5160; shopsins.com

'wichcraft

A sandwich shop from Tom Colicchio, the guy who owns craft and Craftbar. Very tasty, slightly expensive.
49 E. 19th St., bet. Park Ave. and Broadway; 212-780-0577

Peanut Pros

Wherever he is, Elvis is smiling down on a little shop in the Village. **Peanut Butter & Co.** is the Grand Central Terminal of the peanut world. If you have a hard time choosing between smooth and chunky, be prepared for total peanut paralysis: This shop offers 21 homemade varieties of the sticky spread. You can buy the mixtures by the jar or, better, stop by for lunch. The kitschy café offers an incredible array of peanut butter dishes, ranging from the sandwiches you grew up with to delicious recipes you never would have imagined.

For the kid in you, try the "Ants on a Log," celery sticks slathered in peanut butter and covered in raisins. You can also make your own s'mores, drink a PB&J milkshake, or take home a chocolate peanut butter pie or peanut butter tiramisu.

Sandwiches are the house specialty, and the range of options is stunning. There's the unlikely "spicy peanut butter sandwich," the calorie-packing "Fluffernutter" (PB and marshmallow fluff), and the simply delicious, "Peanut Butter Cup" (PB with Nutella chocolate spread). All sandwiches come with chips and carrot sticks, but if you really want to be transported back to your elementary school cafeteria, you can ask to have the crusts cut off.

Of course, the shop offers the best rendition of the "Elvis," an artery-clogging sandwich with generous layers of peanut butter, banana, honey, and bacon. Truly, it's a sandwich fit for a King.
240 Sullivan St., bet. Bleecker and W. 3rd Sts.; 212-677-3995

Delicious Knishes

Photo: Daniel Hood

Turning the potato into a work of art for more than a century, **Yonah Schimmel's Knishes** on Houston Street is one of the city's best-kept food secrets. If your experience with these doughy treats begins and ends at the hot dog cart, have some self-respect: take a trip to the Lower East Side where it all started.

About this time last century, a Romanian rabbi named Yonah Schimmel, fresh off the boat, began selling produce on the beaches of Coney Island. Fellow immigrants were his main customers, and potatoes and kasha – the heart and sole of the inexpensive knish – were his top sellers. He put two and two together, and began selling his wife's samples of the Eastern European Jewish treats.

In 1910, Schimmel opened the store that still stands today. Baked in brick ovens in the basement and transported to customers by dumb-waiter, his knishes soon stood as the definition of the dish: a real knish was always handmade; baked, not fried; and filled with vegetables only. Schimmel's store also came to represent the period itself. An oil painting of its façade today hangs in the Museum of the City of New York.

Through the decades big names ranging from Nelson Rockefeller to Barbra Streisand have gone to Schimmel's for their knishes. Today, you can still choose from the original menu of fillings: kasha, spinach, cabbage, mushroom, and, of course, potato.
137 E. Houston St., bet. Forsythe and Eldridge Sts.; 212-477-2858

Never on White

Legend has it that pastrami was introduced to New York by kosher deli owner Sussman Volk in 1888, after a Romanian friend who was returning to the Old World gave him the recipe. However it happened, the pastrami on rye became the city's ideal sandwich, and opened non-Tribe-members' eyes to the meaty delights of Jewish deli. Remember, you can always ask for extra fat.

Artie's Delicatessen
2290 Broadway, bet. 82nd and 83rd Sts.; 212-579-5959

Barney Greengrass
An Upper West Side institution, the "Sturgeon King" is famous for its smoked salmon and eggs.
541 Amsterdam Ave., bet. 86th and 87th Sts.; 212-724-4707

Ben's Kosher Restaurant
209 W. 38th St., bet. Seventh and Eighth Aves.; 212-398-2367
211-37 26th Ave., Bayside, Queens; 718-229-2367

Carnegie Deli
Like the nearby Stage Deli, a huge draw for tourists, less so for locals.
854 Seventh Ave., bet. 54th and 55th Sts.; 212-757-2245

The Fuss about Guss

Katz's Delicatessen
Where Sally faked it for Harry. Watch out for the very confusing ticket-ordering system, which may well date from the place's founding in 1888.
205 E. Houston St., at Ludlow St.; 212-254-2246

Pastrami Queen
1269 Lexington Ave., bet. 85th and 86th Sts.; 212-828-0007

Second Avenue Deli
156 Second Ave., at 10th St.; 212-677-0606.

Stage Deli
834 Seventh Ave., bet. 53rd and 54th Sts.; 212-245-7850

Everyone knows that New York put the pickle on the map; but few realize that the pickle prime meridian runs right through a 91-year-old shop on the Lower East Side.

Guss' Pickles serves up some of the tastiest varieties of the city's favorite side dish. Just look for the giant barrels out on the sidewalk, or follow the aroma of those sweet, sour, salty snacks.

The history of the New York City pickle, like so many of its culinary wonders, is the history of immigrants. Izzy Guss, who came here from Russia at the turn of the last century, eked out a living pushing a cart full of produce through the Lower East Side. Pickles were his specialty, and when enough money came in he opened the store that still bears his name.

The recipes for his famous full-sour pickles, half-sour pickles, and pickled green tomatoes are still used today. Here are some of the secret ingredients: the full-sour variety contains a mix of coriander, mustard seed, bay leaves, red peppers, and extra garlic and dill. The half-sours get their crunch and sweetness with a milder blend of the same. The tomatoes are immersed in cold saltwater filled with herbs and spices, not boiled. This keeps them firm and delicious.

If you're an aspiring pickle gourmand, but don't know where to begin, let the half-sour be your starting point: that's what you get at most delis and restaurants.
85/87 Orchard St., 516-569-0909; closed Mon. and Sat.

Diamond in the Rough

Talk about a gem of a restaurant. If you want some great Jewish cooking, take a stroll down to the Diamond District. The famous strip on West 47th Street between Fifth and Sixth Avenues is home not only to 2,600 gem businesses, but also the **Diamond Dairy Restaurant** – one the city's best-kept secrets for incredible kosher cuisine.

Without signs or storefront, this eatery is truly a buried treasure. To find it, enter the National Jewelers Exchange near Fifth Avenue. Climb one of the two narrow staircases in the back, where the restaurant juts out of the mezzanine and overlooks the exchange floor. The service is fast and the food is fantastic – especially the grilled eggplant and roasted chicken.

If you wait to get a seat by the window, you can enjoy a bird's-eye view of dealers from around the world haggling for diamonds and antique jewelry. Take note: every transaction is closed with a handshake only.
4 W. 47th St.; 212-719-2694

Visionary Vegan

Strict herbivores know that **Angelica Kitchen** in the East Village is the pole star of the vegan cuisine universe. But few know that the eatery's owner, Leslie McEachern, has been an outspoken advocate of the sustainable agriculture movement for more than 25 years. She even wrote the book on it: her cookbook, *The Angelica Home Kitchen*, is available everywhere, including the restaurant that started it all.

The cheerful place promises that at least 95 percent of all ingredients are organically grown, with sustainable agriculture and responsible business practices. The restaurant's signature piece is the "Dragon Bowl," a heaping dish of rice, beans, tofu, and steamed veggies. The place also keeps customers coming back for its seasonal features, including the baked tempeh with mushroom gravy, the lemon-herb baked tofu with fresh pesto, and the spicy three-bean chili, which is so much like its meaty counterpart that non-vegetarians often confuse the two. Perhaps best of all, the cozy restaurant is a perfect place to introduce a friend to vegan cuisine. Also: the place is frequented by numerous celebrities, so keep an eye out, but try not to wreck the low-key, anonymous vibe that keeps them coming back.
300 E. 12th St., 212-228-2909

The Vegetarian Option

A small sampling of the city's many offerings for the nutritionally evolved.

Bliss Cafe
191 Bedford Ave., bet. N. 5th and N. 6th St., Williamsburg, Brooklyn; 718-599-2547

Candle Cafe
Vegan and organic.
1307 Third Ave., at 75th St.; 212-472-0970

Dojo
Inexpensive and popular with the NYU crowd.
14 W. 4th St., bet. Broadway and Mercer St.; 212-505-8934; 24-26 Saint Marks Pl., bet. Second and Third Aves.; 212-674-9821

Tea Me

Photo: Daniel Hood

What else would you call a tiny café owned by a big star? Moby's **Teany** not only serves up some of the most unusual vegetarian food in the city, it also offers an exhaustive array of herbal teas. It's relatively cheap, it's largely unknown, and best of all, there's not a single picture of the techno celeb in the entire place.

Moby, who's been a denizen of the Lower East Side for 15 years, finally opened the café he had always dreamed about in 2000. Awash in lime green and bright yellow, Teany stands out like a neon beacon on Rivington Street; wander in any day of the week and

you'll see that the Grammy winner has achieved the environment he always envisioned: an easy-going, sedate hangout where you can play a round of Go while sipping a cold nectarine and cantaloupe soup or munching on a faux turkey club.

Don't forget the shop's namesake: tea. There are more than 90 varieties from around the world ready to be brewed. The menu walks you through the various healing properties associated with each kind, and recommends brews for specific ailments. In addition to those that clear the more spiritual channels of your body, there are teas geared for more mundane tasks such as helping you recover from a rough hangover.
*90 Rivington St., bet. Orchard and Ludlow Sts.;
212-475-9190*

Great American Health Bar
*Vegetarian and kosher, too!
35 W. 57th St., bet. Fifth and Sixth
Aves.; 212-355-5177*

Herban Kitchen
*Organic, with some chicken and fish.
290 Hudson St., bet. Dominick and
Spring Sts.; 212-627-2257*

Sacred Chow
*Vegan.
522 Hudson St., bet. 10th and
Charles Sts.; 212-337-0863*

Dinner de Sade

Talk about bad service. These waitresses will tie you up, blindfold you, and give you the whipping of your life – and then charge you $20 for it. And that's all before the appetizers have come.

La Nouvelle Justine is the first and only S&M-themed restaurant in New York City. Taking its name from a Marquis de Sade novel, the dining dungeon employs abusive, whip-wielding waitresses (the dominants) and submissive leather-clad busboys (the slaves). You eat alongside the bondage equipment and full torture-chamber decor, and watch as house slaves and patrons get lavishly "disciplined" by the wait staff.

To be sure, the place is as harmless as a theme park. And although only those customers who want to be humiliated get humiliated, it usually only takes a couple of the house's "necrophiliac" martinis and some persistent goading from friends for most patrons to partake in the abuse. In addition to the regular menu, you'll get a "Special Fare" list from which you can order house specialties such as a spanking or a trip to the rack. If you're lucky, the waitress might let you kiss her knee-high leather boots.

La Nouvelle Justine's owner also runs **Lucky Cheng's**, the renowned Asian restaurant where drag queens put on racy cabaret shows. The restaurants are next to each other, and the owner recently knocked down a wall to create an interior passageway. If you can't decide between wearing a choker and being walked like dog or watching a bunch of transvestites strut their stuff, now you can have the best of both worlds.
24 First Ave.; 212-673-8908

More Culinary Invasions

You can't call yourself the capital of the world and not serve their food. All the usual suspects are represented – Chinese, Indian, Vietnamese, Italian, and so on – so here's a selection of the more esoteric.

Photo: Daniel Hood

A Salt and Battery
Hard-core English fish-and-chips shops, famous for their deep-fried Mars bars. *112 Greenwich Ave., bet. 12th and 13th Sts.; 212-691-2713; 80 Second Ave., bet. 4th and 5th Sts.; 212-254-6610*

Aquavit

Scandinavian food, from hot
Swedish/Ethiopian chef of the
moment Marcus Samuelsson.
Getting in won't be easy.
13 W. 54th Street, bet. Fifth and
Sixth Aves.; 212-307-7311

Cambodian Cuisine

Like the name says; a popular
Brooklyn spot.
87 S. Elliot Pl., bet. Lafayette Ave.
and Fulton Pl., Brooklyn;
718-858-3262

Caracas Arepa Bar

Venezuelan. (Arepas are corn
buns Venezuelans use somewhat
like tortillas.)
91 E. 7th St., at First Ave.;
212-228-5062

Invaded ... by Belgium?

Maybe the city's restaurateurs ran out of cool countries from which to steal cuisines, or maybe they ran through the alphabet and got back to the Bs. Either way, the last ten years have seen an improbable mushrooming of Belgian cuisine. Yes, Belgian.

You can load up on *moules frites* and waterzooi at swank resto **Markt** in the Meatpacking District *(401 W. 14th St., at Ninth Ave.; 212-727-3314)*, a nabe that for a time seemed likely to become Manhattan's Little Belgium, what with the opening of the **Petite Abeille** across the way *(400 West 14th St.; 212-727-1505)*. The "little bee," run by Belgian expat siblings the Jadot Brothers, favors Tintin prints and more homey food (think *croque monsieur* and waffles); with three other Manhattan locations, it's threatening to become a chain. *(107 W. 18th St., bet. Sixth and Seventh Aves.; 134 W. Broadway, bet. Duane and Thomas Sts.; 466 Hudson St., near Barrow St.)* For an old-school Belgian bistro experience, there's the respectably pricey **Café de Bruxelles** *(118 Greenwich Ave., at W. 13th; 212-206-1830)*, with a fantastic beer selection.

But what's really brilliant about Belgian food are the *frites* and the waffles, and they're what's really taken off. **Pommes Frites** *(123 Second Ave., bet. 7th St. and St. Mark's Pl.; 212-674-1234)* started the trend around 1997, selling big greasy cones of fries with an authentic range of non-ketchup sauces – everything from garlic mayonnaise on up – to hungry East Village types. The Belgian couple who owned the place did so well they've opened another storefront *(724 Seventh Ave., bet. 48th and 49th Sts.)*, and created an appetite for

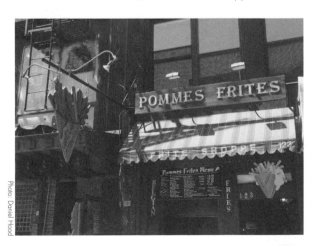

Photo: Daniel Hood

double-cooked fries at places like **B. Frites** (1657 Broadway, bet. 51st and 52nd Sts.) and **Pomme Pomme** (191 E. Houston St., bet. Orchard and Ludlow Sts.; 646-602-8140).

As for waffles, the place to go is one of the many outposts of **Le Pain Quotidien**, a Belgian chain of upmarket bakery/ restaurants that sell the real thing, loaded with sugar crystals that melt when you toast them. In Brussels, these come out of vending machines for around a buck; in Manhattan, they're rare treats at around $3 – when they're not in stock. When they're not, try the croissants, the fantastic pastries, or the truffle-bomb cakes; better yet, plunk yourself down at the big communal table, order a sandwich on their great bread, and borrow your neighbor's *Times* (1131 Madison Ave., bet. 84th and 85th Sts.; 212-327-4900; 1336 First Ave., bet. 71st and 72nd Sts.; 833 Lexington Ave., bet. 63rd and 64th Sts.; 50 W. 72nd St., bet. Columbus and Central Park West; 38 E. 19th St., bet. Broadway and Park Ave.; 100 Grand St., near Mercer St.; painquotidien.com).

Photo: Le Pain Quotidien

Casa La Femme
Egyptian and Middle Eastern, with tents and belly dancers.
150 Wooster St., bet. Houston and Prince Sts.; 212-505-0005

Eight Mile Creek
Australian, complete with seared kangaroo.
240 Mulberry St., bet. Prince and Spring Sts.; 212-431-4635

Lakruwana
Sri Lankan.
358 W. 44th St., at Ninth Ave.; 212-957-4480

Rectangles
Yemeni/Israeli.
159 Second Ave., at 9th St.; 212-677-8410

Photo: Daniel Hood

Mighty Duck

Who doesn't love a good Peking duck? Next time you're in the mood for one of these delicious, crispy, succulent birds, fly down to Chinatown and sample the best variety this side of the Yellow River. At the **Peking Duck House**, the name says it all. If you're not up for duck, don't bother. Otherwise, come in, sit down, and prepare for a fantastic, if somewhat pricey, feast.

Here's how they do duck in Chinatown: first, chefs

pump air into the duck to stretch and loosen its skin. Then they pour boiling water over it several times, delicately dry it, then rub it lovingly with maltose. Now the bird is ready for roasting: just enough to tenderize the meat and crispify the skin.

The delicacy is wheeled out to your table, where a nimble chef carves it in front of you and serves it homestyle, which at the Peking Duck House means with the bird's flesh is still attached to the skin, as opposed to banquet style where only the skin is served.

The traditional side dishes include homemade pancakes, green scallions, fresh cucumbers, and a special hoisin sauce. There's also a tangy sauce that brings out the flavor of the duck meat, just as the cucumber and scallions counter the richness. The skin is crisp, airy, and delicious, which balances the texture of the meat. The experience is best enjoyed by large groups.
22 Mott St., 212-227-1810

Rinconcito Peruano
Peruvian.
803 Ninth Ave., bet. 53rd and 54th Sts.; 212-333-5685

St. Andrews
Scottish. Insert your own haggis joke here.
120 W. 44th St., bet. Sixth and Seventh Aves.; 212-840-8413

Tibet on Houston
Tibetan.
136 W. Houston St., bet. Sullivan and Macdougal Sts.; 212-995-5884

Photo: Daniel Hood

Veselka
Great Ukrainian. (It seems like Russian or Polish to us, but it's in Little Ukraine, and they're touchy about that kind of thing.)
Open 24/7.
144 Second Ave., at St. Mark's Pl.; 212-228-9682

Asian Garden

The back garden is a delightful feature of New York City bars and restaurants. Because Manhattan simply can't spare the space anywhere else, a whole crop of charming back patios have sprung up over the years, sandwiched between brownstones, tucked into corners, yet offering a sliver of sky, a garden of plants, and a dose of fresh air.

One of the best examples is **Café Asean** in Greenwich Village. Serving fresh, authentic Vietnamese and Malaysian cuisine, the restaurant is a charming, little room resembling a country kitchen and done up in burnished colors. But the best place to grab a seat is in the small garden in the back.

Try the curried shrimp, the delicious Gado Gado salad with rice cakes smothered in peanut sauce, the lemongrass-crusted snapper in coconut lime sauce, or the Thai red curry with beef and pumpkin. No matter what your pleasure, Café Asean is a great place to relax, unwind, and sample one of the city's best little outdoor eating areas.
117 W. 10th St., at Sixth Ave.; 212-633-0348

Peep Show

If your last experience with a two-way mirror was picking someone out of a police lineup, you should check out the super-chic Thai restaurant **Peep** in SoHo, where the view behind the glass is truly different.

Sure, the pink-neon-infused place has charming mirrors on its ceilings and walls, but Peep earns its name from the interesting interior-design scheme of its bathrooms: the wall contains a full-size, two-way mirror that lets you spy out into the dining room while you, er, conduct your affairs. The people at the bar, who are literally three feet away from you, can't see a thing.

But it's more than odd, restroom voyeurism that keeps the crowds coming to this hot spot; the drinks are as unusual as the décor. The "Frisk" is a tasty cocktail made with ginger, honey liqueur, and Absolut Citron, while the "Crush" is basically a smashed fruit salad with ice and vodka poured over it. The cuisine, which also benefits from clever architecture thanks to a wide-open, viewable kitchen, is delicious, tapping everything that's great about Thai food: curries, stir-fries, peanuts, seafood, and so on. Try the Ebi and Crab Croquettes or the Emperor Dumplings, followed by a main course of the Baked Crustacean Claypot.

No matter what you order, be sure to load up on the beverages, alcoholic or otherwise. You haven't experienced Peep until you've used the restrooms.
177 Prince St., 212-254-7337

Sushi

OK, OK — **Nobu** (*105 Hudson St., at Franklin St.; 212-219-0500*) may be the best place in the city to eat sushi (which isn't the same as the best sushi in the city, if you see what we mean), but it's phenomenally difficult to get in, so we'll probably never know. In the meantime....

Jewel Bako

Tiny, with beautiful presentation. Owners Jack and Grace Lamb are gradually building an empire.
239 E. 5th St., bet. Second and Third Aves.; 212-979-1012

Kuruma Zushi

Pricey and difficult to find.
7 E. 47th St., Suite 2, bet. Fifth and Madison Aves.; 212-317-2802

Photo: Daniel Hood

Sushi of Gari
Creative and popular; best when Gari himself is on hand.
402 E. 78th St., at First Ave.; 212-517-5340

Sushi Yasuda
Huge variety.
204 E. 43rd St., bet. Second and Third Aves.; 212-972-1001

Tomoe Sushi
Reasonable prices, good quality.
172 Thompson St., bet. Bleecker and Houston Sts.; 212-777-9346

Yama
Big portions, reasonable prices.
122 E.17th St., at Irving Place; 212-475-0969; 92 W. Houston St., bet. Thompson St. and LaGuardia Place; 212-674-0935; 38-40 Carmine St., bet. Bedford and Bleecker Sts.; 212-989-9330

Tucked away below the Manhattan side of the Brooklyn Bridge is a little corner building packed with history. The appropriately named **Bridge Café** is not only the oldest continuously run restaurant in New York City, but it's also housed in the oldest wood-frame structure below Canal Street. If that's not distinguishing enough, it still serves some of the best New England-style food this side of the East River.

Established in 1794, about a century before the Brooklyn Bridge was constructed high above it (and compelled a name change), the Bridge Café shows its age in wonderful ways. The ancient tin-plated ceilings, the over-painted moldings, and the dark wooden bar bring you back to another era – the bar itself is rumored to be the oldest one in Manhattan. If you're lucky (or Type-A enough to reserve in advance) you'll get a table over-looking the East River, which in this setting almost takes on the sepia tones of an old photograph.

Though rich with history, this charming old eatery spares nothing in the kitchen. Its classic dish "Green Eggs and Ham" is a Sunday brunch special, and its proximity to the South Street Seaport provides delicious seafood, like the scrumptious soft-shelled crabs. Best of all, the Bridge Café offers plenty of libations: the bar boasts 120 wines and more than two dozen varieties of scotch malt.
279 Water St., 212-227-3344

blame Disney

Terrifying but true: there's an Olive Garden restaurant in New York. In *Manhattan*. And that's not all – there are Outback Steakhouses, Applebees', and a T.G.I. Fridays or two, and, we're told, there will soon be a Red Lobster. As this is an affront to all right-eating New Yorkers, we won't give you their addresses or phone numbers. We'll just say that most of them seem to be part of a wave of chain restaurants that mostly started with the 1990s' Disneyfication of Times Square, and caters primarily to tourists and nostalgic immigrants from the heartland.

Don't get us wrong – bloomin' onions are a great thing. Here's our point: if you want to eat in a chain, why not try one that's homegrown? There are a number of local restaurants with at least three locations – and you have to know, if they've got more than one, there's a reason.

Baluchi's

Nicely priced Indian, without all the kitsch of those places on 6th Street. Take-out available.
193 Spring St., bet. Sullivan and Thompson Sts.; 212-226-2828; 104 Second Ave, at 6th St.; 212-780-6000; 361 Sixth Ave., near Waverly Pl.; 212-929-2441; 283 Columbus Ave., bet. 73rd and 74th Sts.; 212-579-3900; 240 W. 56th St., near Broadway; 212-397-0707; 1149 First Ave., at 63rd St.; 212-371-3535; 1565 Second Ave., at 81st St.; 212-288-4810; 113-30 Queens Blvd., at 76th Rd., Queens; 718-793-5858; baluchis.com

Mary Ann's

For reasonably priced, pretty decent Mex, Mary Ann's cactus-and-sombrero logo is unavoidable. Nice margaritas, plentiful chips, and a post-work festive

Photo: Daniel Hood

atmosphere. Plus, you can get takeout or delivery.

Artisanal
A restaurant dedicated to the glories of hand-crafted cheese.
2 Park Ave., at 32nd St.;
212-725-8585

Atomic Wings
Buffalo wings with official levels of spiciness ranging from Sane to Abusive, Nuclear, and Suicidal. Plus, they deliver.
184 First Ave., bet. 11th and 12th Sts.; 212-0505-7272; 528 Ninth Ave., bet. 39th and 40th Sts.; 212-760-9090; also in a few bars; atomicwings.com

Carl's Steaks
Philly cheesesteaks, the product of Carl's serious research into the subject.
507 Third Ave., at 34th St.;
212-696-5336

Photo: Daniel Hood

Crif Dogs

Cheap, delicious chili dogs.
113 St. Mark's Place, bet. First Ave.
and Ave. A; 212-614-2728

Photo: Daniel Hood

Golden Krust

Jamaican patties of all descriptions.
Dozens of locations across the city;
goldenkrustbakery.com

Photo: Daniel Hood

104

Shanghai Cooking

Great fried dumplings.
106 W. 32nd St., bet. Sixth and
Seventh Aves.

Two Toms

Brilliant pork chops, in a bare-bones
hole in the wall in Brooklyn.
255 Third Ave., at Union St.,
Brooklyn; 718-875-8689

107 West Broadway, at Reade St.; 212-766-0911;
86 Second Ave., at 5th St., 212-475-5939;
116 Eighth Ave., bet. 15th and 16th Sts., 212-633-0877; 1503 Second Ave., bet. 78th and 79th Sts.,
212-249-6165; 2452 Broadway, bet. 90th and 91st
Sts.; 212-877-0132

Penang

Of all things to multiply – a chain of tasty
Malaysian restaurants.
109 Spring St., bet. Greene and Mercer Sts.;
212-274-8883; 240 Columbus Ave., at 71st St.;
212-769-3988; 1596 Second Ave., at 83rd St.;
212-585-3838

Zen Palate

This popular, design-conscious mini-chain of
vegetarian restaurants makes it easy to go meatless.
And they'll deliver to limited areas.
663 Ninth Ave., at 46th St.; 212-582-1669;
34 Union Square East, at 16th St.; 212-614-9345;
2170 Broadway, at 76th St.; 212-501-7768;
zenpalate.com

Photo: Daniel Hood

The Wonderful Wizard of Tavern on the Green

It's the culinary jewel of Central Park, serves dinner to half a million people a year, and is the city's highest-grossing restaurant. But **Tavern on the Green** wasn't always so charmed. It took a true magician to transform this 1870 sheep stable into one of America's most lavish and beloved restaurants.

Warner LeRoy was born into one of the first royal families of film. His father, Mervyn LeRoy, directed *The Wizard of Oz*, and his mother, Doris Warner, was the daughter of Warner Brothers Studios' founder. In their glitzy mansion, his parents feted the silver screen's finest and frolicked with the Hollywood elite. Young LeRoy's first dog was a terrier named Toto, the same canine celebrity from his father's movie. To him, the whole world was an Emerald City.

He grew up and moved to New York, where he spent the better part of a decade realizing that directing and acting on Broadway was not his calling. Instead, he opened a restaurant where the artistic elite soon gathered and the rest of the world gaped in awe. It was called Maxwell Plum, and it became the highest-grossing restaurant in the country.

He followed this extraordinary success with another. In 1974, LeRoy bought the financially distraught Tavern on the Green, which had been converted to a restaurant four decades earlier, and spent more than $10 million transforming it into a fairy tale.

He connected the six dining rooms with spiraling halls of mirrors, and anointed each of the three main dining areas with a new identity: the Chestnut Room is bathed in warm, cozy wood and stages live entertainment; the Park Room offers stunning views of the garden and its frothy fountain; and the Crystal Room is awash in amazing chandeliers.

Outside, he commissioned a pageant of topiary animals, including a giant gorilla and a prancing horse, and wrapped the large trees with thousands of tiny white and blue lights. To all this, he added an exquisite menu from the most-acclaimed chefs in the world. The formula worked: Tavern on the Green, now a city

Other Seafood Spots

Aquagrill
210 Spring St., bet. Sullivan St. and Sixth Ave.; 212-274-0505

Atlantic Grill
1341 Third Ave., bet. 76th and 77th Sts.; 212-988-9200

Blue Water Grill
31 Union Square West, at 16th St.; 212-675-9500

Docks Oyster Bar
2427 Broadway, bet. 89th and 90th Sts.; 212-724-5588

Le Bernardin
One of the city's classiest — and priciest.
155 W. 51st St., bet. Sixth and Seventh Aves.; 212-554-1515

Mary's Fish Camp
64 Charles St., bet. W. 4th and Bleecker Sts.; 646-486-2185

Oceana
In midtown (read: expensive).
55 E. 54th St., bet. Park and Madison Aves.; 212-759-5941

Pearl Oyster Bar
18 Cornelia St., bet. Bleecker and West 4th Sts.; 212-691-8211

HE SCREAMED FOR ICE CREAM

George Washington had a weakness for ice cream that would have ruined a poorer man.

While living in New York City as president, during the brief time the city served as the nation's capitol, Washington fell so in love with this novel dessert that he paid dearly and often for samples, recipes, and devices to prepare it himself. According to records from a shop on Chatham Street (today known as Park Row) in downtown Manhattan, the president ran up a $200 tab on ice cream in the summer of 1790. That's the equivalent of about $96,000 today.

His addiction didn't cease after he left the city. After his death, inventory records taken at Mount Vernon revealed that the first president had accumulated "two pewter ice cream pots." Legend has it he even once paid $200 for a single ice cream recipe.

landmark, remains one of New York's biggest destinations for tourists and locals alike.

LeRoy took all the excess and extravagance of his Hollywood childhood and remade it in Central Park. For him, there really was no place like home. *Central Park W., at 67th St.; 212-873-3200*

Decline on the Half-Shell

With all due respect to pizza and bagels, the original New York food is, without question, the oyster. In the 1800s, people ate oysters morning, noon, and night, harvested from beds that covered the sea- and riverbottom from the lower bay south of Staten Island to points far up the Hudson. Liberty Island was once called Oyster Island, and Pearl Street got its name from being paved with oyster shells. In 1880, 765 million oysters were taken out of city waters; oysters from Gowanes Creek were said to be as big as dinner plates. Of course, the creek's descendant, the Gowanus Canal, is legendary for its filth, and no sane person would oyster there, making it emblematic of the fate of the city's oysterbeds: by the early 1900s, they had pretty much been overharvested and poisoned out of existence by raw sewage, and ever since the city has had to import anything it wanted on the half-shell.

In his 1999 survey of the health of New York's waters, *Heartbeats in the Muck*, ichthyologist John Waldmann makes a case for reseeding the bottom with oyster beds, not for eating — definitely not for eating — but for cleaning the water, since the bivalves can effectively filter enormous quantities of water.

Until that happens, your best bet for finding oysters is (naturally) the landmark **Oyster Bar**, the cavernous seafood hall beneath the main 42nd Street entrance to Grand Central. *212-490-6650; oysterbarny.com*

The Beginning of Romance –
and the End

Start at **Drip Cafe**, which began as a coffee shop on the Upper West Side that started putting couples together in 1996, fist through a plain old bulletin board, and more recently on the Internet. They've dropped the original café, but they still set up matches online: they let you browse through the profiles of eligibles that they've collected and select the ones that strike your fancy – or post your own profile and try to strike someone else's – and when there's mutual interest, they'll set up a less-than-usually awkward blind date for you at one of their affiliated cafés around town. Meet, get to know one another over a nosh or a cuppa or a cocktail. See if sparks fly. Drip claims to be the founding memory of lots of couples – and more than few marriages.

If romance is flourishing and you're ready to turn your Dripmate into a lifemate, it's time to head downtown, where Aaron Burr's 18th-century carriage house has been converted into **One If By Land, Two If By Sea**, an elegant, intimate restaurant with very good food that just happens to be Manhattan's Engagement Central. They claim to see as many as 10 proposals a night, and up to 30 on Valentine's Day. No word on how many are turned down, but the place has a reputation, so if you suggest it and your significant other agrees, he or she is probably amenable to what's coming. So dress nice, act romantic, and slip them a ring after the Beef Wellington. When they say yes, you're ready to get married – which means the romance is pretty much finished.

Drip Cafe: *dripcafe.com*

One If By Land, Two If By Sea: *17 Barrow St., bet. Seventh Ave. and W. 4th St.; 212-647-9385*

Note: You don't have to be on a date or about to be engaged to go to either; normal people frequent them too.

Meals with a View

As in real estate, a view generally jacks up the price.

Above

"New American" cuisine and an interesting, if restricted, view of Times Square and the Times Building. Good for a drink before a show, too.
234 W. 42nd St., bet. Seventh and Eighth Aves., in the Hilton Times Square; 212-642-2626

Asiate

Asian fusion and a view of Central Park. New, popular, and monstrously expensive.
80 Columbus Circle, in the Mandarin Oriental Hotel, Time Warner Center; 212-805-8881

Battery Gardens

A nicely refurbished utility building with unequalled view of the harbor to the south. Outdoor eating in warm weather.
South end of Battery Park across from 17 State St.; 212-809-5508

Secret in the Cellar

Photo: Daniel Hood

River Cafe

A great restaurant that just happens to have an unparalleled view of the Brooklyn Bridge and the East Side of Manhattan.
1 Water St., by the Brooklyn Bridge, Brooklyn; 718-522-5200

Terrace in the Sky

French food and an uncommon view of Manhattan from the north, as well as the George Washington Bridge, from atop a Columbia University dorm. Can get a little uneven when it's busy.
400 W. 119th St., bet. Amsterdam Ave. and Morningside Dr.; 212-666-9490

The Water Club

One of the few spots that looks out over the East River to Brooklyn.
500 E. 30th St., on the East River; 212-683-3333

The Water's Edge

Queens' answer to Brooklyn's River Cafe, with free ferry service from 34th Street in Manhattan.
44th Drive, at the East River and Vernon Blvd., Queens; 718-482-0033

Legend has it that Edgar Allan Poe was inspired to write *The Cask of Amontillado* after visiting a creepy old wine cellar in an antiques shop on Bond Street. In the story, a guy gets imprisoned behind a brick wall for all eternity; in real life, that same creepy old wine cellar today houses one of the city's best selections of Italian and Spanish vino.

Il Buco combines delicious Mediterranean cuisine with stunning Old World decor. Transformed in 1994 from an Americana antiques shop into an acclaimed hole-in-the-wall restaurant, Il Buco (literally, "the hole") specializes in succulent dishes from all points Italian to Iberian. Here's a great combo: salt-baked sea bass, langoustines grilled in garlic, and wild boar sausage with corona beans. You can also try the roasted rabbit salad with shaved fennel or the sautéed baby eels on a bed of grilled white polenta. The desserts alone will make a regular out of you: orange bunt cake, home-made macaroons, and mixed berry tarts.

If it's Poe you want, it's Poe you can get. The mysterious wine cellar is available for private parties and select tastings. Just don't go snooping around any suspicious, hastily laid brick walls.
47 Bond St., 212-533-1932

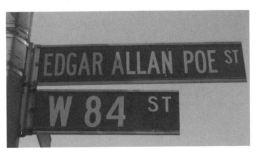

a better Little Italy

Italians once actually lived in Manhattan's Little Italy, we're told, but between rising standards of living and the metastasization of nearby Chinatown, the vast majority of them have long since moved out. All they left behind was the strip of restaurants on Mulberry Street between Canal and Broome – and most of those are mediocre tourist traps. (**Luna**, a hundred-year-old joint at 112 Mulberry, stands out as an exception for its unpretentious lack of kitsch and its great, inexpensive food.)

A better bet, if you want a neighborhood dining experience, is the "other Little Italy" – the Arthur Avenue section of the Bronx near Fordham University. The restaurants here are generally much better than on Mulberry Street, though what really keeps it together as a neighborhood are the many bakeries and food shops, which draw back a steady clientele of Italians from the suburban exodus.

Dominick's

2335 Arthur Ave., bet. Crescent St. and Frank Simeone Pl.; 718-733-2807

Emilia's

2331 Arthur Ave., bet. Crescent St. and Frank Simeone Pl.; 718-367-5915

Mario's

2342 Arthur Ave., bet. Crescent St. and Frank Simeone Pl.; 718-584-1188

The City at Night

It's not that it never sleeps, it's that it has insomnia, and eating something sometimes helps. These restaurants are there to fill the gap, 24/7.

Anytime
For late-hanging hipsters.
93 N. 6th St., bet. Bedford Ave. and Berry St., Williamsburg, Brooklyn; 718-218-7272

Brasserie Pigalle
French bistro.
790 Eighth Ave., at 48th St.; 212-489-2233

Empire Diner
An Art Deco homage in Chelsea, with great pigs-in-blankets.
210 Tenth Ave., at 22nd St.; 212-243-2736

Still, the fact is that there's great Italian all over New York, and you don't need to go to an Italian neighborhood to find it.

Angel's

A neighborhood fave, always a line.
1135 First Ave., bet. 62nd and 63 Sts.; 212-980-3131

Babbo

Mario Batali's headquarters.
110 Waverly Pl., bet. Washington Square Park and Sixth Ave.; 212-777-0303

Barbetta

Housed in a couple of townhouses, with a great backyard area.
321 W. 46th St., bet. Eighth and Ninth Aves.; 212-246-9171

Bar Pitti

A Village trattoria.
268 Sixth Ave., bet. Houston and Bleecker Sts.; 212-982-3300

Photo: Daniel Hood

Cucina di Pesce

87 E. 4th St., at Second Ave.; 212-260-6800

Ecco-La

1660 Third Ave., bet. 92nd and 93rd Sts.; 212-860-5609

Esca

402 W. 43rd St., at Ninth Ave.; 212-564-7272

Filli Ponte Ristorante

39 Desbrosses St., near Washington St.; 212-226-4621

Florent
A Belgian bistro in the Meatpacking District.
69 Gansevoort St., bet. Greenwich and Washington Sts.; 212-989-5779

French Roast
458 Sixth Ave., bet. W. 10th and W. 11th Sts.; 212-533-2233

Kang Suh
When you absolutely, positively must have Korean barbecue at 4 a.m.
1250 Broadway, at 31st St.; 212-564-6845

Kiev
Pierogies and kielbasa in a Ukrainian restaurant. It doesn't get as much play as Veselka up the street (also open 24 hours a day), but many prefer it.
117 Second Ave., at 7th St.; 212-674-4040

L'Express
French bistro on the right bank of Park Avenue.
249 Park Ave. South, at 20th St.; 212-254-5858

Il Mulino

Expensive, extensive, and worth it.
*86 W. 3rd St., bet. Sullivan and Thompson Sts.;
212-673-3783*

'ino

*21 Bedford St., bet. Houston and Downing Sts.;
212-989-576*

L'Impero

Refined, with goat.
*45 Tudor City Pl., at 42nd St., bet. First and
Second Aves.; 212-599-5045*

Lupa

Try the crudo.
*170 Thompson St., bet.
Houston and Bleecker Sts.;
212-982-5089*

Tre Pomodori

*210 E. 34th St., bet.
Second and Third Aves.;
212-545-7266*

Photo: Daniel Hood

Via Emilia

Remarkably reasonable
prices for that stretch of Park.
*240 Park Avenue South, bet.
19th and 20th;
212-505-3072*

Photo: Daniel Hood

McDonald's of Times Square

One of the busiest in the world,
they say.
*1560 Broadway, bet. 46th and
47th Sts.; 212-921-8900*

Sarge's Deli

Deli restaurant founded by a police
sergeant for those on the late shift.
*548 Third Ave., bet. 36th and
37th Sts.; 212-679-0442*

7A Cafe

The usual late-night menu, with
healthy and vegetarian options.
*130 Ave. A, at 7th St.;
212-673-6583*

Photo: Daniel Hood

Skylight Diner

A nice, normal diner.
*402 W. 34th St., bet. Ninth and
Tenth Aves.; 212-244-0395*

Mad for Cow

Photo: Daniel Hood

Tom's Restaurant
Yes, the one from *Seinfeld* and the
Suzanne Vega song. It's open all
night from Thursday to Sunday.
*2880 Broadway, at 112th St.;
212-864-6137*

Westside Restaurant
A neighborhood place with
American/Greek food.
*2020 Broadway, at 69th St.;
212-724-4000*

Photo: Daniel Hood

Yaffa Café
Popular vegetarian-leaning East
Village stop.
*97 St. Marks Pl., bet. First Ave.
and Ave. A; 212-674-9302*

There's a certain sameness to New York's upscale
steakhouses – the brusque, white-aproned waiters, the
sawdust, the creamed spinach, the general turn-of-the-
century feel – and that's all well and good, since places
like **Peter Luger's** *(178 Broadway, bet. Courtland and
Dey Sts., Brooklyn; 718-387-7400)*, **Smith &
Wollensky** *(797 Third Ave., at 49th St.; 212-753-
1530)*, **Keen's** *(72 W. 36th St., bet. Fifth and Sixth
Aves; 212-947-3636)*, and **Ben Benson's** *(123 W.
52nd St., bet. Sixth and Seventh Aves.; 212-581-8888)*
serve damn fine steaks.

But if you'd rather have a little fun when you pay
exorbitant prices, head to the Lower East Side to
Sammy's Roumanian *(157 Chrystie St., bet. Rivington
and Delancey Sts.; 212-673-0330)*. In a panelled
basement straight out of the 1970s, with syrup
dispensers full of schmaltz (liquid chicken fat) on the
tables and the waiters doing their best Woody Allen
and Don Rickles impressions, this is about as far from a
WASPy old New York
steakhouse as you can
get. But the meat is
amazing, so order a
bottle of vodka frozen
in a block of ice, stuff
yourself, have an egg
cream to top it off,
and learn that
steakhouses don't
need to be stuffy to
justify high prices.

Photo: Daniel Hood

Literature & the Arts

Don't talk to us about Paris. No city in the world draws more artists — be they painters or writers, sculptors or musicians, poets or opera divas — than New York. And if the place can be hard on them while they're alive, at least it celebrates them royally when they're dead, with a host of museums, galleries, concert halls, and enduring legends.

London's New York

Every English major knows that many of America's most notable writers have had to grapple with New York City in some way at some point in their careers — but few know that a young **Jack London** went through some particularly hard times in the city. He even lived homeless in City Hall Park for several weeks.

Born John Griffith Chaney in 1876, Jack London broke into the writing world as a teenager in his hometown of Oakland, California. He then pursued a peripatetic career as a journalist, war correspondent, short story writer, and columnist. In his early 20s, he landed in downtown New York virtually penniless. Instead of looking for work, he spent long, lazy days in City Hall Park reading voraciously from books he bought from street peddlers. At night he stayed in the park, and tried to write novels.

Though it's very unlikely that his most-famous short story, "To Build a Fire," was inspired by his homeless experiences in City Hall Park, London spent several cold, snowy nights in the park before finally drifting on to better fortunes.

But Can He Get into Soho House?

Ex-pat Brits have always found Manhattan pretty comfortable, and that may be because it holds an important part of their childhood: the original Winnie the Pooh (as well as the original Eeyore, Kanga, Piglet, and Tigger, too).

A.A. Milne gave the stuffed toys to his son, Christopher Robin, and then, when they'd inspired the massively successful book series, took them away and gave them to his publisher, E.P. Dutton, for publicity purposes in 1947. Dutton sent the animals on tour, and much later gave them to the New York Public Library. They now live at the Central Children's Room in the **Donnell Library Center** *(20 W. 53rd St., bet. Fifth and Sixth Aves., 212-621-0636)*, where Pooh and his crew are the heart of a fantastic collection of kids' books.

In 1998, a Labor MP of very little brain named Gwyneth Dunwoody declared that the stuffed animals looked "unhappy" where they were and demanded their return to the U.K. The INS offered the animals green cards, the Public Library made some intemperate remarks about the Elgin Marbles, and in the end Pooh and the rest stayed here. Maybe they're waiting for Lorne Michaels to invite them on *SNL*.

The City of Wise Fools

Every comic book geek knows Gotham City is New York, and vice-versa, but not many know where the city got its most enduring nickname. The story goes back to **Washington Irving**, who referred to his hometown by that name in a pre-*Spy* literary/humor magazine called *Salmagundi* that he published in the early 1800s. Irving got the name from the semi-mythic medieval English village of Gotham, whose residents put off a ruinously expensive visit from King John by pretending to be crazy when the royal advance men came to town (a tactic that might come in handy the next time the president drops into town for a fundraiser or an address to the U.N., and brings traffic to a grinding halt). Apparently, Irving thought New Yorkers had something in common with the legendary "wise fools" of Gotham, though he tended to see more foolishness than wisdom in the Gothamites of the 19th century.

Incidentally, Irving also popularized "knickerbocker" as nickname for New Yorkers and roundballers in his 1809 spoof *Diedrich Knickerbocker's History of New York*. The word referred to the short pants worn by the Dutch colonists who founded the city, and whose descendants were a pretty reliable source of humor at the time.

Photo: Daniel Hood

THE COMPROMISE OF THE MAGI

Wander into **Pete's Tavern**, a grand old New York saloon and restaurant on Irving Place at 18th Street, and you may notice a sign announcing that **O. Henry** wrote his wonderfully sentimental classic *The Gift of the Magi* in one of the booths by the front door. The tin-ceiling bar still looks much the way it did then, so it's nice to imagine him there, scribbling a classic over a pint.

If you then head across the street and down a block, however, to 55 Irving, you may notice a problem: the building sports a plaque announcing that *Magi* was written there.

Literary Lions

Next time you're at the NYPL, spare a thought for its mascots, the two marble lions outside the main branch at 42nd Street and Fifth Avenue. Born Leo Lenox and Leo Astor, after two of the private foundation libraries that were combined to create the NYPL, they were renamed Patience and Fortitude by Mayor Fiorello LaGuardia, because he claimed to see in them the same qualities with which his constituents were weathering the Great Depression. And here we thought it was because they have to put up with the library staff dressing them in different headgear – including Santa hats and scarves around Christmas, construction hardhats, and Yankees or Mets caps when either team wins the World Series.

Big Time=Big Apple

While we're on the subject, we may as well dig into the murky history of the more tabloid-friendly "Big Apple." The most common explanation is that it was first used by black stablehands from New Orleans on the racing circuit. Turn-of-the-century Big Easy slang, we're told, borrowed the Spanish phrase *matanza principal* ("main orchard") and used it to refer to the place where things were happening – the big time. New York being the big time in racing, stablehands called it the Big Apple. Sportswriter John J. Fitzgerald heard the phrase and liked it so much he called his 1920s column in *The Morning Telegraph* "Around the Big Apple." (In 1997, the city designated the southwest corner of West 54th Street and Broadway, where Fitzgerald lived for years, "Big Apple Corner" in his honor.)

Black jazz musicians also used the phrase in the 1930s and '40s, since New York's jazz scene, particularly in Harlem, was definitely the big time, but like so much else here in the 1950s and '60s, the nickname was sadly neglected until Charles Gillette repopularized it as the centerpiece of a tourism promotion in the 1970s. Since then, it's been going strong.

OK – that's good enough for the kids. Now consider this more colorful (though admittedly more questionable) hypothesis: in the early 1800s, French emigre Evelyn Claudine de Saint-Evremond established a high-class brothel at 142 Bond Street. The locals shortened her name to Eve, and started referring to her girls as "Eve's Apples," with all the requisite Edenic connotations. Over time, apples and apple trees became synonyms not just for prostitutes and whorehouses, but for corruption and decadence in general, and New York, with more whorehouses per capita than any other city in the country, was naturally the Big Apple – or, as William Jennings Bryan described it in an 1892 campaign speech, "the foulest rotten apple on the tree of decadent federalism." Apples may have since lost most of their sexual overtones, but the nickname stuck.

So which is it?

The answer, according to those with no commercial interest in the matter, is a compromise the Magi would approve of: O. Henry apparently conceived the idea while drinking in Pete's (then known as Healy's), and ran across the street to 55 Irving (where he lived from 1903 to 1907) to write it up in a single three-hour session.

O. Henry, by the way, was born William Sidney Porter in North Carolina, and only came to Manhattan in 1902, after a five-year stretch in an Ohio prison for embezzlement. Over the next eight years he turned out over 300 short stories and became one of America's most popular writers before dying, in 1910 at the age of 47, a penniless alcoholic (a point not mentioned on the sign in Pete's).

Photo: Daniel Hood

The **New York Public Library** is the largest public library in the U.S., with over 11 million books. The second largest? The **Queens Borough Public Library**, with around 9 million. And only a little further down the list you'll find the **Brooklyn Public Library**. If you put them together, they'd be bigger than the Library of Congress – but that's not likely ever to happen.

Three separate public libraries for one city may seem excessive, but the excess is rooted in history. Each system was established before the consolidation of the five boroughs in 1898, and the libraries found themselves at the bottom of the city elders' list of services that needed conglomeration. Then, in 1901, library-loving philanthropist and robber baron Andrew Carnegie made large individual donations to all three, on the understanding that the city would continue funding them all, which effectively made their independence official. Since then, borough pride and local interests have foiled all attempts to bring the three together.

BIBLE BELT

John Lennon called America the new Roman Empire, and New York the new Rome. He may have said more than he knew: New York possesses a major hand-me-down from Rome that few people know about.

The largest collection of Latin bibles in the world is kept in a library in Chelsea. The **General Theological Seminary** at 175 Ninth Avenue is not only the oldest seminary in the Episcopal Church (founded in 1817), it is also reputed to have the nation's greatest ecclesiastical collection of tomes: the St. Mark's Library.

Rare Recipes

That copy of *The Joy of Cooking* in your kitchen may have a few dog-eared pages, food stains, and other signs of age. But if you want to see a real relic, stop by the **New York Academy of Medicine**. Because of its name, few people know that it houses one of the largest and oldest collections of ancient cookbooks in the world.

With more than 10,000 volumes and pamphlets documenting the history of cookery and nutrition, the academy's special collections offer an unprecedented view into the eating habits of various societies. The jewel of the collection is a 9th-century edition of Apicius' *De re culinaria*, which is one of two known copies of what is believed to be the earliest cookbook in the Western world. Who was Apicius? None other than the most-reputed culinary expert of the Roman Empire, who served under Augustus and Tiberius. Apparently, Apicius was a real gourmand's gourmand; he invented the art of the odd dish, with memorable appetizers such as flamingo tongues, camel heels, and stuffed pig's womb. His recipes were widely recorded and shared, and finally compiled into one collection in the 4th century.

If a view into a Roman kitchen doesn't impress you, maybe one of prized pieces from the academy's other collections will. Its oldest relic is an Egyptian papyrus dating from 1700 B.C. that depicts the techniques for head and brain surgery – representing the oldest surgical document in the world.

Speaking of old recipes and eating habits, the academy also boasts George Washington's lower denture, as well as his last natural tooth, which was preserved and mounted on his dentist's watch chain. *1216 Fifth Ave., at 103rd St.; 212-822-7200*

Though the block-long seminary is a showcase of exquisite Gothic Revival architecture, including its stunning Chapel of the Good Shepherd with its 161-foot bell tower, the 210,000-volume library is housed in the institution's most modern building. The 1960s-era main building that faces Ninth Avenue between 20th and 21st Streets is open to the public daily from 10 a.m. to 8 p.m. and on weekends from 10 a.m. to 5 p.m.

Of course, although the ancient Latin bibles aren't exactly available for check-out, you can see some of the seminary's artifacts on display.

Joe Mitchell's Secret

Few writers have delved as deeply into this city as **Joseph Mitchell**, the North Carolinan who, as a writer for *The New Yorker* from the 1930s on, helped create the notion of literary journalism. His work chronicled many of the city's odder aspects and characters, from its tenements and seedy bars to circus freaks, gypsy scams, the (literal) underside of the harbor, and – most unhappily – a Greenwich Village mystery man named Joe Gould, who was responsible, many believe, for the end of Mitchell's brilliant writing career.

In 1942's "Professor Seagull," Mitchell presented a picture of a man who looked like a bum but might just be a genius: Gould was a Harvard grad and one-time literary wannabe who subsisted on cadged drinks and bowls of ketchup, while claiming to be able to speak with seagulls and to be accumulating a vast oral history of his time, the impenetrable notebooks for which he stashed in various friends' apartments around town. Mitchell's article made Gould a minor celebrity, allowed him to borrow money from a more select crowd (including e.e. cummings), and even led to some potential publishing deals for the Oral History, though these never seemed to pan out. Delighted with his measure of fame, Gould stumbled through the next decade-and-a-half, always looking for a drink and always talking up the Oral History, until his death in an asylum in 1957.

In 1964, Mitchell published a sequel of sorts called *Joe Gould's Secret*, in which he revealed the sad truth he'd discovered since writing the first article: Gould wasn't a genius, but an unstable alcoholic whose Oral History consisted of nothing more than unintelligible ramblings and one or two insignificant pieces endlessly repeated. From then until his death in 1996, though he continued to draw his salary and the sounds of typing still came from his office, Mitchell never wrote another word.

Much of Mitchell's early work is still in print, in collections like 1992's *Up in the Old Hotel*, and it holds up beautifully. Gould's legacy has held up less well: it consists of a number of his near-illegible diaries kept in a special collection at New York University, and is rarely looked at.

Photo: Spencer T Tucker/NYC Dept of Parks & Recreation

CONCRETE CUBISM

Not long after its unveiling in 1970, *The New York Times* called it the "ugliest piece of public art in the city." Still, few people even realize that Manhattan lays claim to one of the largest Picasso sculptures in the world. **Bust of Sylvette** (pictured at the beginning of this chapter) is a 36-foot-tall, 60-ton concrete monolith that juts out of the otherwise unadorned lawn in the center of a New York University apartment complex. The artwork is an enlargement of Picasso's 1934 sculpture, and though roundly abused by the media at its opening, the piece is all but forgotten by anyone who doesn't actually live in the modernist apartment buildings.

The crown jewel of Central Park is **the Mall**, the 40-foot-wide wonderful walkway flanked by giant, cathedral-like American elm trees. At one end of the Mall is the colossal concrete bandshell; at the other is colossally misnamed "Literary Walk."

As Central Park designer Frederick Law Olmsted labored to turn a raw parcel of land into the dynamic outdoor jewel that it is today, the city began receiving request after request to install sculptures throughout Central Park. Concerned that the park would soon be littered with sculptures, the commissioners decided to allot the southern end of the Mall as the unofficial sculpture dumping ground in 1873.

Approved statues started to appear overnight, and right away a theme took hold: literary figures. There was William Shakespeare, Sir Walter Scott, and Robert Burns — enough for the new name "The Literary Walk" to stick. Though the entrance to the Mall was literary enough, the walkway changed themes quickly from there.

A sculpture of Christopher Columbus went up in 1894, accompanied by composers Ludwig van Beethoven and Victor Herbert. There was a sculpture called "The Indian Hunter" and another called "Eagles and Prey," both depicting less-than-literary subjects. Despite the shift in the sculptural landscape, and its consequently outdated name, the Literary Walk remains one of the highlights of Central Park to this day.

Rockefeller Saw Red

On May 22, 1933, **Diego Rivera**, the world-famous muralist, was called down from his scaffolding at **Rockefeller Center** while working on his latest colossal project. He was given a check, escorted off the premises, and barred from returning. His 63-by-17-foot mural was concealed with tar paper, and several months later a group of workmen demolished it with axes in the middle of the night.

Why? Nelson Rockefeller had commissioned Rivera to create a mural with the subject "human intelligence in control of the forces of nature." Rivera embarked on what he titled "Man at the Crossroads," and along the way included a small portrait of Vladimir Lenin. Critics railed. Politicians screamed. Newspapers called it willful propaganda.

Rockefeller insisted that Rivera erase the Red Revolutionary. The artist refused, but offered to add a portrait of Lincoln to balance the imagery. Rockefeller was incensed, and not only fired him but prevented him from moving the work to the Museum of Modern Art. Rivera never worked in the United States again.

But Rivera's mural wasn't the only piece of art in Rockefeller Center that evoked a public outcry. Another one is still standing today. The mammoth bronze statue of Atlas across the street from St. Patrick's Cathedral was picketed after its unveiling in 1937.

This time, critics and politicians saw the face of Benito Mussolini, Italy's fascist dictator, in the visage of the Greek god. The artists, Lee Lowrie and Rene Chambellan, insisted no such tribute was made, and the issue was eventually forgotten.

It's definitely worth a look, however. Scandinavian sculptor Carl Nesjaar used Norwegian black stone and concrete to magnify Picasso's 24-inch, sheet-metal "Sylvette." He first covered the stone in concrete, then etched away the outer layer to reveal the dark lines of the aggregate underneath. The sculpture was installed in the center of modernist architect I.M. Pei's 30-story apartment complex off the corner of Bleecker Street and LaGuardia Place, where it languishes almost completely unobserved to this day. Only in New York could a Picasso possibly be forgotten.

Art You Can Use

Photo: Daniel Hood

Alamo

Our Alamo is a giant (eight feet to a side) cube standing on one point in Astor Place. Created by sculptor Bernard "Tony" Rosenthal in 1966, it's now a magnet for skate rats, drunken NYU students, and the St. Marks Comics crowd. It's also a frequent venue of choice for anti-Christopher Columbus rallies, and in 2002 was briefly turned into a giant Rubik's Cube. The best thing about it? It spins on its point — provided you have enough drunken NYU students to push.

If given 3,600 square feet of prime loft space in the heart of SoHo, how would you decorate it? Artist **Walter De Maria** apparently preferred earth tones: he simply dumped soil all over the floor until it was 22 inches deep wall-to-wall.

His resulting interior sculpture, **The Earth Room**, is far more stunning than you might imagine. Ring the buzzer at 141 Wooster Street, walk up a flight of stairs, and observe how the sight and smell of 280,000 pounds of rich loam can soothe your entire nervous system. The ground emanates moisture and warmth; the silent serenity eases your mind; the patches of mushrooms embody a fertility uncommon to the city. Though in a second-floor loft in the middle of Manhattan, the room is the antithesis of all things urban.

Commissioned by the Dia Center for the Arts, the Earth Room received a lot of press when it opened in 1980, but has since become an unknown treasure in a neighborhood now packed with purveyors of chic. If you go, chances are good you'll have the stretch of soil to yourself.

De Maria has never offered a statement on the meaning of his primeval earth room. But hints of its genesis may be found in the names of the rock bands that he was involved with in the 1960s. De Maria was the drummer in a group with Lou Reed called The Primitives, a forerunner to The Velvet Underground.

Bad Day for Dalì

Talk about surreal; in March 2003, news broke that a sketch by **Salvador Dalì** had been stolen from a New York institution. Which would be only mildly interesting, except that the institution in question wasn't a museum – it was **Riker's Island**, the city's main detention center and one of the largest prison complexes in the country. Who hangs a painting worth hundreds of thousands of dollars in a place that, on any given day, is temporary home to as many as 15,000 criminals?

Dalì himself, that's who. In 1965, the corrections commissioner invited him to give a talk to the prisoners on the redemptive power of art, but when the day came, he found himself too sick to attend, and dashed off a picture (of Christ on the cross) by way of apology, with a note suggesting the sketch be displayed in the prisoner's dining room. And so it was until 1980, when an inmate splashed coffee on it, and the authorities ordered it removed to the lobby for safekeeping.

Still, prison is a precarious place for priceless portraiture, and no one could really pretend to be surprised to discover in 2003 that the original had been stolen from its display case in the prison lobby and replaced with a copy (among the giveaways was the fact that it had been stapled in place). After all, with all those criminals around....

Prisoners, though, aren't allowed in the lobby, so here's the final bit of surrealism: the police arrested four prison guards for the crime. After seeing the valuable painting day after day for years, the guards allegedly staged a fire drill in another part of the prison, using the diversion to install their fake. They were arrested only a few months later.

The painting, sadly, met an all-too-mundane fate, according to the testimony of one of the guards who turned state's evidence: sensing that the police were closing in, the mastermind of the plot destroyed it.

Photo: Daniel Hood

Metronome

The huge sunburst and flashing numbers on the wall of the Virgin Megastore at the bottom of Union Square are all part of a "sculpture" by Kristen Jones and Andrew Ginzel that's also supposedly the city's most accurate clock. It tells the phases of the moon, and emits steam on the hour and at noon and midnight. In 2000, the *New York Post* voted it one of the city's ugliest buildings. *1 Union Square South, bet. Broadway and Fourth Ave.*

The Unicorn Tapestries

Photo: Brad Dunn

BLUE LOO

In 1989 pop artist **Keith Haring** gave new meaning to the term "Men's Room." Commissioned to create a mural inside the second-floor men's restroom at the **Lesbian, Gay, Bisexual and Transgender Community Services Center** at 208 West 13th Street, Haring painted a graphic cartoon orgy of gay sex and dancing penises. The mural, which was hailed as "a powerful, black-and-white festival of sex," became one of the Center's main attractions for its boldness and celebration of homosexuality during the height of the AIDS crisis.

The Center, which recently completed an intense, three-year renovation, offers the gay community a wide range of services, including cultural programs, counseling, and recreational events such as bingo nights and dances.

The racy bathroom mural gained even more importance less than a year after it was completed: in 1990, Haring died of AIDS at the age of 31.

One of the greatest treasures of the Metropolitan Museum of Art goes unappreciated by thousands of museum visitors for one simple reason: it's not located at the main museum.

The Hunt of the Unicorn Tapestries hang in the quiet retreat of the **Cloisters** at the upper tip of Manhattan, in Fort Tryon Park *(212-923-3700)*. They are more than worth the haul north; woven between 1495 and 1505, the seven pieces are widely accepted as some of finest medieval tapestries in the world.

Though art historians do not know for whom the tapestries were made, each one has the initials A and a reverse E woven into them. Designed in France and made in Belgium, they were handed down through the generations, looted during the French Revolution, and finally were bought in 1922 by John D. Rockefeller, who donated them to the Met in 1937.

On the surface, the tapestries simply tell the story of the hunt and capture of a unicorn, but they also offer numerous hints of religious allegory. The myth of the

LITERATURE & THE ARTS   **131**

unicorn has been around since ancient China, but the fascination of this magical creature that never existed has spread across several civilizations.

The theme of these remarkable tapestries is the fight between a unicorn and the humans who hunt it. Not to spoil the story, let's just say it doesn't end well for the unicorn. Here's the title and quick summation of each of the seven tapestries:

1. Start of the Hunt: Only the hunters here, dressed to kill.
2. Unicorn at the Fountain: Uses his horn to remove snake venom from water.
3. Unicorn Leaps the Stream: Chased by furious hunting party.
4. Unicorn Defends Himself: Makes a stand, gives as good as he gets.
5. Unicorn Is Captured by the Maiden: There's an apple tree here, with a nod to Eve.
6. Unicorn Is Killed and Returned: Hunters are now sad about the dead animal.
7. Unicorn in Captivity: Alive again, though he's forever chained to a gate.

The Rest of the Mile

They don't call it Museum Mile because of the long lines outside the **Metropolitan Museum of Art** – there really is a mile of museums stretching north from 82nd Street. Struggle free of the Met's enormous gravitational pull, resist the impulse to spiral through Frank Lloyd Wright's giant flowerpot at the Guggenheim at 89th Street, and try some of these lesser-known Fifth Avenue mileposts.

El Museo del Barrio
Started in 1969 to highlight Puerto Rican art and culture; it now covers Latin America and the Caribbean too. *1230 Fifth Ave., at 104th St.; 212-831-7272; elmuseo.org*

Photo: Daniel Hood

Photo: Cooper-Hewitt National Design Museum

Cooper-Hewitt National Design Museum

The only museum in the U.S. devoted to historic and contemporary design, with innovative and funky exhibitions. (The building, once robber baron and steel magnate Andrew Carnegie's mansion, was the first residential structure to have a steel frame.)
*2 E. 91st St., at Fifth Ave.;
212-849-8400*

The Jewish Museum

One of the largest in the world devoted to the Jewish experience, housed in the mansion of mid-century financier Felix Warburg.
*1109 Fifth Ave., at 92nd St.;
212-423-3200; jewishmuseum.org*

Museum of the City of New York

A vast array of all things New York, including a great collection of urban landscape art and a toy collection with over 10,000 items.
*1220 Fifth Ave., at 103rd St.;
212-534-1672; mcny.org*

If Indiana Jones turned archaeology into a thrill ride, then the **South Street Seaport Museum** has turned it into an art form. **New York Unearthed** is one of the city's best-kept art secrets; established in 1990, the permanent exhibit reveals the fascinating underworld of a city that has been built and rebuilt innumerable times. Enter across the street from Battery Park at 17 State Street and walk through 6,000 years of urban and pre-urban history displayed in 10 delightful dioramas created by renowned graphic artist Milton Glaser (famous for his "I Love New York" logo).

Since skyscrapers began growing like weeds in Manhattan, millions of interesting objects have been discovered as foundations were laid. Glaser's dioramas include everything from ancient medicine vials and crucibles to cannonballs and clay pipes.

Sex on Display

The **Museum of Sex** *(233 Fifth Ave., 212-689-6337; museumofsex.com)* may sound like a porn shop, but it's really a serious, artistic institution on Fifth Avenue. Treating pornography as both art form and historical reference, the Museum of Sex, or MoSex, as its owners call it, celebrates New York's leading role throughout the sexual revolution. Though some visitors have raved about the power of its exhibits and others railed that they're more profane than profound, the institution remains a largely unknown destination to New Yorkers and tourists alike.

The museum's official mission is "to preserve and present the history, evolution, and cultural significance of human sexuality." To that end, the institution's displays include everything from explicit pornography to tributes to important historical figures like birth-control advocate Margaret Sanger. Of course, most exhibits are restricted to adults over 18, which gives you an idea of how blue they tend to be.

In a recent show, the museum showed the pornographic film *A Free Ride (aka A Grass Sandwich)* which was made between 1915 and 1919 and is widely considered the earliest surviving porn movie. Permanent exhibits include 19th-century erotica, featuring graphic paintings and sketches, and a section devoted to early sexual literature, including racy comic strips, erotic essays, and lesbian pulp novels.

According to one exhibit, early pornography was made for the nobility and upper classes. What few people know is that the first real erotica made for and distributed to the general masses was produced in New York; *The Tijuana Bibles* was an illegal comic strip sold underground in the early 1900s. MoSex features an interactive display paying tribute to this ground-breaking publication, which put real celebrities in fictional sexual situations. Strips include "Laurel and Hardy in 'Doing Things,'" and others based on everyone from Joe Louis and Cary Grant to Ginger Rogers and Wonder Woman.

National Academy of Design

1083 Fifth Ave., at 89th St.; 212-369-4880; nationalacademy.org

Neue Galerie New York

Exclusively early 20th-century German and Austrian art, including original works by Klee, Klimt, and Kandinsky, with a great café.

1048 Fifth Ave., at 86th St.; 212-628-6200; neuegalerie.org

Photo: Neue Galerie

Where Forbes Laid Eggs

DEMATERIALIZING

The *new* new thing in art museums is not to have a museum at all. At least, that's what the **Alternative Museum** decided when it gave up its lease at Broadway and Prince Street in 2000 in exchange for an address entirely in cyberspace *(alternativemuseum.org).* When it was founded in 1975, it was one of the few outlets available for artists who weren't being appreciated in the mainstream; such outlets are far more common now, and its founder, Geno Rodriguez, decided that the Web was the next art frontier. Rent, he says, had nothing to do with it.

If you had billions of dollars, would you blow a chunk of it on Faberge Eggs? Why not? That's what the Forbes family did, and now they can boast the largest collection of imperial eggs in the world, as well as the second-largest overall collection of Faberge Eggs (first is Queen Elizabeth II). Who wouldn't want to lay claim to that?

The **Forbes Magazine Galleries** *(60 Fifth Ave. at 12th St.; 212-206-5548)* will make you ask yourself these hypothetical questions, and many others. The free museum is packed with the kinds of luxury items that only the unthinkably wealthy would buy – pricey trinkets that the Forbes family has collected over the years. Though the highlight is certainly the precious Faberge Imperial Easter Egg collection, which were gifts from Russia's Czar Nicholas to his wife, the gallery also contains more than 500 toy boats that the Forbes have hoarded.

In addition, you'll see first-edition Monopoly sets, presidential memorabilia, and artifacts relating to Abraham Lincoln's assassination, including the opera glasses he was holding in his final minutes, his autopsy report, and his signature stovepipe hat. There's also more than 12,000 vintage toy soldiers, all engaged in various battles.

If the Forbes ever have a yard sale, you're looking at the main attractions.

Pity the **Brooklyn Museum**. In almost any other city, this would be the pre-eminent art museum, a cultural monolith that provides good reason for a swell of civic pride. In New York, though, it plays also-ran to the Met. Which may explain why, despite its world-class Egyptian collection, its 58 Rodin statues, and its paintings by Degas, Matisse, Sargent, Homer, and others, the museum feels obliged to try a little harder.

That means hosting exhibits like "Sensation," the 1999 show that included Damien Hurst's piece featuring cross-sections of a cow, and a Virgin Mary composed partly of elephant dung, by Nigerian artist Chris Ofili. The latter offended many (mostly those who hadn't seen it) as well as Mayor Rudy Giuliani, who threatened to cut the museum's $7 million subsidy from the city.

Then again, don't pity the museum. Their facilities are huge, their building is beautiful, their collection massive, and with all the first-place pressure on the Met, they're free to try shows like "Sensation," or to focus on their unparalleled collections of non-Western art and their 28 fully decorated period rooms.
200 Eastern Parkway, at Washington Ave.; 718-638-5000

More Museum and Archives

American Folk Art Museum
Fighting the good fight to prove that quilts, "tramp art," and things painted on tin really are art since 1961, and winning, particularly in their new building.
45 W. 53rd St., bet. Fifth and Sixth Aves.; 212-265-1040; folkartmuseum.org

Asia Society
John D. Rockefeller's institute for building cultural connections between the U.S. and Asia also houses exhibits on a huge range of Asian art.
725 Park Ave., at 70th St.; 212-288-6400

Photo: Daniel Hood

The Frick Collection

Robber barons are good for two things: endowments and art collections. Coke and steel magnate Henry Clay Frick's daughter left his brilliant collection of Old Masters and Renaissance art to the public, along with his mansion, which is a work of art in itself.
1 E. 70th St., bet. Madison and Fifth Aves.; 212-288-0700; frickmuseum.org

International Center for Photography

Founded by Robert Capa's brother Cornell, the ICP's collection includes their work, as well as that of Roman Vishniac, notorious New York tabloid photog Weegee, and many others. It also offers photography classes and discussions in its school diagonally across Sixth Avenue.
1133 Sixth Ave., at 43rd St.; 212-857-0000

Proud locals knew it all along, but it took the Museum of Modern Art's temporary relocation across the East River to clue many Manhattanites in to the wealth of art, particularly sculpture, already available in Queens, much of it drawn in by the cheap rents and large industrial spaces available in places like Long Island City and Astoria.

Photo: Daniel Hood

In good weather, a great place to start is the **Socrates Sculpture Park**, a reclaimed landfill and dump right on the water at Hallett's Cove, with a beautiful view of Roosevelt Island and Manhattan. The outsized outdoor sculptures are often created in place, with no restraints on the artists' wild creativity, so the park often feels like a cross between a construction site and a children's playground – which is fitting, since this is no staid museum gallery, but a great place for kids, sunbathing, and general hanging out. It also offers all sorts of participatory workshops and programs, and outdoor movies in the summer. *(Broadway at Vernon Blvd., Long Island City; 718-956-1819; socratessculpturepark.org)*

Nearby is the **Isamu Noguchi Garden Museum** *(32-37 Vernon Blvd., at 33rd Rd., Long Island City; 718-721-1932; noguchi.org)* which should, by the time you read this, have finished a series of renovations that had forced it to relocate to a spot conveniently close to MoMA's home-away-from-home. A Guggenheim Fellow and near-constant traveller, Noguchi settled into this industrial space in Long Island City in 1961, long before Queens became hip, and used it to create and display his unique blend of modern Western and ancient Eastern designs.

A more recent arrival is **SculptureCenter**, which started in Manhattan in 1928 and only arrived in Long Island City in 2002, in an industrial space redesigned by Maya Lin. *(44-19 Purves St. and Jackson Ave.; 718-361-1750; sculpture-center.org)*

For more than just sculpture, the **P.S. 1 Contemporary Arts Center** *(22-25 Jackson Ave., at 46th Ave., Long Island City; 718-784-2084; ps1.org)* has developed quite a name for itself as a hotbed of the cutting edge. Founded in 1971, the center moved into a century-old public school building in 1976, and since then has remained dedicated to supporting and presenting contemporary artists in a vast range of media, featuring artworks by Jack Smith, Julian Schnabel, and James Turrell. (It also operates the Clocktower Gallery, at 108 Leonard Street in Manhattan.)

So don't let nobody tell you there ain't no *culcha* in Queens....

Photo: PR Capuozzo

Jacques Marchais Museum of Tibetan Art

In a Himalayan-style building, find Tibetan art and cultural exhibits, as well as popular meditation and chanting classes, and an annual Tibetan rug sale.

338 Lighthouse Ave., off Richmond Rd., Staten Island; 718-987-3500

New Museum for Contemporary Art

Small but highly regarded, and ruthlessly contemporary; open to all forms and media. (Note: they're aiming to have a new home on Bowery by 2006.)

583 Broadway, bet. Houston and Prince Sts.; 212-219-1222

NYC's Mini-Me

Photo: Daniel Hood

For a brilliant aerial view of the city without all the expense of hiring a helicopter, trek out to the **Queens Museum of Art** in Flushing Meadows, where a minimal fee gets you entry to the **Panorama of New York**, a complete scale model of the entire city from the

Photo: Daniel Hood

Schomburg Center for Research in Black Culture

A branch of the NYPL, this is one of the largest research libraries in the countries devoted to the experiences of African-Americans. Among five million other things, it possesses the ashes of poet Langston Hughes, buried at the center of the auditorium that bears his name.
515 Malcolm X Blvd, at W. 135th St.; 212-491-2200

The Storefront for Art and Architecture

Uniquely designed small space for innovative looks at art, architecture, and design.
97 Kenmare St., bet. Mulberry St. and Cleveland Pl.; 212-431-5795

Studio Museum in Harlem

An impressive collection of works by artists of African descent, with a strong program for emerging artists.
144 W. 125th St., bet. Lenox and Seventh Aves.; 212-864-4500

Whitney Museum of American Art

Dedicated to American art from the 20th century on, this is home to the often-controversial Whitney Biennial, which showcases current trends and artists.
945 Madison Ave., at 75th St.; 800-WHITNEY; whitney.org

Outerbridge Crossing to Pelham Bay, from Van Cortlandt Park to the Rockaways. And we mean complete: The entire model is around 9,300 square feet, with almost 900,000 individual buildings and structures and a remarkable level of detail.

The largest architectural model in the world, the Panorama was commissioned for the 1964 World's Fair by planning czar Robert Moses, who thought it would be useful as a development tool (and also, we imagine, slipped in at night to play Godzilla, or maybe just God). After its stint as a popular attraction at the Fair, the model quickly fell behind the development of the real city, and was finally given a serious updating in 1992. Given the speed with which New York changes, there is always a bit of time lag before the model catches up with real life, but it's still a spectacular way to see the city.

Apart from the Panorama, the QMA also runs regular art shows and workshops, and has a great exhibition on New York's two World's Fairs.
New York City Building, Flushing Meadows Corona Park, Queens; 718-592-9700; queensmuseum.org

Photo: Bengt Wasellius/BAM

Head of the Glass

As the Village underwent its counter-culture sea change in the late 1960s and early '70s, so much new music, poetry, philosophy, and pop culture was born that few people know that another renaissance in the art world was also being hatched.

Glass blowing and glass sculpting were resurrected as a fine art, thanks in large part to a tiny shop called the **Heller Gallery**. Devoted to artists who worked exclusively with glass, the gallery celebrated the material in all its forms and in all its interactions with color, light, shape, and texture.

For three decades, the Heller Gallery has displayed sculptures that have since been acquired by major art institutions around the world, including the Metropolitan Museum, the Museum of Modern Art, the Louvre, and the Hokkaido Museum. Not only are few people aware that these inroads were made in New York, they don't know that the gallery is still open today in its new, larger studio, featuring 7,000 square feet of space devoted to nothing but breathtaking glass sculptures.
420 W. 14th St.; 212-41-4014; hellergallery.com

Words and Music (and Dance and Film and...)

Dublin's a long way away, but every June 16 for the past 20 years or so it surfaces in a little corner of the Upper West Side, when **Symphony Space** holds its annual "Bloomsday on Broadway" reading marathon from James Joyce's *Ulysses*. Which may not sound very symphonic, but then neither does their nationally broadcast Selected Shorts series of short story readings, or their dance programs, or their film festivals. The fact is, Symphony Space has been dedicated to providing community access to just about every kind of art there is since it was founded in 1978 in an abandoned movie house. It's come a long way since then, with two newly refurbished theaters (one called the Leonard Nimoy Thalia, after the very generous Mr. Spock) to host its eclectic season of readings, performances, and art classes. And yes, there is music in its busy schedule, too – quite a wide range of it, from chamber orchestras and *opera buffa* to Leonard Bernstein marathons and Gilbert & Sullivan revues. *2537 Broadway, bet. 94th and 95th Sts.; 212-864-5400; symphonyspace.org*

OPERA FOR THE REST OF US

Opera is a rich man's entertainment; the Met, remember, was built by upstart millionaires who couldn't get into the old money's opera house. That's where the **Amato Opera Theater** comes in: founded by husband-and-wife Tony and Sally Amato in 1948, the little theater puts on a full season of classics in a cozy theater seating 100 people or so, with tickets costing less than $30.

Over the years, it's gained a reputation as a great place to see young talent and rising stars, with many performers graduating uptown to Lincoln Center. *319 Bowery, at Bleecker St.; 212-228-8200; amato.org*

You Can't Go Home Again

Photo: Daniel Hood

Or so the **New York Philharmonic** found, when it tried to ditch its current digs at **Lincoln Center**. The Philharmonic, America's oldest orchestra – it traces its origins to the band that played for George Washington's funeral in 1799 – lived at **Carnegie Hall** from 1891 to 1962, when it was lured west to the new Lincoln Center complex. There it pays a hefty sum every year for the exclusive use of Avery Fischer Hall, which was a major draw, since at Carnegie Hall it had to accommodate visiting orchestras and all the other programs the hall hosted.

There was only one problem with Avery Fischer Hall: the acoustics weren't so hot. We're still not clear on how a purpose-built concert hall for the country's premiere orchestra can have so-so acoustics, but that's been the running joke about the Philharmonic for over 40 years. So when Carnegie Hall neared the completion of a major renovation and expansion in 2003, the board of the Philharmonic entered into secret negotiations to come back home, and announced over the summer that it would be back in its old stomping grounds by 2006.

In October 2003, though, the whole deal fell apart as quickly as it had come together. Carnegie Hall still planned on a full slate of non-Philharmonic programming, after all, and the Philharmonic still had a contract with Lincoln Center. The winner is clearly Lincoln Center, which gets to keep the $2.5 to $2.75 million the Philharmonic pays over every year – though they have promised a $250 million renovation soon. Presumably some of that will go to the acoustics.

Photo: Dan Perdue/Carnegie Hall

More Opera

DiCapo Theatre

A professional outfit that performs a full season of opera and musical theater on the Upper East Side. They also have a renowned Children's Chorus.
184 E. 76th St., bet. Third and Lexington Aves.; 212-288-9438; dicapo.com

New York City Opera

Just across the plaza from the Met, the "people's opera company" offers cheaper seats and a more eclectic repertoire, with a special dedication to fostering American opera. (They also introduced the first supertitles.) Placido Domingo and Beverly Sills started here.
New York State Theater, Lincoln Center, Columbus Ave. at 63rd St.; 212-870-5630

New York Philharmonic: *Lincoln Center, Broadway bet. 62nd and 65th Sts.; 212-875-5656; newyorkphilharmonic.org*
Carnegie Hall: *881 Seventh Ave., at 57th St.; 212-247-7800; carnegiehall.org*

Lore and Behold

Though New York is a famously self-infatuated town, there is really only one private organization that is devoted exclusively to putting the place – and its people – on a pedestal. Founded in 1986 "to produce programs and publications that convey the richness of New York City's cultural heritage," **City Lore** is a celebration of the city, by the city, and for the city.

Instead of focusing on all the glamour of New York and its obvious influence on the world, this conscientious nonprofit seeks to highlight the everyday human side of the five boroughs. Located in a beautiful old brownstone at 72 East First Street near First Avenue, City Lore offers photo archives, audio tapes, and historical documents to curious city lovers.

The group is staffed by devoted folklorists, historians, anthropologists, and ethnomusicologists, who all host open discussion groups and music and film festivals. A mix between a public poetry forum and a more-artistic Ellis Island, you can visit the gallery and learn more about the diversity of the city, or you can become a member and participate in countless city events all year long.

To give you an idea of the type of subjects that City Lore celebrates, check out its People's Hall of Fame online, which lists all the winners of the annual accolade. Instead of heaping more honors on the usual suspects, the organization recognizes the truly unsung folks who really have made a difference in New York. Past winners have included Ralph Lee, for creating the Greenwich Village Halloween Parade; Hovey Burgess, for his decades of mentoring young circus performers; Deborah Edel and Joan Nestle, for founding the Lesbian Herstory Archives; Rudy King, for bringing the steel drum to New York City; Bob Wilson and Cleve Jones for creating the AIDS quilt; and Peter Schumann, for creating the Bread & Puppet Theater.
72 East 1st St. near First Ave.; 212-529-1955; citylore.org

New York Grand Opera
Concentrating on Verdi and Puccini, they do free, fully staged productions in Central Park in the summer, as well as performances in other spaces like Carnegie Hall.
212-245-8837; newyorkgrandopera.org

Opera Orchestra of New York
Concert versions of rarely performed operas at Carnegie Hall.
212-799-1982; oony.org

JOEY'S VINYL
ROCK • R&B • SOUL • JAZZ
RARITIES • COLLECTORS ITEMS

Since the days when $24 bought an entire island, New York's been the place where everything is for sale – even the Brooklyn Bridge. From the country's first condom store to a service that will page you about a last-minute sample sale, the city takes shopping very seriously, and the only limit is the one on your credit card.

City Treasures

You can pay around $280,000 for a New York City taxi medallion from the Taxi & Limousine Commission, or you can spend around $20. The cheap ones aren't knockoffs; they're just decommissioned and sold at New York's very own city-run store. The store also has horseshoes once worn by NYPD mounts, the Department of Environmental Protection's alligator-in-the-sewer t-shirt, and all sorts of Department of Sanitation gear, as well as the more common kinds of tchotchkes you might expect, including NYPD and FDNY gear. To top it off, from time to time they sell seats from Yankee Stadium. And if you don't want to enter the city (or if you're already here but don't want to leave your apartment), try the **CityStore** online.
Municipal Building, North Plaza, 1 Centre St., at Chambers St.; 212-669-7452; nycitystore.com

New York's Thriving Rubber Industry

It's fitting that the shop that bills itself as "America's First Condom Store" should open in the city that never sleeps. Established in 1991 in the heart of Greenwich Village, **Condomania** today boasts over 3 million condoms sold. The company has even gone online with its catalogue of sensational (and sometimes deliberately less-sensational) latex contraceptives.

While roaming through the Village, check out the extra-large range of products for yourself. There's the camouflaged, the lollipop, and of course the glow-in-the-dark varieties. If edible condoms are more to your taste, then you're a kid in a candy store: There's mint, chocolate, banana, and strawberry, to name a few. The shop also boasts Gene Simmons-endorsed KISS Kondoms, as well as "Madonna Condoms" that come in packs featuring rare, lurid photos of the Material Girl.
351 Bleecker St., 212-691-9442

shopping as war

People ask what happened to roller derby – we suspect it morphed into the **sample sale**. Once or twice a year, designers and fashion houses take their prototype designs and unsold stock, mark it way down, and throw open the doors to hordes of bargain-crazed shoppers. It's ugly and it's hectic, but the opportunity for a serious score can't be beat – if you have the stomach for it.

And if you can find it. Sample sales are often held in secret spots away from the designer's regular location, or at undisclosed times; some are practically invitation-only. To get a jump on the competition, you need to be in the know (see Intelligence), and once you get there, you need to be ready for battle (see Strategy).

To practice your maneuvers, you can try **SSS Sample Sales** *(134 W. 37th St., bet. Sixth and Seventh Aves., 2nd floor; 212-947-8748)*, where labels send overstock on a regular basis. Nothing, though, can prepare you for the real thing: Fighting hand-to-hand over a wedding dress at **Vera Wang**'s sale, grappling for affordable cashmere at the semi-annual **TSE** sales, or struggling for control of a $10 rack at **Chaiken & Capone**.

INTELLIGENCE

Both *New York* and *TimeOut New York* print lists of sample and regular sales, but they're weeklies, and you need to know *now*. Turn to the Web, where a number of sites offer frequently updated lists; many will even e-mail you when news of a sale pops up.

budgetfashionista.com

Sales lists, and advice for the budget-conscious.

dailycandy.com

The inside scoop on sales, products, and lots, lots more.

Beauty in the Rubble

As a city that devours itself, New York has plenty of architectural ornaments and fixtures to recycle. Be warned, though: as more and more people learn to appreciate the hand-crafted feel of the old, prices can only get higher. Some places to check out:

Manhattan Castles and Props

An outdoor lot with old signage and statuary.
76 East Houston St., at Elizabeth St.; 212-505-8699

Olde Goode Things

Run by the Church of Bible Understanding, a controversial sect out of Philadelphia, and the inspiration for *Seinfeld's* "Carpet Cleaning Cult."
124 W. 24th Street, bet. Sixth and Seventh Aves.; 212-989-8401; 19 Greenwich Ave., at W. 10th St.; 212-229-0850; 400 Atlantic Ave., near Bond St., Brooklyn; 718-935-9742

girlshop.com

They have sales of their own on many designers.

lazarshopping.com

Its S&B Report is considered the most complete – but they charge for it.

nymetro.com

New York Magazine's Web site.

nysale.com

They'll page you for an important sale.

STRATEGY

Never like anything.

Your fellow shoppers can smell desire, and it makes them desire, too.

Buy 'em all – let God sort 'em out.

When in doubt, buy. You'll end up with some duds, but you'll miss out on less.

Grab.

With both hands.

Don't be self-conscious.

There often aren't changing rooms, so be prepared to flash (or be flashed) if you insist on trying things on. Some hardcore samplers suggest wearing a body stocking.

Schmuck Bros.
Hands-down winner for the best store name in antiques. *205 E. 125th St., bet. Second and Third Aves.; 212-369-6400*

Urban Archaeology
Salvaged items as well as lines of reproduction fixtures and bathroom accessories. *143 Franklin St., bet. Hudson and Varick Sts.; 212-431-4646; 239 E. 58th St., bet. Second and Third Aves.; 212-371-4646*

Photo: Daniel Hood

You can't keep a good shopping district down: in the late 1800s and early 1900s, Sixth Avenue in Chelsea was **Ladies' Mile**, the shopping destination of choice and home to some of the city's greatest stores, from the original Macy's at 14th Street, to B. Altman's at 19th Street opposite Siegel-Cooper's "Big Store," a veritable palace of a department store, all the way up to Stern Brothers at 23rd Street.

For a generation, that's where any New Yorker of note shopped, brought in by the Sixth Avenue El (notice how the exteriors of many of the buildings are more elaborate on the second floor, the only part train passengers would see). But as the city grew north, so did the retail trade, beginning with Macy's departure for 34th Street in 1902, after which many other big names decamped for Fifth Avenue above 42nd Street. For most of the century, the old Mile languished, until rezoning and the relentless churn of New York real estate made many of the old buildings attractive to retailers in the 1990s.

Nowadays, Siegel-Cooper's gorgeous old palace at 620 Sixth Avenue is home to not one but three stores: **T.J. Maxx**, **Filene's Basement**, and **Bed, Bath and Beyond**, and there's an **Old Navy** just down the street at 610 Sixth Avenue. There's a giant **Barnes & Noble** at 675 Sixth at 21st Street, a **Burlington Coat Factory** and a **Baby Depot** up at 707 Sixth, and a **Sports Authority** at 636 Sixth.

Consignment Stores

Sure, someone else wore it — but we're not talking Goodwill here. In New York there's an awful lot of designer togs sloshing around, and the original owners often send them to consignment stores in hopes of raising some cash. For classier duds, think uptown; hipsters head downtown. Most of these stores concentrate on women's fashions, unless otherwise noted.

Tokyo Joe
Nobody knows funky fashion like the Japanese — and they shop here a lot. *334 E. 11th St., bet. First and Second Aves.; 212-473-0724*

Children's Resale Clothing
303 E. 81st St., at Second Ave.; 212-734-8897

Designer Resale
324 E. 81st St., bet. First and Second Aves.; 212-734-3639

Mirage on 34th Street

Photo: Daniel Hood

Encore
*1132 Madison Ave., near 84th St.,
2nd floor; 212-879-2950*

Fisch for the Hip
*153 W. 18th St., bet. Sixth and
Seventh Aves.; 212-633-6965*

Gentlemen's Resale Clothing
*322 E. 81st St., bet. First and
Second Aves.; 212-734-2739*

INA
*101 Thompson St., bet. Prince and
Spring Sts.; 212-941-4757
21 Prince St., bet. Mott and
Elizabeth Sts.; 212-334-9048
208 E. 73 St., bet. Second and Third
Aves.; 212-249-0014
Men's: 262 Mott St., bet. Prince and
Houston Sts.; 212-334-2210*

Michael's
*1041 Madison Ave., near 79th St.,
2nd floor; 212-737-7273*

A Second Chance
*1109 Lexington Avenue,
bet. 77th and 78th Sts.,
2nd floor; 212-744-6041*

At a glance, the first and still most famous department store in the world takes up an entire city block in midtown Manhattan, flanked by Seventh Avenue on one side, Herald Square on the other. But a look at city property records reveals a tiny inconsistency.

The miracle of **Macy's** is that it has managed to hold on to the title of largest department store on the planet, despite being located in a city with one of the highest prices per square foot on earth. Still, it does not own the entire block. Ironically, the ground beneath the giant "Macy's" sign near its southeast entrance is held in non-Macy's hands.

The missing card in an otherwise perfect hand is the product of a failed gambit played out long ago between Macy's and its competitor, the Siegel-Cooper department store.

When Macy's relocated to 34th Street in 1902, Henry Siegel desperately wanted to move his store into Macy's old location at 14th Street. To add incentive to the deal, Siegel quickly purchased a small chunk of land on the northwest corner of Broadway and 34th Street, which clearly lay in Macy's block-wide ambitions. Macy's didn't budge, didn't do business with Siegel, and ultimately built around the parcel of land. Today, the hold-out property houses a Sunglass Hut, and Macy's leases the space above it for its enormous ad.
151 West 34 St., at Seventh Ave.

Deal of the Century

Though not exactly unknown to many New Yorkers, one of the greatest discount stores in the city, and possibly the continent, has been dubbed by its salivating patrons "the best-kept shopping secret in New York."

Century 21 not only sells everything from real-deal designer clothes and cosmetics to brand-name housewares and electronics, it also sells them all for at least 40 percent less than regular stores (many items up to 70 percent off). How? The emporium buys unsold, high-end European and American merchandise by the barge load. Bulk means cheap prices, and cheap prices on chic labels like Prada, Versace, and Ungaro mean people with fashion sense and financial savvy line up by the hundreds.

With its flagship location just across the street from the World Trade Center site, Century 21, like many downtown businesses, suffered a major blow after the terrorist attacks of 9/11. The place was hit with tons of falling debris and had to close down for a five-month renovation. But it bounced back in a big way. Thousands of bargain hunters showed up on its reopening in February 2002, which was hosted by none other than Mayor Michael Bloomberg. The doors were opened at 11 a.m. and by 12:30 p.m. the doors had to be closed because the four-story store was filled to capacity.

Though you might expect a vendor of so many svelte goods to occupy an equally glamorous space, Century 21 is actually a pretty ragged place. The deals may be sweet, but the shopping experience itself falls a little on the sour side. Bargain-hungry patrons swarm the bins, and with rolled-up sleeves tear through the merchandise like a pack of wild boars. The fitting rooms have no doors, and the lighting throughout the building seems more suitable to an interrogation room. Still, the

Comic Opera

Comic book stores are odd places to begin with, but there can be none odder than **Funny Business Comics** (660B Amsterdam Ave., bet. 92nd and 93rd Sts.; 212-799-9477), a tiny retailer with a wide selection of back issues of Marvel and DC comics that shares its space with **Live Opera Heaven**, which sells old opera recordings. The sign alone is worth the trip.

Forbidden Planet
A heavy emphasis on science fiction and fantasy.
840 Broadway, at 13th St.;
212-473-1576

Jim Hanley's Universe

The whole spectrum, from superheros to Harvey Pekar.
4 W. 33rd St., bet. Fifth and Sixth Aves.; 212-268-7088; 325 New Dorp Lane, Staten Island; 718-351-6299

Midtown Comics

Two floors and 200,000 back issues.
200 W. 40th St., at Seventh Ave.; 212-302-8192

St. Mark's Comics

Famous for Comic Book Guy-style attitude.
11 St. Mark's Pl., bet. Second and Third Aves.; 212-598-9439; 148 Montague St., bet. Clinton and Henry Sts., Brooklyn; 718-935-0911

Village Comics

More underground, with a big adult section.
214 Sullivan St., near Bleecker St.; 212-777-2770

unbelievable finds and jaw-dropping prices keep Century 21 a regular destination for shopping-savvy New Yorkers.
22 Cortlandt St., bet. Church St. and Broadway; 212-227-9092

If the Shoe Fits

Footwear fetishists around the world swoon over the name **Peter Fox**, but the fact that one of the most renowned shoe designers on the planet runs his flagship boutique in the Village is lost on many New Yorkers.

Treating the shoe as a work of art, Peter Fox has sparked more lasting fashions than Gianni Versace or Donna Karan. Since the late 1970s, his designs have captured the imagination of chic pop culture, including the Granny boot, the platform shoe, and the ultra-modern boots now seen all over fashion show runways. Give the man laces, leather, buckles, and straps, and he'll give you a glimpse of what the ultra-hip will be wearing next year.

Born in London in 1933, Fox found his calling as an assistant in the footwear department of the world-famous Harrod's. After learning the trade from master shoemakers, he moved to Vancouver in 1954, got married, and decided to launch his own line of shoes. Success followed success, and in 1981, he opened his first store. Today, the shop is more art gallery than footwear emporium, and his talents continue to receive attention from not only the fashionistas, but also the entertainment world.

If you don't believe the shoe can be a work of art, swing by his store and behold his current efforts. Otherwise trust the judgment of the curator at the Brooklyn Museum: many Peter Fox designs were selected for a permanent art exhibit there entitled "Fancy Feet: A Historic Collection of Ladies' Footwear."
105 Thompson St., near Prince St.; 212-431-7426

Alley of the Dolls

At the **Manhattan Dollhouse** in Chelsea, you can't swing your arms without hitting an expensive doll or doll house. That's not only because the store is small, but also because it offers an incredible range of collectibles for hobbyists and toddlers alike.

The shop at 176 Ninth Avenue is worth checking out even if you've never given antique dolls a second thought. You'll be amazed by the detail of its Colonial mansions and classic New York City brownstones. The store sells them assembled or in build-it-yourself kits, and you can augment any of these scaled-down homes with additional rugs, furniture, trim, and lighting fixtures. The place is truly the Home Depot for doll houses.

Then there's the dolls themselves. Antiques, collectibles, moderns, you name it. The shop is most famous for its unmatched collection of Madame Alexander dolls. Best of all, the store boasts an in-house doll doctor: If any afflictions strike your collectibles, such as chipped eyelids or dislocated shoulders, they'll fix your little one right up.
428 Second Ave., bet. 24th and 25th Sts.;
212-725-4520

Tina Fey Sat Here

Why get a sofa like the one you saw on TV, when you can have the actual sofa? **Props for Today** rents furniture to TV and movie sets, and then sells the used stuff off. The best part are the tags, which tell what show or movie the piece was used on — and also have very low prices on them. Stock sells fast, and the provenance isn't always electrifying (your friends may not be impressed by the couch from the second-to-last sketch of last week's *Saturday Night Live*), but cool things do show up, and it's still the closest we've been to being on TV.
330 W. 34th St., bet. Eighth and Ninth Aves.;
212-244-9600

Recycled Tunes

If you have any shred of guilt about downloading songs for free, you can make yourself feel slightly better by buying a used album for a fraction of the new cost.

The city is host to dozens of excellent used music shops. Among the best of the best, however, is **Etherea** at 66 Avenue A in the East Village *(212-358-1126)*. The small store with huge windows maintains an impressive inventory of rock, hip-hop, electronica, and easy-listening. About two-thirds of the shop is CDs, while the other third is vinyl. You can also pick up some rare and interesting music documentaries and other related videos. Best of all, the shop will pay top dollar for that album collection you want to retire (up to $6 a CD, anyway), as long as your tastes hit the mark.

Here are some other terrific used music shops, mostly in the Villages, East and West, which take their music very seriously, and where you're likely to bump into the DJ from the club last night.

Academy
Cheap for all kinds of used CDs and vinyl.
12 W. 18th St., bet. Fifth and Sixth Aves.; 212-242-3000

Bleecker Bob's Golden Oldies
Rock up to punk.
118 W. 3rd St., at Macdougal St.; 212-475-9677

Breakbeat Science
Drum 'n' bass; popular with DJs.
181 Orchard St., at Stanton St.; 212-995-2592

Dance Tracks
Vinyl; named best underground record store by *Billboard*.
91 E. 3rd St., bet. First and Second Aves.; 212-260-8729

The Diamond District of Cameras

Photo: Daniel Hood

It's not the fact that professional photographers and photo-journalists like to hang out there that makes **B&H Cameras** interesting, nor is it the vast array of nicely-priced equipment. It's not even the Diamond District feel that comes from the fact that it's owned and run by Orthodox Jews (though that does mean you should check before going over, since they're closed on Jewish holidays you may have never even heard of). No, what really makes it interesting is the Rube Goldberg-esque system of ceiling-hung conveyor belts that send your basket of camera equipment zigging and zagging overhead from the counters where you pick it out, past the cashiers where you pay for it, and to the counter where you pick it up.
420 Ninth Ave., bet. 33rd and 34th Sts.; 212-444-6615

Photo: Daniel Hood

You know when they put up special street signs that say "Bargain District" that it's less of a bargain than it used to be, but that shouldn't keep the serious clothes hound away from Orchard Street between East Houston and Delancey Streets. After all, around the turn of the last century, the Lower East Side launched a thousand tailors, dressmakers, and pushcart salesmen (back when pushcarts were sort of like rolling discount stores) – most of them Jewish immigrants who made the neighborhood a sort of ur-Garment District.

The LES is less Jewish these days than Latino (and cheap-living artsy types), but many of the stores still close on Saturday to observe the Sabbath, so don't go then; try Sunday instead, when Orchard is closed to traffic and the bargains roll out into the street on racks.

It's all there, from discount women's wear at places like **Forman's** *(82 Orchard St.; 212-228-2500; also 145 E. 42nd St. bet. Lexington and Third Aves. and 59 John St., at William St.)* and **Klein's of Monticello** *(105 Orchard; 212-966-1453)*; handbags or luggage at **Fine & Klein** *(119 Orchard; 212-674-6720)*, **Grace Bags** *(190 Orchard; 212-228-6118)*, and **Altman's Luggage** *(125 Orchard; 212-254-7275)*; women's underwear of all descriptions and sizes at the **Orchard Corset Discount Center** *(157 Orchard; 877-267-2427)*; furs and leathers at **Arivel Fashions** *(150 Orchard; 212-673-8992)*; and the general free-for-all at **Ben Freedman** *(137 Orchard; 212-674-0854)*. Plus, there are more fabric and linen shops than you can shake a stick at – so many, in fact, that they spill over into the surrounding streets, so don't limit yourself just to Orchard.

Also, keep an eye open for chic boutiques like **anastasiaholland** *(184 Orchard; 212-777-1999)*, **DDC Lab** *(180 Orchard; 212-375-1647; also*

Finyl Vinyl
Great rare and out-of-print selections.
204 E. 6th St., bet. Second and Third Aves.; 212-533-8007

Footlight Records
Musicals, soundtracks, and scores.
113 E. 12th St., at Fourth Ave.; 212-533-1572

Photo: Daniel Hood

Gryphon Record Shop
90,000 rare records.
233 W. 72nd St., bet. Amsterdam and West End Aves.; 212-874-1588

Halcyon
Club music of all kinds, and a coffee bar.
227 Smith St., bet. Butler and Douglass Sts., Brooklyn; 718-260-9299

427 W. 14th St., at Ninth Ave.) and **Jelena Behrend**'s all-handmade jewelry shop *(188 Orchard; 212-995-8497)*. A number of these decidedly non-discount places have infiltrated the nabe from the pricier latitudes of Soho and Nolita, but what they lack in wallet-friendliness, they make up for in bleeding-edge fashion.

If you plan shopping expeditions like they're the Normandy landings, you'll want to drop by the **Lower East Side Visitor Center** *(261 Broome St., bet. Orchard and Allen Sts.; 212-226-9010; (lowereastsideny.com)* for a local shopping guide, but the best tip we can offer is to remember that the key at the real bargain places is haggling, for which you only really need one real skill: the ability to walk away. Haggle in good faith, though – these guys are professionals, and you don't want to waste their time.

The Pants-Matcher

Photo: Daniel Hood

If you tear your eyes away from the bargain racks on Orchard Street long enough to look up, you may notice the name **Beckenstein** in huge letters on the front of a few buildings. An Orchard Street mainstay, Beckenstein's was a famous "pants-matcher" – if, say, the knees of your suit pants wore out, they'd match the fabric from the thousands of samples in their vast collection, and make you a new pair. They've bounced around a lot of locations in these few blocks, but their men's fabrics are currently at 133 Orchard Street *(212-475-6666)*. Their main branch, though, has moved uptown and out of the old neighborhood. **Beckenstein Fabric & Interiors** *(4 W. 20th St., near Fifth Ave.; 212-366-5142)* concentrates on upholstery and other furniture fabrics; they've got over 7,000 samples in stock.

House of Oldies
Vinyl oldies.
35 Carmine St., bet. Bedford and Bleecker Sts.; 212-243-0500

Jammyland
Ska and reggae.
60 E. 3rd St., bet. First and Second Aves.; 212-614-0185

Jazz Record Center
236 W. 26th St., Room 804, bet. Seventh and Eighth Aves.; 212-675-4480

Joe's CDs
11 St. Mark's Pl., 212-673-4606

Mooncurser Records
Old vinyl only; over 100,000.
229 City Island Ave., near Scofield St., City Island, the Bronx; 718-885-0302

NYCD
426 Amsterdam Ave., near 80th St.; 212-724-4466

Replacing the Irreplaceable

Photo: Daniel Hood

Architectural salvagers are usually the only people who are happy when a building collapses – unless the building that collapses is theirs. That's what happened to Evan Blum, one of the city's best-known salvagers, when the four-story warehouse that housed his **Irreplaceable Artifacts** store came tumbling down in the summer of 2000. The collapse endangered the building's neighbors at Second Avenue and Houston Street, forced the evacuation of the low-income co-op for formerly homeless people, closed a subway station, and landed Blum in a whole lot of hot water.

The city moved in to demolish the remains of the building, claiming that the collapse was a direct result of renovation work that Blum had conducted despite a work-stop order. Blum, who in 1992 had been evicted from a city lot on the Bowery for not paying his rent, fought back to no avail, and soon found himself indicted for reckless endangerment. In late 2003, he and his father were convicted on the misdemeanor charge.

Fortunately, for those in search of antique architectural details, Irreplaceable Artifacts has a replacement: Blum's Harlem outpost at **The Demolition Depot**, another four-story warehouse on 125th Street that's jam-packed with gorgeous doors, mantels, windows, fixtures, and everything else that can be rescued from buildings slated for destruction.
214 E. 125th St., bet. Second and Third Aves.; 212-860-1138; demolitiondepot.com

Other Music
Underground and experimental.
15 E. 4th St., bet. Broadway and Lafayette St.; 212-477-8150

Rockit Scientist Records
43 Carmine St., at Bleecker St.; 212-242-0066

Rocks In Your Head
157 Prince St.; 212-475-6729

Shrine
441 E. 9th St.; 212-529-6646

Sonic Groove
Techno and electronica.
206 Ave. B, bet. 12th and 13th Sts.; 212-675-5284

Photo: Daniel Hood

Sounds

Just about everything. Seriously.
16 and 20 St. Mark's Pl.,
bet. Second and Third Aves.;
212-677-2727

Temple Records

Techno.
29A Ave. B, bet. 2nd and 3rd Sts.;
212-475-7552

Village Jazz Shop

163 W. 10th St., bet. Waverly Pl.
and Seventh Ave. South;
212-741-2635

Vinylmania

Dance music from disco on.
60 Carmine St., bet. Bedford and
Bleecker Sts.; 212-924-7223

You don't have to be a Wiccan to appreciate the incredible variety of herbs, oils, incense, and spices at one of the best-kept shopping secrets in the Village. But it might make you love the store even more.

As its name suggests, **Aphrodisia** is an exotic feast for the senses. The shop is worth browsing if just for the aromas. The air is perfumed by more than 800 spices from around the world – from Jamaica to Jordan, Vienna to Vietnam. Most are sold in glass jars like dry goods, which means you can not only see, taste, and smell them before you buy them, you can also purchase exactly how much you want.

There are also plenty of unusual items you're not likely to find elsewhere: lobster mushrooms, exotic dried fruits, and rare erotic oils, to name a few. The owner also keeps purveyors posted on its spice imports. A sign recently posted inside read: "Due to crop failure there will be no arrowroot until spring."

Moreover, whether you're an aspiring gourmand or an experienced potion maker, Aphrodisia offers a range of books on aroma therapy, Chinese medicine, and magical herbalism. With everything from sickness remedies to romance inducers, the store will have something desirable every time you visit.
264 Bleecker St.; 212-989-6440

Button Gluttons

TENDER BUTTONS

You'd think it would be difficult to pay the rent by selling buttons. But, amazingly, that's all they do at **Tender Buttons** on the Upper East Side – and they not only pay the rent, they're known as the best button business in the country. Stop by their large, gallery-like store and you'll be overwhelmed by the mind-boggling expanse of buttons: they line the shelves like a pebble beach stretching for miles. There's the blazer buttons, the French and Italian couturier buttons, the Edwardian cuff links, the tuxedo shirt studs. From floor to ceiling, there are buttons representing every style and age and function since the dawn of humanity. You might even find a belt buckle or two.

The white, standard-issue dress shirt button will run you 50 cents, while you can expect to shell out a couple of C-notes for a single, antique gold button inlaid with a precious stone. Your kids will love it too: the place has a slew of cute, colorful, silly buttons that they can sew on their dolls' clothes or their own.

Of course, if you don't have time to gaze through the entire button genome, and simply want to replace one that fell off your favorite shirt, the staff will find a perfect match for you in no time.

143 E. 62nd St., near Lexington Ave.; 212-758-7004

Flea Circus

Sure, you can find some nice things at Tiffany's or Bloomingdale's, but where can you get a pile of Gordon Lightfoot albums on vinyl or an umbrella stand from the 1940s? Manhattan is host to some of the best permanent and seasonal flea markets around. Whether you want a piece of antique jewelry or a velvet Elvis portrait, walk the rows of some of these.

Annex Antique Fair & Flea Market

Furniture, decorations, jewelry, clothing, silver, and works of art.
$1.00 admission fee
Sixth Ave. from 24th to 27th Sts.; 212-243-5343; Saturday and Sunday, sunrise to sunset

Columbus Avenue Flea Market

Vintage furniture, antiques, jewelry.
162 W. 72nd St.; 212-721-0900

On a budget? Credit cards maxed out? There's hope yet, and help, in some of the city's giant discount emporia. For housewares, dishes, toys, and assorted knick-knackery, try **Jack's World** *(110 W. 32nd St., bet. Sixth and Seventh Aves.; 212-268-9962)*, **Odd-Job Trading** *(169 E. 60th St., at Third Ave.; 212-893-8447; locations in all five boroughs; oddjobstores.com)*, or **National Wholesale Liquidators** *(632 Broadway, bet. Houston and Bleecker Sts.; 212-979-2400; locations in Brooklyn, Queens, and Staten Island; nationalwholesaleliquidators.com)*. This is not brand-name stuff, but it's a few steps above doing all your shopping from blankets on St. Mark's Place.

For clothes, your best bet may be the strip of 34th Street from Sixth Avenue to Eighth Avenue, where most of the stores sell cheap, Macy's excluded. Worth a try is the similar section of West 14th Street, where there are bargain bins to be pawed through.

The Garage

Indoor antiques market.

112 W. 25th St.; 212-647-0707;

Saturday and Sunday, 7 a.m.- 5 p.m.

Greenflea

Imports, handmade crafts, antiques and books. Also: fresh produce.

Columbus Ave., bet. 76th and 77th

Sts.; Sunday, 10 a.m.- 6 p.m.

Noho Market

Clothing, jewelry, tapes, sunglasses, bongs.

Broadway and W. 4th St.; open

seven days a week.

Coin Operators

The world's rarest and most unusual coins, like its rarest and most unusual people, tend to find their way to New York eventually. Whether you're a numismatic fanatic or are in the market for a few high-price tokens of history, the city has at least two shopping destinations for you.

Stack's Coin Co. *(123 W. 57th St.; 212-582-2580)* is the largest dealer of rare coins in the United States. A coin shop ironically founded in the middle of the Depression, Stack's has handled some of the most valuable coins in the world. Among recent lots handled was a piece from the Roman Republic, stamped in 42 B.C., which depicted the bare head of Brutus on one side and the "cap of liberty" flanked by daggers on the other. The shop also advertised an almost flawless, 1794 U.S. half-dollar, which shows "Miss Liberty with flowing hair" on the front and a thinner American eagle on the back. The rarest coin to go through its doors was a 1933 U.S. $20 gold piece, which was never released by the Mint, and sold for $7.5 million at Sotheby's.

Another terrific coin destination is **Donald Brigandi** *(60 W. 44th St.; 212-869-5350)*, which sells a slightly more affordable range of vintage coins, mostly originating from North America. It also sold a $20 gold piece, though this one was circulated in the 1850s, for $75,000 at a recent auction.

Don't think there aren't deals for the lighter spenders: at Brigandi, you can walk away with some pretty cool classic coins for less than a C-note.

Upstart Oldtimers

If Kiehl's seems like an upstart to you, try **Caswell-Massey**, "America's Oldest Chemist," for bath and body products; George Washington bought cologne from them and Sarah Bernhardt liked their cold cream, so you know you're in good company. They're not a New York original, unfortunately, having been founded in Rhode Island in 1752, and they only arrived in the city at the very late date of 1860.
518 Lexington Ave., at 48th St.; 212-755-2254; caswellmassey.com

Specialty Bookstores

If you can't find it in Manhattan, you won't find it anywhere. Here's where to look for those unusual titles, ancient tomes, rare collections, and one-of-a-kind books that you can't get anywhere else. Sorted by specialty, but first:

TWO UNKNOWN GEMS

United Nations Bookshop

Huge selection of books on world affairs, hard-to-find reports, and surveys and studies performed by the United Nations since its inception.
General Assembly Building, E. 45 St. and First Ave., Room 32; 800-253-9646

U.S. Government Bookstore

Official publications from the U.S. Government Printing Office, with titles on agriculture, business, consumer aids, transportation, and best of all, space exploration.
Room 110, Federal Building, 26 Federal Plaza; 212-264-3825

USED

Argosy

Used hardcover fiction, old prints, Americana, antique and used books, maps, and prints.
116 E. 59th St.; 212-753-4455

Gotham Book Mart

Since 1920. Jacqueline Kennedy Onassis once said, "I cannot imagine New York City without it." Supplied James Joyce books to U.S. readers, including those banned under U.S. obscenity laws. Rumor has it the store may relocate soon.
41 W. 47th St.; 212-719-4448

Gryphon Bookshop

Enormous literature and history sections, and probably the world center for *Wizard of Oz* books.
2246 Broadway, bet. 80th and 81st Sts.; also at 233 W 72nd St.; 212-362-0706

Housing Works Used Book Cafe

Huge selection, lovely wood-library setting, and all profits go to Housing Works, which supports homeless people with HIV and AIDS.
126 Crosby St., bet. Houston and Prince Sts.; 212-334-3324

Strand Book Store

The one, the only. The new and used bookshop that defines New York. Smaller branches at 95 Fulton Street, and Second Avenue between 59th and 60th Streets.
828 Broadway, at 12th St.; 800-366-3664

Vanity Since 1851

Photo: Kiehl's

Fashions in clothes and shoes may come and go, but smooth skin and a sweet smell are always in demand, which neatly explains the longevity of **Kiehl's**, the East Village pharmacy that has been dispensing its unique skin creams, shampoos, lipsticks, perfumes, and the like from the same location since 1851. The shop itself is old-fashioned fun, and though the upscale products aren't cheap, Kiehl's is famed for its good-sized free samples and friendly staff. Budding metrosexuals take note: almost half of the clientele is male, and even if you haven't gone all Beckham yet, there's a collection of vintage motorcycles to keep you occupied while your significant other loads up.

Though it was bought by L'Oreal in 2000, Kiehl's has kept its individuality, and recently reaffirmed its deep neighborhood roots by rededicating the nearby intersection Pear Tree Corner, after the fruit tree that had stood there for 200 years before being plowed down by an out-of-control wagon in 1867.
109 Third Ave., at 13th St.; 212-677-3171; kiehls.com

Flower Power

In one of the grittiest, most disheveled parts of midtown lies a brilliant swath of color and life, where the commonplace smells of the city are beat out by strong, soothing fragrances. By rounding a single corner, you can cross the border between a dilapidated commercial neighborhood and Oz.

The **Flower District** is the smallest, and one of the last, of New York's single-trade districts. Stretching west of Sixth Avenue between 26th and 29th Streets, this 100-year-old floral oasis is clinging to its roots despite relentless market forces that would drive it out.

Offering virtually every variety of flower and innumerable arrangements, these shops have given color to almost every New York institution: Broadway theaters, Fifth Avenue boutiques, five-star restaurants, public parks and gardens, and city monuments, to name a few. But time may be running out to enjoy this secret shopping gem.

The collective of dealers, florists, wholesalers, and retailers is wilting under the pressure of rising real estate costs, stifling car traffic, and increasing pedestrian congestion from Herald Square. Though several of the businesses have banded together to scout out possible locations for a new flower district, many of them are choosing go it alone.

With thousands of colorful blossoms and wonderful aromas, the Flower District is a requisite destination not only for amateur botanists, exhausted shoppers, and celebrating couples, but also – because it's sadly shrinking – urban historians.

ARTS & SCIENCE

Applause Books
Specializes in theater and film.
211 W. 71st St.; 212-496-7511

Book Scientific
Excellent selection of physics, chemistry, engineering, mathematics, and computer texts.
10 W. 19th St., 3rd floor; 212-206-1310

Drama Book Shop
Almost every play ever written is in stock.
723 Seventh Ave., at 48th St., 2nd floor; 212-944-0595

International Center of Photography Bookstore
Unbeatable selection of photography books.
1133 Sixth Ave.; 212-860-1767

Patelson's House of Music
Books about music, classical music scores.
160 W. 56th St., at Sixth Ave.; 212-582-5840

MYSTERY

Murder Ink
2486 Broadway, bet. 92nd and 93rd Sts.; 212-362-8905

The Mysterious Book Shop
129 W. 56th St., 212-765-0900

Partners & Crime
44 Greenwich Ave., near
W. 10th St.; 212-243-0440

RARE

Antiquarian Book Arcade
Vintage, rare and antiquarian books.
110 W. 25th St., 9th floor;
212-678-6011

Ursus Books Ltd.
New and out-of-print art
books and catalogues.
981 Madison Ave., bet. 76th and
77th Sts.; 212-772-8787

CULTURE

Fil Caravan
Middle Eastern history,
culture, and philosophy.
240 E. 56th St., Suite 2E;
212-421-5972

J. Levine Jewish Books and Judaica
Huge Judaica selection,
over 100 years old.
5 W. 30th St.; 212-695-6888

Kinokuniya Bookstore
Japanese books, origami paper,
and art supplies.
10 W. 49th St.; 212-765-7766

Macondo Books
The king of Spanish-language
bookstores.
221 W. 14th St.; 212-741-3108

A Bad Trade

Photo: Daniel Hood

Every Christmas, **Cartier** wraps its flagship store at Fifth Avenue and 52nd Street in a big red ribbon, as if the whole thing was a gift – which, in some ways, it was. Back in 1917, the building was the townhouse of railroad tycoon Morton Plant, who sold it to Cartier for a two-strand string of natural pearls worth $1 million that he gave to his wife, a swap that made everyone happy at the time. When she sold the pearls in the 1950s, though, Plant's wife Mae may have wished she'd kept the building, because in the meantime cultured pearls, which tend to be more uniformly round than natural ones, had become widespread, and the necklace brought her a little less than a tenth of its original value.

Bridal Dress for Less

As many parents of brides and grooms can tell you, weddings tend to come in over-budget – often scandalously so. But a little shop in Midtown helps make the big day a little easier on the pocketbook, while, best of all, it doubles as the city's most novel, charitable fund-raising outfit.

The Bridal Garden carries hundreds of designer bridal dresses, offers them at ridiculously steep discounts, and then gives all the profits to underprivileged children. Sounds too good to be true? The system works only because all the dresses are donated.

Most of the Bridal Garden's inventory comes from local designers who donate their overstocked wedding gowns and floor samples. About 15 percent of the dresses are donated by individuals after their weddings – and the store insists that no dress has been worn more than once. All donations are tax deductible. The resulting collection includes a fabulous range of gowns from top-name designers, including Carolina Herrera, Priscilla of Boston, Vera Wang, Yumi Katsura, Ulla Maija, Richard Glasgow, and Nancy Issler.

Opened in 1998, the super-discounted shop became an instant success. In its first year, it raised more than $130,000 for the Sheltering Arms Children's Service. Today, it typically raises even more. The shop sees about 35 women a day via appointments, and continues to receive the latest fashions from chic designers across the city.
54 W. 21st St., Suite 907; 212-252-0661(by appt.)

OAN-Oceanie Afrique Noire Books
Books on African art, history, and culture.
15 W. 39th St.; 212-840-8844

Oriental Culture Enterprises Co.
Best bookstore in Chinatown.
13-17 Elizabeth St., 2nd floor; 212-226-8461

Rizzoli Bookstore
Italian art, design and architecture books.
31 W. 57th St., near Fifth Ave.; 212-759-2424

GAY & LESBIAN

Creative Visions
Books, as well as performances, readings, and art showings.
548 Hudson St.; 212-645-7573

Oscar Wilde Bookstore
Small but well-stocked. Probably the first store of its kind in the city, and coincidentally, near Gay St.
15 Christopher St.; 212-255-8097

HISTORY & PHILOSOPHY

East West Books
Buddhism, Taoism, Sufism, Indian religions, and New Age.
78 Fifth Ave., bet. 13th and 14th Sts.; 212-243-5994

Photo: Daniel Hood

Pathfinder Bookstore

Books on the Cuban revolution, South Africa, union struggles, black history, women's liberation, Russia and Eastern Europe.
167 Charles St.; 212-366-1973

Revolution Books

Books on Marx and the like.
9 W. 19th St.; 212-691-3345

St. Mark's Bookshop

Fiction, philosophy, art, small-press literary magazines, and best of all, open until midnight.
31 Third Ave., near 9th St.; 212-260-7853

Three Lives Book Store

Women authors, and reissues of books from the 1920s and 30s.
154 W. 10th St.; 212-741-2069

TRUE SPECIALTIES

Biography Bookshop

All biographies, all the time.
400 Bleecker St., at 12th St.; 212-807-8655

Bluestockings

A Lower East Side destination for radical and feminist books, and a hotspot for readings, discussions, and all sorts of countercultural happenings.
172 Allen St., at Rivington St.; 212-777-6028

If you have children, this is the place to turn them loose. If you don't, it's the place that will make you feel like one all over again. **Books of Wonder** is the city's largest independent children's bookstore, and it's heaven for kids of any age who like to read. The store offers dozens of sections for your children to browse – from pop-up books to Harry Potter titles – as well as tons of places for them to curl up and read. Parents can thumb through the Old & Rare Books Department, which showcases an amazing collection of out-of-print classics. The store's specialty is L. Frank Baum and his entire *Wizard of Oz* oeuvre; one of the first editions is priced at $9,500.

Authors and illustrators make frequent appearances to read from their latest works and sign copies, and every Sunday at 11:30 a.m., the store hosts a free half-hour story time.
16 W. 18th St., near Fifth Ave.; 212-989-3270

Any Witch Way

Also known as "Ye Olde Religion School & Supply Store," the **Lady in the Moon** *(212-473-8466)* is a serious magick shop for people who are serious enough about magick to spell it with a "k."

With two locations on St. Mark's Place – hit the one at 111 first, then go down to 94 – this dark, gritty, ominous shop sells products for witches, warlocks, gothics, and vampires without a shred of novelty, or irony. Not one of the countless occult books, tarot decks, incense sticks, oils, or odd pieces of jewelry is marketed for mere recreational use. These are the real deals.

The mysterious proprietress behind Lady in the Moon is the Rev. Lady Armida, an accredited High Priestess who teaches classes on witchcraft, tarot, and candle magick, and has written numerous books on the subjects. She'll explain to new customers the workings of pentagrams and covens and modern-day initiation rites. But she's not so thrilled when passersby pop in for a set of glow-in-the-dark vampire teeth and fake blood. So, before you walk in on a lark, consider this: Lady Armida is known to cast spells right there in the store. The shop may sell eerie capes, cloaks, and dresses, but if you show up and browse the racks for something to wear to your office Halloween party, be prepared for a clash with the occult.

Another serious shop of magick is **Prophecy** *(213 W. 80th St.; 212-799-3000)*, a charming establishment whose Upper West Side location is the least of its differences with its East Village brethren. Clean, airy, and far more expensive, Prophecy is a pleasant place to learn about all things Wiccan. The shop feels more like a new age gift store than a den of the paranormal. The standard dream-catchers are the giveaway. You can also pick up crystals, candles, and other enchantments, as well as the requisite oils, incense, and witchcraft recipes. Prophecy also offers a spectacular range of statues of religious figures from around the globe – Christ, Buddha, and Vishnu included.

Complete Traveller Bookstore
Every map and guidebook thinkable.
199 Madison Ave., at 35th St.;
212-685-9007

Kitchen Arts & Letters
All books on food and wine.
1435 Lexington Ave., at 93rd St.;
212-876-5550

The Military Bookman
Specializes in military books.
29 E. 93rd St.; 212-348-1280

New York Nautical Instrument and Service Corp.
Maritime charts for the whole world, almanacs, tide tables.
140 West Broadway; 212-962-4522

Printed Matter, Inc.
Chockful of art books and artists' monographs, in the heart of Chelsea's gallery district.
535 W. 22nd St.; 212-925-0325

Urban Center Books
Architecture/planning/ urban design books.
457 Madison Ave., bet. 50th and 51st Sts.; 212-935-3592

Fred Wilson Chess Books
Chess books, chess sets, chess everything.
80 E. 11th St.; 212-533-6381

INDEPENDENT BOOK STORES

Coliseum Books

This beloved fixture survived the loss of its lease further uptown, and is now bringing its famously huge selection and a lot of signings and readings to the Bryant Park area.
11 W. 42nd St., bet. Fifth and Sixth Aves.; 212-803-5890

Posman Books

Posman mostly runs bookstores at colleges around the city; this branch caters to the well-read commuter.
9 Grand Central Terminal, Vanderbilt and 42nd St.; 212-983-1111

Shakespeare & Co.

Urban legend held that, in the days before computer inventory, *The Times* compiled its bestseller list from the sales at this serious booklovers' bookseller's branches.
939 Lexington Ave., at E. 68th St.; 212-570-0201
137 E. 23rd St., at Lexington Ave.; 212-505-2021
716 Broadway, at Washington Pl.; 212-529-1330
1 Whitehall St., at Beaver St.; 212-742-7025

Photo: Daniel Hood

You can either eat, or buy art supplies (which may explain the whole "found object" idea), and a good place to spend your lunch money is **Pearl Paint**, a 60-year-old, five-story stockpile crammed full of everything an aspiring artist could need – including valuable lessons on the proper artiste attitude from the clientele, and knowledgeable help from the friendly staff.
308 Canal St., bet. Church St. and Broadway; 212-431-7932

Stuffed Animals

If you're in the market for a stuffed zebra or lion's head, the city's got just the stop for you. **Schoepfer Studios**, near Madison Square Garden, is New York's best and strangest taxidermy. The family business has operated out of the location for 86 years, and the shop's current head taxidermist, Jim Schoepfer, is the founder's grandson.

The place is a veritable zoo, albeit a very silent and eerie one. You can buy stuffed armadillos, anteaters, and antelope – and that's just the As. There's also all manner of fish and fowl, as well as crocodiles, snakes, and lizards. Though Schoepfer's draws in thousands of passersby off the street, the place does not want to be a museum. A sign on the door welcomes customers, not browsers. If that deters your entrance, don't worry, there's plenty to see in the windows.
138 W. 31st St.; 212-736-6939

Photo: Daniel Hood

Wandering through the giant **ABC Carpet & Home** on Broadway is like going to the apartments of dozens of people with much more money, taste, and imagination than you'll ever have. It's both inspiring and intensely annoying – all that gorgeous furniture and those beautiful accessories, with prices you can never afford. Yes, they have clearance sales, but how often do those happen?

There's help for you. Head on out to ABC's warehouse outlets in the Bronx or Dumbo in Brooklyn, where the discounts can get pretty steep. It's not cheap as mere mortals might understand the word, but certainly cheaper. And no one needs to know where you got it.
888 Broadway, at 19th St.; 212-473-3000; 20 Jay St., bet. Plymouth and John Sts., Dumbo, Brooklyn; 718-643-7400; 1055 Bronx River Ave., by the Bruckner Expwy., the Bronx; 718-842-8772. If you're really far afield, they've got outlets in Hackensack, N.J., and Florida, too. Visit abccarpet.com

Stores that Make You Wish...

If Tannen's makes you want to be a magician, these will turn your thoughts in other directions.

Capitol Fishing Tackle
An angler's paradise that makes you wish the fish in New York's waters didn't have three eyes.
218 W. 23rd St., bet. Seventh and Eighth Aves., in the Chelsea Hotel; 212-929-6123

Evolution
"Natural history collectibles" – that's bones and bugs to laymen – that make you wish you'd become a paleontologist.
120 Spring St., bet. Broadway and Mercer St.; 800-952-3195

The Big Trick

Disappearing isn't the big trick for a magic shop – staying in business is. West 42nd Street, for instance, used to be littered with them, all serving the vaudeville and theater circuits, but most are gone now, while **Louis Tannen's** has stuck around since 1929, and is now one of the oldest and largest shops in the world. It's a Mecca for professional magicians – David Copperfield, among others, got his start at one of Tannen's annual Jubilees – and the staff still perform tricks and demonstrations in the aisles.
24 W. 25th St., bet. Fifth and Sixth Aves, 2nd floor; 212-929-4500; tannens.com

Garret Wade

High-end tools that makes you wish you were handy.
161 Sixth Ave., bet. Spring and Broome Sts.; 212-695-3358

Kate's Paperie

Beautiful and imaginative stationery that makes you wish you wrote thank-you notes.
561 Broadway, bet. Prince and Spring Sts.; 212-941-9816. Also 8 W. 13th St., near Fifth Ave.; 1282 Third Ave., bet. 73rd and 74th Sts.; and 140 W. 57th St., bet. Sixth and Seventh Aves.

Five-Finger Discount

Forget about candy bars and the odd pair of socks: shoplifting here is serious business, particularly in the ritzier sections of Fifth Avenue and on Madison and Lexington in the Upper East Side of Manhattan. A plague of well-organized groups has taken to hitting high-end clothing and jewelry stores for thousands of dollars worth of merchandise. They often start the day with lists of specific items – the hot new shoe, say, or the must-have handbag – and many of the items end up in special "stores" set up in the outer boroughs, where (perhaps willfully) clueless shoppers can't believe their luck.

Stuffing loot in your pants, by the way, is for amateurs. If you want to set up your own shoplifting ring, here's how the pros do it: first, line a regular shopping bag (preferably from a chi-chi store, but not the one you're going to hit) with aluminum foil and duct tape. We won't go into specifics, but if they're properly lined, these "booster bags" will foil those pesky security tags; plus, they make it look as if you've already done some serious shopping. Then get two friends – one to distract the store employees while you fill your booster bag, and another to wait on the street and relieve you of the incriminating evidence the minute you walk outside. It beats window shopping.

Media & Entertainment

Photo: Spencer T. Tucker/NYC Dept. of Parks & Recreation

There's too much. There – we said it. There's too much – too many Broadway shows (On-and-Off) that must be seen, too many live bands that must be heard, too many newspapers and magazines that must be read, too many media barons and theater festivals and cabaret acts and shock jocks, too many movies and TV shows that want to be a part of New York. Is it any wonder we send the shows on the road, and let other cities impersonate us on the screen?

Photo: Museum of Television and Radio/Norman McGrath

The Past in Pictures

Before California stole them away, TV and movies were weaned here, in studios at Rockefeller Center, studio lots in Queens, and soundstages in the West 20s. There's a lot of history there, and there's a lot of history at the **Museum of Television & Radio** and the **American Museum of the Moving Image** – the good kind of history, though, with lots of pictures and no tests.

CBS head honcho and general TV legend William Paley founded the MT&R *(25 W. 52 St., bet. Fifth and Sixth Aves.; 212-621-6600; mtr.org)* in 1975 as a place to preserve broadcast programming, and that makes it a couch potato's dream: You can basically walk in and ask for anything that has ever aired, and hear or watch it in your own little cubicle. OK, not *everything*, but just about, from the earliest broadcasts to the Beatles on *Ed Sullivan* to that elusive episode of *Small Wonder*. They also put together some innovative exhibitions, particularly in radio.

In the 1920s, Paramount's Astoria Studio in Queens was the biggest movie production facility between London and Hollywood – then the Army took it over to make training films. Now it's landmarked, and one of its buildings is home to the AMMI *(35 Ave., at 36 St., Astoria, Queens; 718-784-0077; ammi.org)*, which has movies, naturally, but also a Smithsonian's worth of movie artifacts, like Chuck Heston's chariot from *Ben-Hur*.

We Now Begin Our Broadcasting Era

Since the "Golden Age" of 1950s TV, when *Playhouse 90* and Milton Berle were beamed across the U.S. from studios in Manhattan, the island has been New York's face on TV, crowding the other boroughs out of the spotlight. Manhattan wasn't first to the small screen, though – that honor goes to Queens, which on April 30, 1939, hosted the inaugural commercial TV broadcast as part of the just-opened World's Fair in Flushing Meadows. In fact, the broadcast was really only viewable *at* the World's Fair, since TV was pretty brand-spanking new, but the lineup was still impressive: President Franklin D. Roosevelt, Albert Einstein, and RCA chief David Sarnoff (there to pitch his company's TV sets, which may constitute the first commercial on a commercial broadcast). The borough wouldn't get this much airtime again until January 1971, when Archie Bunker started spouting off from his living room on (fictional) Hauser Street. After that, Queens natives may have preferred to leave the spotlight to Manhattan.

Unholy Sex

Question: How can a little bit of lovin' lead to misdemeanor charges for one couple, pink slips for three radio personalities, and a $357,000 fine for a major broadcasting company?

Answer: When the little bit of lovin' takes place in New York's most famous cathedral – during mass.

Attempting to win a public-sex competition run by shock jocks "Opie" Hughes and Anthony Cumia, a Virginia couple copulated in a vestibule at St. Patrick's Cathedral on Aug. 15, 2002, while a show employee narrated the events on live radio via cell phone. Police heard the program, rushed to the church, and arrested the couple – Loretta Lynn Harper, 36, and Brian Florence, 38 – on charges of public lewdness.

According to the misdemeanor complaint filed against Florence and Harper, the couple was seen having sex

Off, Off, Off Broadway

Though generally classified as a venue with less than 100 seats, the real identifier of an Off-Off or an Off-Off-Off Broadway theater is its staging of highly experimental plays, musicals, and other shows. If you're tired of the Tony-Award-tilting ilk of theater, call or stop by one of these venues – you just might see the work of the next century's Samuel Beckett or Jean Genet.

Bouwerie Lane Theatre
330 Bowery St.; 212-677-0060

Broome Street Theatre
559 Broome St.; 212-226-6213

Courtyard Playhouse
39 Grove St.; 212-765-9540

El Porton Del Barrio
172 E. 104th St., 212-246-7478

La Mama Experimental Theatre
74A E. 4th St.; 212-475-7710

Photo: Daniel Hood

in a church vestibule, "rocking their pelvises back and forth." Harper, with her back to Florence, was naked from the waist down and "her genitals were open to view by the public." The sacrilegious sex sparked outrage from the Catholic community, which sent the radio station into profuse-apology mode and prompted the immediate firing of Opie, Anthony, and their field reporter.

Though the debacle made headlines for weeks, the competition was actually in its second year. Known as the "Sex for Sam" contest, because winners received a free trip to Boston paid for by Sam Adams Brewing Co., participating couples won points for having sex in various public settings (St. Pat's was worth a whopping 25 points).

They were given extra points for specific sex acts, and Opie and Anthony developed an on-air slang describing them, such as a "two-point conversion" or "balloon knot," for anal sex. During the St. Pat's stunt, Opie excitedly announced what the Virginia couple had won: "Oh my God, 25 points, a two-point conversion, and eternal damnation."

Before the scandal occurred, the radio station even posted a list of notable New York spots and the points awarded to any couple who could prove they had sex there. Among them:

The *Intrepid*	15
NBC's *Today Show*	20
Times Square	15
Tiffany's	20
Central Park	10
Gracie Mansion	20
ATM (any)	15
Museum (any major)	15
FAO Schwartz	15
On live TV	50
NY Public Library	10
Hansom cab	15
Double-decker tour bus	15
City Hall	30
Bill Clinton's office in Harlem	30

black and white and blood-red all over

Every morning there's a war on the newsstands over which tabloid can produce the cleverest headline (or the cheapest pun) and the most shocking photo. Our picks for the three best:

"Dead!" (Jan. 13, 1928)

At the time, the *Daily News* was just one struggling newspaper among many, until photographer Tom Howard hid a camera under his pants leg and snapped pics of the electrocution of Ruth Snyder, a Queens housewife who had murdered her husband and was the first American woman sent to the chair. The full-page photo and single-word headline were a sensation, selling out millions of copies from two extra print runs. They also catapulted the *News* to prominence, and launched a trend toward ever-more graphic newspaper photography focused on gruesome murders, accidents, and suicides.

"Ford to City: Drop Dead" (Oct. 30, 1975)

It's not that clever, but in the midst of an enormous fiscal and social crisis, the city felt unloved and unwanted by the rest of the country, and the *Daily News* perfectly summed up that feeling. The story itself was about a speech by President Gerald Ford, in which he refused to back the loan guarantees the city needed to refinance its massively swollen debt. Fact was, the debt and near-bankruptcy were largely self-inflicted, and Ford was just hoping to force some fiscal discipline on the profligate city.

"Headless Body in Topless Bar" (April 15, 1983):

Easily the most famous headline in tabloid history, this was a score for the *Post*. When they heard that a would-be robber had cut off the head of a bartender at a seedy joint, they sent a lowly staffer out to find out if the bar by any chance featured strippers. When she reported that it did, cheers went up in the newsroom, and a legend was born.

Theater Festivals

FringeNYC

A hodge-podge of over 100 different theater and dance productions spread mostly around the Lower East Side and the Village throughout August, the New York International Fringe Festival had been doing its thing under the radar for a few years, when the surprise success of *Urinetown* turned it into the place to hunt for the next big thing. Don't let that turn you off; there's plenty of exciting and avant-garde stuff for everyone.
Fringenyc.org; 212-279-4488

Howl! Festival

A recently created celebration of arts in the East Village, in the spirit of Beat poet Allen Ginsburg, with new plays, poetry readings, jazz performances, and much more, in August.
howlfestival.org

First Editions

Raiding other cities for journalistic talent is a long-standing tradition – think of the *Post*'s current editor, a transplanted Australian – so it should be no surprise that the city's first newspaperman should be an Englishman named **William Bradford**, who established himself here as a printer in 1693, after falling afoul of political debates in Philadelphia. He started New York's first newspaper, the *New-York Gazette*, in 1725, and soon after began complaining about costs and subscription rates.

Even before he started the paper, though, he had made two decisions that would prove momentous. In 1710, he accepted German immigrant John Peter Zenger as an apprentice. Zenger went on to found a newspaper of his own in 1733, and in 1734 was put on trial for slandering the power-hungry governor of the time. His trial and eventual acquittal (by jury nullification) are considered landmarks in the fight for the freedom of the press.

Bradford's second decision was something of a disappointment. In 1723, a young man from Boston approached him for work, but Bradford had a full shop, and sent the would-be printer on to Philadelphia – and that's why Ben Franklin got famous in Philly, not New York.

Bradford's gravestone, by the way, is in the Trinity Churchyard, and it has a typo – he was born in 1663, not 1660.

Playwrights Theater Festivals of O'Neill

Each summer and winter, the Playwrights Theater group stages productions of O'Neill's plays in the Provincetown Theater (his old stomping grounds). The plan is to perform all of his plays, in order; thus far they're about a quarter of the way through, sometimes drawing big names.

Provincetown Playhouse: 133 Macdougal St., bet. W. 3rd and W. 4th Sts.; playwrightstheater.com

The 24 Hr. Plays

The name says it all: from time to time, this group writes, produces, and stages a number of plays, all in a day. Since 1995, they've done over 300 short plays, and now they're spreading the love around the country.

24hourplays.com

Visitors to Roosevelt Island often make a point of seeing the remains of the once-breathtaking Octagon Tower. Few know, however, that this stonemasonry marvel was single-handedly brought to ruin by a 23-year-old woman more than a century ago.

Nellie Bly (aka Elizabeth Cochrane) was perhaps the most ambitious young journalist of the 19th century, and her courage and drive not only led to the invention of "investigative reporting," but also inspired thousands of women to enter what was then the man's world of newspaper publishing.

Fresh in from Pittsburgh, Bly hit the pavement for a reporter job for six months before finally landing an interview with the managing editor of the popular *New York World*. John Cockerill didn't know what to do with the 23-year-old fireball, and decided to give her a dare. He asked if she would be willing to pose as a lunatic and allow herself to be carted off to Blackwell's Island (today known as Roosevelt Island), where New York City's notorious insane asylum stood. To Cockerill's surprise, Bly not only agreed, but had herself committed in a matter of days.

Posing as Nellie Brown, a Cuban immigrant, Bly spent 10 days in the winter of 1888 discovering how abusive the institution was towards its inmates. The asylum itself had already received some bad press from Charles Dickens about 40 years earlier. After touring the grounds, he wrote, "Everything had a lounging, listless, madhouse air, which was very painful."

But when Bly returned to the world of the sane, the *New York World* ran a series of her articles, written in the first-person, which recounted the cruel beatings, ice-

New York Movies

It would probably be easier to compile a list of famous films that *didn't* take place in New York. But sometimes when you're scanning the shelves at the video store, the titles of great Manhattan movies escape you. Here's a bare-minimum list of the city's essential screen appearances.

The Thin Man (1934)
William Powell and Myrna Loy star as detective couple Nick and Nora Charles, who solve a murder on a lark while delivering one-liners and downing martinis.

The Lost Weekend (1945)
Billy Wilder's vivid portrayal of a chronic alcoholic who sinks to new lows during a four-day drinking binge. Shot all along Third Avenue, and at the renowned bar P.J. Clarke's.

Miracle on 34th Street (1947)
Yuletide at Macy's. A young lawyer stands up for a nice old man who is institutionalized after he claims to be the real Santa Claus.

Easter Parade (1948)
The teaming of Judy Garland and Fred Astaire delivers outstanding

song and dance in this classic New York musical.

On the Town (1949)

Sailors Gene Kelly and Frank Sinatra let loose during a 24-hour pass in Manhattan and dazzle every destination they hit.

Marty (1955)

Ernest Borgnine took the Oscar for his portrayal of a lonely Bronx butcher approaching middle-age, who finally finds love and moves out of his mother's house.

Blackboard Jungle (1955)

Young Sidney Poitier and Vic Morrow stars in this classic about a school teacher who goes to teach in an unruly high school filled with thugs.

An Affair to Remember (1957)

Cary Grant and Deborah Kerr fall in love and agree to meet in six months at the Empire State Building in this oft-referenced classic.

The Apartment (1960)

Jack Lemmon hopes to climb the corporate ladder by letting his boss use his apartment as a love shack. Instead, Lemmon falls in love with Shirley MacLaine, his boss's mistress.

cold baths, and forced meals of often-rancid food that the inmates had to endure. The searing exposé gripped readers and got the attention of City Hall.

"The insane asylum on Blackwell's Island is a human rat-trap," she wrote. "It is easy to get in, but once there it is impossible to get out." She went on to describe the tortuous routines that the mentally ill patients faced every day: "The water was ice-cold. My teeth chattered and my limbs were goose-fleshed and blue with cold. Suddenly I got, one after the other, three buckets of cold water over my head – ice-cold, too," she wrote. "I think I experienced some of the sensations of a drowning person as they dragged me, gasping, shivering, and quaking, from the tub. What, excepting torture, would produce insanity quicker than this treatment?"

Bly's undercover reporting sparked quick action from municipal leaders. The asylum was investigated and shut down. Her articles alone sparked a revolution in the treatment of mental illness in New York.

Superhero Central

No city has served as backdrop to more **comic books** than New York. Almost every classic superhero battled crime in some fictional form of New York, and many were born and developed their superpowers here. Batman had his Gotham; Superman his Metropolis.

There's an old saw that Metropolis is New York by day, and Gotham City is New York by night. But an editor at DC Comics once said it was more than that: "Gotham is Manhattan below 14th Street at 3 a.m., November 28, in a cold year. Metropolis is Manhattan between 14th and 110th Street on the brightest, sunniest July day of the year."

But the Man of Steel and the Dark Knight are not the only New Yorkers. Peter Parker grew up in Forest Hills, Queens, before he was bit by a radioactive spider and became Spider-Man. Matt Murdock grew up in Hell's Kitchen, before he was hit by a radioactive truck and became Daredevil.

And don't forget Thor, Iron Man, Dr. Strange, the Hulk, and all of those X-Folks: They're all denizens of the city that never sleeps – or its suburbs.

Old Amsterdam News

In addition to some of the nation's first newspapers, New York City also lays claim to the oldest continuously published black newspaper in the country. Founded in 1909, the **Amsterdam News** has been covering local and national stories for the black community in Harlem for four generations. Established by Wilbert Tatum, who set up an editorial office at 124th Street and Amsterdam Avenue, the paper was widely read throughout most of its history by overtly catering to a black audience. Many black luminaries were offered space in the paper to spread their messages, including W.E.B. DuBois, Malcolm X, and Adam Clayton Powell.

Today, the *Amsterdam News* is run by Tatum's daughter, Elinor, who faces a dwindling circulation and severe competition from cable TV and the Internet. Despite the trials of newspaper publishing in the 21st century, the younger Tatum has vowed to keep the focus of the publication the same: To present a fair view of blacks in the media.

She summed it up in a recent interview by comparing her paper to another ancient city tabloid: "If you took the *New York Post* and the *Amsterdam News* for a week, and read them both in a hundred years, you'd think you were in two different places," she said. "They have to show what sells. We show all sides, because, guess what: Our folks are not just rapists, drug dealers, and murderers."

Butterfield 8 (1960)

Elizabeth Burton plays Gloria Wandrous, a call girl with a disturbing past, who hooks up with a philandering lawyer. Shot throughout the Village and SoHo.

West Side Story (1961)

Classic Bernstein. The Jets and the Sharks battle it out for territory and respect in Hell's Kitchen as two star-crossed teens fall in love despite belonging to rival gangs.

Breakfast at Tiffany's (1961)

Audrey Hepburn portrays Holly Golightly, a young jet-setter in New York who searches for a rich, older man to marry, while unavoidably falling for the poor writer in her building.

The Hustler (1961)

Small-time pool hustler "Fast" Eddie Felson takes on the legendary Minnesota Fats, falling in love and almost losing his soul in the process. Paul Newman at his best.

Valley of the Dolls (1967)

Three remarkable women look for fame, fortune, and fast times in the city in this controversial book-turned-Hollywood smash hit.

Barefoot in the Park (1967)

Adapted from Neil Simon's play, this light comedy follows Robert Redford and Jane Fonda in their first days of marriage and setting up home in a small pad off Washington Square Park.

Funny Girl (1968)

Barbra Streisand picked up an Oscar for her portrayal of comedienne Fannie Brice, whose rise to fame as a singer begins in the Jewish slums of the Lower East Side.

Midnight Cowboy (1969)

Jon Voight plays a naïve male prostitute who struggles to survive in the big city with his sickly friend Ratso Rizzo, played by Dustin Hoffman.

The Out-of-Towners (1970)

Jack Lemmon and Sandy Dennis star as a hapless couple whose trip to New York turns into a nightmare including a hellish train ride, a mugging, a police chase, and a broken tooth.

Great Names, Not Listed

A lot of great names have come out of **The New Yorker** – writers like E.B. White and James Thurber, and cartoonists like Charles Addams and William Steig (who, like White, turned his hand to children's literature and produced the book on which *Shrek* was based) – but arguably the magazine's most important name of all almost never appeared in its pages.

Harold Ross, the gap-toothed newspaperman who launched the magazine from 25 West 45th Street in 1925, wanted to create a unified voice for what would become one of the most influential magazines of the 20th century, so he made a point of relegating writers' names to the end of their pieces, and refused to include a masthead listing the editors. Unlike today's relentlessly self-promoting magazine editors (we're looking at you, Tina Brown and Michael Wolff), Ross stuck to the notion of anonymity so strictly that his own name was never printed in *The New Yorker* during his tenure, and didn't appear in the magazine until 1951 – in his obituary.

While we're here, we'll note a few things: the magazine's distinctive font was designed for it by art director Rea Irvin, and is called Irvin in his honor (it's also been used, among many other places, in the credits for TV's *Frasier*). For the cover of the first issue, Irvin also created the top-hat-wearing, monocle-toting fop who became the magazine's mascot; the sophisticate's name – Eustace Tilley – came later, from a staff writer.

And the magazine still doesn't have a masthead.

Musical Sensation

What do you get when you mix a stranded ballet troupe, a hack playwright, an empty theater, and a producer ready to spend a fortune to attract a crowd? You get the world's first musical — a concoction that was cooked up on lower Broadway right after the Civil War.

The Black Crook, by many accounts, was the first musical as we know them today. It was a trite, tawdry, unintelligible mess, but it attracted New Yorkers by the thousands, broke the record for the longest-running show, and set the stage for a new form of American entertainment that would be mimicked around the world.

It started in 1866, when producer William Wheatley watched one of his much-anticipated new plays go belly up before it hit the stage. He needed a replacement fast. Fortunately for him, the New York Academy of Music burned to the ground in a sudden fire and left a traveling troupe of French ballet dancers without a venue. At the same time, he was sitting on the rights to a mediocre melodrama written by a depressed playwright named Charles Barras.

Wheatley decided to make a stew: he built the most lavish sets ever seen, hired an enormous orchestra, and then basically shuffled the musical score and scenes from the play like a deck of cards. The result was a wild, unwieldy extravaganza, running an unheard of five-and-a-half hours, but audiences couldn't get enough of it.

Here are the plot essentials: the evil Count Wolfenstein woos the beautiful Amina after capturing her lover, Rudolph, and giving him to the nefarious necromancer Hertzog (whose crooked back and black magic give the show its title). Incidentally, Hertzog can only stay alive by giving Zamiel, aka Satan, a new soul to devour every New Year's Eve. This year, it's shaping up to be Rudolph. But lucky for him, he casually rescues a dove, which instantly transforms into another woman — Stalacta, the Fairy Queen of the Golden Realm. Stalacta is grateful to Rudolph, and delivers him from all his troubles. The bad guys are dragged off to hell and

The French Connection (1971)

Two of New York's Finest stumble onto an international drug-smuggling operation that leads Gene Hackman into one of the most famous car chases in cinema history.

The Godfather Trilogy (1972, 1974, 1990)

After arriving in America via Ellis Island, Vito Corleone builds a "family" Mafia organization that he hands off to his son Michael. Little Italy never looked better than in Part II.

Serpico (1973)

Al Pacino plays Frank Serpico, the real-life cop who blew the whistle on rampant corruption in the New York City Police Department only to have his friends stab him in the back.

The Great Gatsby (1974)

Fitzgerald via Coppola (the screenwriter) puts Robert Redford in the role of the lovelorn Jay Gatsby who builds a showy estate on Long Island only to impress the love of his life played by Mia Farrow

Dog Day Afternoon (1975)

Godfather alumni Al Pacino and John Cazale try to stage a quick bank robbery that instead transforms into a hostage situation and a media circus.

Marathon Man (1976)

Dustin Hoffman chases an infamous Nazi war criminal known as the "White Angel," played by Laurence Olivier, who is smuggling diamonds and settling old scores.

Taxi Driver (1976)

Martin Scorsese directs Robert DeNiro as a mentally unstable Vietnam vet who lashes out against the decadence and sleaze he witnesses while driving a cab at night.

Rudolph is reunited with Amina forever.

The show was staged at Niblo's Garden, a 3,200-seat venue at the corner of Broadway and Prince Street, which was torn down in 1895. At a time when a good play ran for two or three weeks, "The Black Crook" lasted for more than a year and was revived eight times after that. A version was even staged in London, where it was equally popular with the public.

Hearst, Rehearst

Not long after William Randolph Hearst made a mint selling the *New York Journal* (at the same time selling the Spanish-American War), the media mogul set out to build a complex of modern skyscrapers at Columbus Circle that would be called "Hearst Plaza."

He never got further than one building, which itself never got higher than six floors. The Depression postponed his plans and World War II scuttled them. Until 2003, that is, when his magazine empire began rebuilding his dream.

The strange-looking **Hearst Building** at Eighth Avenue and 57th Street was designed as the base of an 18-story tower. Today, marked by enormous pylons that rise far above the roofline, the stubby Art Deco landmark is finally getting the addition it's been waiting for.

After gutting the old building and leaving only the façade, steel workers began assembling what will become a 42-story, geodesic-type office tower, featuring triangular steel bracing. From the tenth floor up, the unusual structure will have no vertical columns at all. Moreover, the steel framework will be visible both from inside and outside the building.

The modern project will combine style elements from two disparate eras, creating what London-based architect Lord Norman Foster hopes will become known as one of the city's most stunning buildings. Either way, with construction starting up again after a 80-year hiatus, William Randolph is certainly smiling down on the project, which should be complete by 2006.

Show Time

In addition to everything else, New York City may be the prerecorded-message capital of the world. You're reminded to watch your step getting on the subway, offered connecting-train information, and cautiously urged to keep an eye on your personal belongings in major stations. But one of the longest-running public reminders in the city goes unnoticed by many visitors, as well as life-long New Yorkers. The **Paramount Building** on 43rd Street in Times Square plays chimes at 7:45 p.m. every night save Wednesday. The prerecorded tune is "Give My Regards to Broadway," and the carillon reminds theater-goers that the curtains go up in 15 minutes.

Time Over Time

Photo: Daniel Hood

With all the hoopla over the new **Time Warner Center** on Columbus Circle (the most expensive condo ever! a food court where all the restaurants are run by five-star chefs!), it's easy to forget that *Time* Magazine's previous home, the **Time-Life Building** at Sixth Avenue and 50th Street, was something of a landmark in its way, too. Apart from lobby treatment, it wasn't much architecturally, but it was the first extension of Rockefeller Center across to the shabby side of Sixth Avenue, and led the way for the other tall towers that now line the west side of the street, in the same way as the Time Warner Center is pioneering the rehabilitation of the area around 59th Street and Eighth Avenue.

And with all that, it's easy to forget the place where it all started – the humble little building at 141 East 17th Street between Third Avenue and Irving Place, from which Henry Luce and Briton Hadden launched *Time* (and the whole idea of weekly newsmagazines) on March 3, 1923.

Saturday Night Fever (1977)
John Travolta delivers his world-famous portrayal of a Brooklyn youth who feels his only chance to get somewhere is as the king of the disco floor.

The Goodbye Girl (1977)
Marsha Mason and Richard Dreyfuss bring to the big screen Neil Simon's award-winning romantic comedy about reluctant roommates who fall in love.

Annie Hall (1977)

Woody Allen's Best Picture Oscar winner, in which the neurotic New Yorker falls in and out of love with the kooky title character played by Diane Keaton.

Hair (1979)
Milos Forman's tribute to long locks follows the journey of a young man from Oklahoma to New York where he is indoctrinated into the youth subculture and subsequently drafted.

The Warriors (1979)
After the Warriors are mistakenly accused of killing a big-time gang leader named Cyrus, they have to navigate from the Bronx to Coney Island, with every gang in the city after them to get revenge.

Kramer vs. Kramer (1979)

Dustin Hoffman plays a newly divorced man who must learn to care for his young son by himself, and then fight to keep custody of him.

Manhattan (1979)

In what is arguably Woody Allen's best film, a divorced New Yorker looks for love in all the wrong places, first with a high-schooler, then with the mistress of his best friend, played by Diane Keaton.

Raging Bull (1980)

DeNiro's portrayal of real-life boxer Jake LaMotta tracks the self-destruction of a legend, whose rage not only makes him unstoppable in the ring, but also destroys everything in his life.

Escape from New York (1981)

Manhattan of the future is transformed into a maximum-security prison, and ex-con Kurt Russell is sent in to rescue the president after his plane crashes in the middle of it.

The Other White Way

Photo: Daniel Hood

Broadway didn't always have a lock on big theatrical productions in New York. Sure, a large proportion of the town's theaters have been located there – moving with the mass of the population from the earliest stages down below Canal, up into the Teens and 20s, and finally coming to rest in the 40s around Times Square – but for most of the 19th century, the Great White Way competed for pre-eminence with another broad street: **The Bowery.**

Before it was the Street of Forgotten Men, the Bowery was home to dozens of boisterous theaters, concert halls, and proto-burlesque houses, where Lower East Side roughs could go to enjoy a show or heckle the performers. The quality of the actors, the plays, and the audience might have been lower than on Broadway, but there was plenty of spectacle, from elaborate recreations of earthquakes, to sea stories complete with ships floated in giant tanks of water, to dramatizations of the lives and misdeeds of local heroes and villains.

In the 1880s, when other venues for mass entertainment had drawn off much of the old crowd,

Bowery theater thrived anew with the coming of large numbers of Jewish immigrants, and the Yiddish theater they brought with them. Theaters like the Roumania Opera House, at Grand Street and the Bowery, and the Thalia and Windsor Theaters, which squared off on opposite sides of the Bowery at Canal Street, offered hundreds of original works in all forms, from comedy to operettas, in a language the newcomers could understand – even Shakespeare was translated into Yiddish.

Between the Yiddish theater and the rise of variety and vaudeville, the Bowery managed to hang on as a theatrical locale until World War I before population changes, political meddling, and, perhaps most important, the coming of the movies killed it off.

Which isn't to say there isn't an alternative to the high prices and decorum of Broadway – Off-Broadway theater is alive and well throughout the city, and burlesque has recently enjoyed a mini-revival. You just won't find much of it in its old home on the Bowery, whose mainstay these days seems to be restaurant supply shops.

Voodoo Macbeth

Long before *War of the Worlds* and *Citizen Kane* took the world by storm, a 20-year-old **Orson Welles** took Harlem by storm. Barely out of his teens, the future film genius took a stab at directing *Macbeth* using money from Roosevelt's Depression-fighting Works Progress Administration. And as if it weren't risky enough to take on Shakespeare's notoriously haunted play with taxpayer dollars, Welles reset the tragedy in 19th-century Haiti and cast all black actors.

Welles' wife, Virginia, came up with the idea of a "Voodoo *Macbeth*," suggesting that the witches be replaced by voodoo priestesses and the evil Hecate be played by a male voodoo drummer. Welles loved it, and rewrote Shakespeare's play to accommodate lavish jungle settings and pounding percussion – that is, he rewrote it almost beyond recognition.

The production had troubles from the start. First, most black performers had experience only in vaudeville and musical shows. Out of his 150-person cast, Welles could only find four professional black dramatic actors. Next, many critics in and out of Harlem doubted the

Night Shift (1982)

Kooky comedy in which Henry Winkler and Michael Keaton star as two ambitious young men who turn the City Morgue into a thriving business.

The Muppets Take Manhattan (1984)

Kermit and his friends go to the Great White Way to get their musical produced only to find it's a more difficult task than they anticipated. Tons of cameos.

The Brother from Another Planet (1984)

John Sayles's cult classic is a loosely veiled allegory of the immigrant experience, as a mute extraterrestrial who looks like a black man tries to fit in on the streets of Harlem after he crash-lands on Earth.

Ghostbusters (1984)

Out-of-work parapsychologists Dan Aykroyd and Bill Murray set up a ghost-removal service that ultimately saves Sigourney Weaver, and the city, from a bunch of unruly phantoms.

Quicksilver (1986)

A young stock market hotshot played by Kevin Bacon makes one bad decision, loses his nerve, quits his job, and becomes a bike messenger who races through gridlock traffic all day.

Crocodile Dundee (1986)

Paul Hogan leaves the Outback for a week in Manhattan, where he struggles against wildlife in the steel jungle while falling in love.

Hannah and Her Sisters (1986)

Three sisters sort out their tangled-up, interconnected love lives in Woody Allen's masterful drama, part of which was shot in Mia Farrow's fantastic Central Park South apartment.

Wall Street (1987)

Charlie Sheen plays Bud Fox, a Wall Street hotshot who learns the trade from a ruthless, high-powered broker played by Michael Douglas, who delivers the 1980s creed, "Greed Is Good."

Bright Lights, Big City (1988)

Michael J. Fox stars as a young kid from Kansas who moves to New York and gets snared in a downward spiral of booze and drugs.

ability of a 20-year-old white man to write and direct what was quickly known as "Shakespeare in blackface." One outspoken opponent of the production in Harlem accused Welles of deliberately trying to make blacks look ridiculous, and even attacked Welles with a razor in the theater on opening night. Welles escaped the assault unhurt.

The director tackled these criticisms by establishing trust and respect between himself and his actors. He approached his two talented stars, Edna Thomas and Jack Carter, as their personalities required. Thomas was known for her professionalism and dignity, while Carter for his hard drinking and wild nights on the town. Welles handled Thomas delicately and quickly won her respect. To win over Carter, however, he accompanied him after rehearsals for benders on the town that would end at dawn. For all the others, Welles won their affection by providing food and drink during rehearsals, paid for out of his own pocket. The personal touches paid off; Welles forged his vision into a rich, loud, heart-pounding tale of how one man's ambition fueled his ruin.

The show opened in April 1936 at the Lafayette Theater on Seventh Avenue near 131st Street. All 1,223 seats were taken when the curtain rose at 9:30 p.m. and revealed a lush jungle scene filled with witches and throbbing, voodoo drums. The crowd was rapt until the final scene, when Hecate delivered his famous last line, "The charm's wound up!" Applause filled the theater for 15 minutes.

The next day, the *New York Times* declared that "Excitement ... fairly rocked the Lafayette Theatre." But not all the reviews were so good. In addition to the problem many critics at the time had with an all-black cast, many were enraged that such lavish productions were being paid for by federal money as the country languished in the Depression. The *Herald Tribune*'s Percy Hammond said the production was "an exhibition of de-luxe boondoggling," and carped the Roosevelt's New Deal was squandering taxpayer dollars on a vanity productions. Legend has it that every production of *Macbeth*, going back to Shakespeare's days, brings some sort of tragedy to its cast or producers. This time it struck a critic. Hammond died suddenly a few days after his seething column. A rumor circulated among the actors that he was the victim of malevolent spells cast by the enraged voodoo drummers.

Photo: Amy Della Rocca

There's only one public marionette theater company left in the United States, and it calls a stunning old log cabin in Central Park its home. On the west side of the park near 79th Street, the **Swedish Cottage Marionette Theater** *(212-988-9093)* stages original productions with hand-made puppets for children of all ages. In addition to showcasing their own plays, the puppet-masters perform regular showings of Cinderella, Hansel and Gretel, and Jack and the Beanstalk.

Long before puppets took over, the Scandinavian cottage housed an unusual range of organizations. Built in Sweden in 1875, the quaint, Baltic fir log cabin was designed as a schoolhouse and transported to Philadelphia for the U.S. Centennial Exposition in 1876. The Nordic Romantic style and expert craftsmanship left an unforgettable impression on Frederick Law Olmstead, the chief landscape architect of Central Park. After he successfully urged the city to buy it (for $1,500), Olmstead installed it at its present site.

Since then, the cottage has been used as a tool shed, a library, a lunchroom, an entomology lab, and district headquarters for the Civil Defense during World War II. When the marionettes moved in in 1976, however, they stayed and became a beloved destination for kids and parents from across the city.

Big (1988)

After a bit of magic turns a young boy into a grown-up, he moves to the city to be on his own, get a job, play at FAO Schwartz, and have his first romantic encounter with a woman.

When Harry Met Sally (1989)

Meg Ryan and Billy Crystal play the title characters who get to know each other through their years in New York and eventually fall in love.

Do the Right Thing (1989)

Spike Lee's sets the camera on the hottest day of the year in Bed-Stuy, Brooklyn, where racial tensions comes to a boil between black residents and Italian and Korean shop owners.

GoodFellas (1990)

Based on the true story of Irish-Italian mobster Henry Hill,

Martin Scorsese tells the tale of three friends who work their way up through organized crime.

King of New York (1990)
A former drug lord, played by Christopher Walken, returns from prison to exact gruesome revenge on his old enemies and then redistribute their wealth to the city's poor.

The Freshman (1990)

Matthew Broderick stars as an NYU film student who gets tangled up with a "Godfather"-like boss played by Marlon Brando in this funny parody.

The Fisher King (1991)

Terry Gilliam directs Jeff Bridges and Robin Williams in this colorful tale of personal demons, redemption, and the dark side of the city.

Home Alone 2 (1992)
The sequel has Macaulay Culkin on his own in New York, where he is chased through familiar city landmarks by bungling criminals Joe Pesci and Daniel Stern.

Theater Row

Photo: Robert Davis

"Off-Broadway" leaves an awful lot of city to cover. One good place to start is **Theater Row**, the stretch of 42nd Street between Ninth and Tenth Avenues. Starting in the 1970s, this haphazard group of little theaters helped set the standards for grunginess and lack of comfort that came to be associated with the Off-Broadway experience – until the 1990s, when a little of the sanitizing spirit then at play in Times Square leaked west. Suddenly, the theaters were cleaner, and then, just as suddenly, new ones began to sprout up. The row is now a major destination for new and untried works in theater and dance, at places like the Little Schubert *(422 W. 42nd St.; 212-239-6200)*; Playwrights Horizons *(416 W. 42nd St.; 212-564-1235; playwrightshorizons.org)*, which is dedicated to new work by American playwrights and debuted, among other things, *Driving Miss Daisy* and works by Christopher Durang, Stephen Sondheim, and A.R. Gurney; and the five-theater Theater Row Complex *(410 W. 42nd St.; 212-714-2442; theatrerow.org)*.

The Better Booth

The history of the **Booth brothers** can be summed up in one sentence: one knocked 'em dead on stage; the other shot 'em dead off stage. But while many people know John Wilkes Booth's claim to fame, few know that his older brother Edwin made his own mark on American theater. In fact, the first monument erected to an actor in New York City was in honor of this brother of a presidential assassin.

While John Wilkes shot his way into history at Ford Theater, Edwin spent his life mastering stage acting. He not only became the foremost American Shakespearean performer in the 19th century, but also was the first American ever to perform Shakespeare before the British crown: he played Hamlet for Queen Victoria.

A long-time lover of New York City, Edwin used his good fortune to establish a "Player's Club" in 1888 to give actors a place to meet and improve their craft. He bought a townhouse at 16 Gramercy Park South, moved into the top floor, and refurbished the rest into acting studios and a small theater. Membership was open only to thespians and their patrons.

At the same time, Edwin founded the Theater Library to chronicle the history of the American stage. Over the years the Player's Club became a who's who of notable actors, and membership was practically required for serious actors. A strange range of future members included the Barrymores, Irving Berlin, Frank Sinatra, and Winston Churchill.

When Edwin Booth died, New York decided to honor him with a statue. The sculptor chose to portray him in the pose of his best-known character: Hamlet. The statue at the south end of Gramercy Park depicts Edwin with his head bowed and meditative, with a slight smile – the exact pose he often took before delivering Hamlet's most famous soliloquy.

Today, you can tour the Player's Club by appointment only (212-228-7610).

For those who love historical twists of fate, the brothers Booth shared one other coincidental link besides actions on or near a stage. John Wilkes killed Abraham Lincoln; Edwin saved the life of Lincoln's son. Edwin saw young Robert Lincoln accidentally fall onto train tracks at a Chicago station, and pulled him up on the platform just as an oncoming train rushed by.

Six Degrees of Separation (1993)

A pair of rich New York art dealers, played by Stockard Channing and Donald Sutherland, have a strange encounter with a man who claims to be Sidney Poitier's son, played by Will Smith.

Sleepless in Seattle (1993)

Tom Hanks and Meg Ryan star in Nora Ephron's tale about a hopelessly single woman, a recently widowed man, and their ultimate rendezvous atop the Empire State Building.

Kids (1995)

Larry Clark's disturbing, dark, low-budget indie about teens growing up in poverty in the city. The main character has a goal to sleep with as many virgins as he can, even after he contracts HIV.

Clockers (1995)

Spike Lee zooms in on a housing project in Brooklyn, where an innocent boy gets mixed up in a drug bust that threatens to take everything from him.

City Hall (1996)

After a boy dies from a stray bullet during a shootout between a cop and a mob family member, New York's deputy mayor, played by John Cusack, starts digging for information about his boss, Al Pacino.

Gangs of New York (2002)

Decades in the making, Martin Scorsese's epic follows the violent gang warfare that unfolded in 1863 in the Five Points area of New York City.

25th Hour (2002)

Edward Norton faces his last day of freedom before going to jail in Spike Lee's moving story of a man forced to re-examine his life and how he got himself into his predicament.

Tony or Toni?

Oscar may be a man, but Tony was a woman. Broadway's most prestigious award is named after **Antoinette Perry**, a theatrical whirlwind from the first half of the 20th century. She was, by turns, a knockout actress, an enormously successful director (she staged the hit *Harvey*, among others), a savvy producer and investor, and an enormous force in the theatrical community. She created the Stage Door Canteen, where Broadway stars served servicemen during World War II, and founded what would become the American Theater Wing, which started giving the awards a year after her death in 1946. If they'd started giving it a little earlier, it'd have been called the Toni, but Perry changed the spelling of her nickname after Toni Home Permanents were released.

The Obies, by the way, were created by the *Village Voice* in 1955 to recognize Off-Broadway productions – hence the O and the B. Fortunately, when they added Off-Off-Broadway productions in 1964, they kept the old name.

Moving Pictures

The Empire Theater on 42nd Street has quite a history (including Abbott & Costello's debut in vaudeville in 1935), so when Brooklyn-based developer Bruce Ratner wanted to build a massive movie multiplex on the block in the 1990s, he decided not to knock the venerable old showplace down, but to leave it standing as part of the development. The only problem was, he didn't like where it was standing – so he moved it.

On March 1, 1998, workers jacked up the entire building and moved it 168 feet further west along a special track, setting it down at 236 West 42nd, where it forms the entrance and lobby to a 25-theater multiplex with sky lobbies that look out over Times Square, the Times Building, and the Hudson.

One more thing: not only wasn't the Empire always where it is now, it wasn't always the Empire. When it was built in 1912, the owner called it the Eltinge, after one his most profitable acts, the immensely popular Julian Eltinge, who made a household name for himself as a female impersonator in the first quarter of the 20th century, long before RuPaul and Dame Edna.

Photo: Daniel Hood

There are a few facts about the **Angelika Film Center**
(18 W. Houston St.; 212-995-2000), New York's
beloved independent movie house, that few people
know about. First, despite the common perception that
non-mainstream film venues can barely make then rent,
Angelika is actually one the top-grossing theaters in the
country. Second, the theater's construction was far more
creative than any movie ever shown there.

In the mid-1980s, film producer and distributor
Angelika Saleh wanted to open an indie film house in
Manhattan. She and her partners scoured the city for a
suitable space, but nothing was available. Finally she
got the idea to buy the basement in the charming old,
run-down Cable Car Building on Houston Street, an
unofficial landmark where the motors were housed that
ran the city's long-since-defunct cable-car network. Saleh
saw that the basement rooms where the motors were
stored had extremely high ceilings, which were ideal for
big screens. After a painstaking renovation, which
included removing abandoned, rusted-out cable cars,
the Angelika Film Center opened its doors in 1989. The
theater boasted six screens, 1,200 seats, and a 36-foot
espresso bar on the first floor.

Among its first roster of flicks was Robert Altman's *Let It
Ride*, starring Richard Dreyfuss, and a Danish film titled
Emma's Shadow. It became an instant success with New
Yorkers looking to escape the mainstream. Since then,
Saleh has been looking to open other film centers in
cities including Chicago, Seattle, Minneapolis, and
Pasadena. In an ironic twist that recalled the address of
the Manhattan movie house, the second Angelika Film
Center opened in Houston, Texas.

That's Not New York!

A list of movies and TV shows filmed
or set in New York would take up
more space then we have; instead,
here's a list of those that have
pretended to be filmed here.

American Psycho

This tale of literally murderous
business competition is
quintessentially New York —
but it was filmed in Toronto.

Eyes Wide Shut

Stanley Kubrick notoriously
would not film outside of England.
Though his final film, starring Tom
Cruise and Nicole Kidman, was
set in Manhattan, Kubrick chose
to recreate Greenwich Village and
other city locations in London.

Jackie Chan's Rumble in the Bronx

Filmed in Vancouver. Note the tall mountains in the background.

Rear Window

The famous Alfred Hitchcock thriller starring Jimmy Stewart was set around a courtyard behind several apartment buildings in Chelsea. Though the film's location was convincing, it was nonetheless shot in Hollywood — Hitch had them build the entire courtyard set on a soundstage.

West Side Story

One of the few that at least made an effort — most of the movie was shot in Hollywood, but some exterior shots were filmed in San Juan Hill, the rough tenement neighborhood that was mostly destroyed to build Lincoln Center.

New Movie Palaces

Photo: Daniel Hood

In the early days of movies, the studios built giant palaces in New York like the Roxy and the Rialto, and used them as marketing gimmicks to sell seats at lesser theaters in the sticks. (When they asked, "What's playing at the Roxy?" in *Guys and Dolls*, they really wanted to know.) They were all gone by the 1990s, except for one or two grand ghosts like the Ziegfeld, replaced by a fairly sad set of cramped boxes.

That all changed in 1994, with the coming of the **Loews Lincoln Square** *(1998 Broadway, at W. 68th St.)*, a huge, over-the-top, near-kitsch homage to the old palaces. It looked great and, more important, had comfortable, stadium-style seating, so you didn't spend so much time looking at the back of peoples' heads. Since then, the city has been gifted with a flurry of modern, mainstream movie houses like the **AMC Empire 25** and the **Loews E-Walk** *(opposite each other on 42nd St., bet. Seventh and Eighth Aves.)*, the **UA Union Square Stadium 14** *(Broadway and 13th St.)*, the **Magic Johnson Harlem USA** *(300 W. 125th St., bet. Frederick Douglass Blvd. and Manhattan Ave.)* and many more.

But for our money, the best new place to see movies in New York is the **UA Battery Park City 16** *(102 North End Ave., at Vesey St.)*. It's got all the good points of the other recently built theaters, plus it's so far downtown that it's half empty most of the time. Getting in, even on opening night, is never a problem.

Arguably, no city appears in more films than New York. But at the same time, no city has had more impostors on the silver screen than the Big Apple. From *King Kong* and *Miracle on 34th Street* to *Wall Street* and *Working Girl*, the city has racked up a countless collection of memorable movie moments. But while screenwriters cannot resist setting their plots in New York, many producers have resisted plotting their sets here. With cheaper sites almost everywhere, New York is more often replicated on celluloid, rather than actually represented. In fact, though alternative New Yorks have been used since the dawn of film, the problem has grown worse recently: from 1998 to 2001, movie and television production in New York shrank by 20 percent.

Perhaps the most ironic – and insulting – forgery of recent years is the 2001 cable-television movie *Rudy*. New York's former mayor was one of the most outspoken proponents of New York movies being filmed in New York. However, the company that produced the unauthorized biopic, USA Networks, chose to shoot it in Toronto. Worst of all, the film attempts to play out the tragedy of 9/11, and Rudy's response to it, on clearly Canadian streets.

Today, the city is fighting to get all these errant filmmakers back. During the first Tribeca Film Festival after 9/11, city officials announced a plan to install blue plaques that read "Set in New York" at the sites of famous on-screen scenes to honor a film's authenticity. An online poll was conducted, and the first place chosen for the award was Katz's Delicatessen, where Meg Ryan famously faked an orgasm in *When Harry Met Sally*. "The plaques remind filmmakers of what the city has to offer," said New York City Film Commissioner Katherine Oliver. "New York is the ultimate location."

For his part, former mayor Ed Koch wanted to see the first "Set in New York" plaque installed in a small park in Sutton Place overlooking the East River. It's the iconic scene in *Manhattan* where Woody Allen and Diane Keaton talk on a bench before the sparkling lights of the 59th Street Bridge. "That to me was the most memorable in terms of seeing New York City," Koch said in an interview. "Woody Allen was just the master of it."

Of course, Koch, who writes film reviews, also believes the Empire State Building should be honored for

Midnight Movies

Whether you're a natural nocturne or a chronic insomniac, the city that never sleeps contains a bevy of movie houses where the celluloid keeps flickering into the wee hours. Some of them show current films after midnight, but most rely on unknown indie releases or proven cult classics.

Here's a look at some of New York's stand-by theaters for midnight screenings:

Photo: Brad Dunn

Two Boots Pioneer Theater

Once a pizza shop, now an indie movie house, Two Boot's current midnight movie is *Donnie Darko*, the warped 2001 cult hit about an ultra-perceptive time traveler who saves the universe with the help of a six-foot rabbit.

155 E. 3rd St.; 212-254-3300

its appearance in the original *King Kong*. But though the world-famous building certainly deserves the plaque for other movies, it won't be recognized for the 1933 classic: *King Kong* was made in Hollywood.

Raiding the Craft Services Spread

Photo: Daniel Hood

When the city is otherwise engaged, Toronto and Vancouver may occasionally stand in for New York, but that doesn't mean there isn't plenty of TV and film production going on here. In fact, the Mayor's Office of Film, Theater and Broadcasting estimates that there are about 100,000 locals who make their living in the business, and the city can average as many as 40,000 film, TV, commercial, and still-photography shoots every year. That means lots of chances to spot stars and models at work — and lots of chances to get yelled at by pimply production assistants with clipboards, headsets, and a bloated sense of their own self-importance.

They'll order you to cross the street, or even insist that an entire block is closed off, limiting your opportunities to gawk at the stars' trailers and steal from the catering tables. Here's our favorite trick: unless the cameras are actually rolling, these movie martinets can't keep you off a block if you live or work there. So lie, and peep to your heart's content.

Photo: Daniel Hood

The Very Last Gig

Frank E. Campbell's is popular with the stars, though it usually sees them at their worst – it's the funeral parlor of the rich and famous. In its 100-plus years, it has handled the final arrangements for a great many stars (among them Judy Garland, Dorothy Parker, John Lennon, Jacqueline Onassis, Biggie Smalls, and Aaliyah), but few presented the problems that came along with silent screen legend Rudolph Valentino in August 1926.

A Hollywood man, Valentino was only in town to promote a picture when he fell ill from an ulcer, and then died of complications from surgery. Thousands of hysterical fans mobbed Campbell's funeral parlor on Broadway at 66th Street, fighting police and breaking windows in hopes of a parting glimpse of the Sheik. Fainting women had to be carried out of the pandemonium, and would be again when over 100,000 fans showed up outside St. Malachy's on West 49th Street for his funeral mass.

Fortunately, Valentino soon went west for his final burial, and Campbell's could take out a newspaper ad stating that "dignity and decorum" had returned to the establishment – though it would be mobbed by mourners again as recently July 2003, when 100,000 fans of the late salsa queen Celia Cruz paid their respects outside Campbell's new location at Madison and 81st Street. No ads were required afterward.

A Hit from the 70s

"New York, New York" is the city's official anthem; the question is, what did we do for an anthem before 1977? That's when the song was written by Kander and Ebb, the Broadway geniuses behind *Cabaret* and *Chicago*. It has an older sound because they wrote it for the Martin Scorsese movie of the same name, which was set in the 1940s. The story goes that they presented an early version of the song to Scorsese and the movie's star, Robert DeNiro, and Bobby told them it should be angrier. His interference put them in an angry mood, and the rewrite came close to the version we all know now. Still, the movie was a huge flop, and the song went nowhere until Frank Sinatra re-arranged it, changed a few words, and released the now-classic version on a 1980 album.

The Screening Room

The best movie house in Manhattan, where you can carry a draught beer into the theater, the much-storied Screening Room has elevated unnoticed underground flicks into full-fledged cult classics. The theater recently put *Hedwig and the Angry Inch* in its regular midnight slot, and became a magnet for legions of Hedheads in the tri-state area.
54 Varick St.; 212-334-2100

Sony Lincoln Square Imax

Not exactly your traditional indie art house, this ornate Imax theater makes the list not only because it boasts the largest screen in Manhattan, but also because it shows regular midnight movies — current, classic, and otherwise.
1998 Broadway, at 68th St.;
212-50-LOEWS, #638

Film Festivals

African Diaspora Film Festival
nyadff.com

Big Apple Anime Fest
bigappleanimefest.com

Brooklyn International Film Festival
A sizable event in June; formerly the Williamsburg Film Festival.
wbff.org

Margaret Mead Film and Video Festival
Tons of documentaries, some with an anthropological slant. Held in the fall, and run by the American Museum of Natural History since 1977.
amnh.org/programs/mead/

Native American Film and Video Festival
Biennial since 1979; run by the National Museum of the American Indian.
nativenetworks.si.edu

NewFest
Officially, the New York Lesbian, Gay, Bisexual, & Transgender Film Festival, in June.
newfestival.org

Punk Mecca

In the four letters **CBGB** lie the birth, zenith, and death of punk music in the 1970s and '80s. For hundreds of bands and thousands of fans, the acronym encapsulates one of the most important eras of music history. But to most people – indeed to many who experienced CBGB then and now – the name is a mystery, as is the history of this seminal hotspot in the Bowery.

The club's full name, CBGB OMFUG, stands for Country, Bluegrass, Blues – Other Music for Uplifting Gormandizers, and its founder and still owner, Hilly Kristal, envisioned an entirely different music venue than he ended up with. When asked if punk and other underground music is his favorite, Kristal says, "No!!! I've always liked all kinds, but [when CBGB was founded] half the radio stations all over the U.S. were playing country music, cool juke boxes were playing blues and bluegrass. So I thought it would be a whole lot of fun to have my own club with all this kind of music playing there. Unfortunately – or perhaps fortunately – things didn't work out quite the way I'd expected."

After staging various country and blues acts to minimal success, Kristal began signing on unknown bands that played what he called "screeching noise." With the end of disco and its heavily produced, formula-driven sounds, music lovers were looking for something new and raw. Kristal discovered he could give it to them. By offering all door sales to new bands (he would keep only the bar money), Kristal attracted undiscovered talent from all across the country.

The birth of punk may as well be Aug. 16, 1974, when a band called the Ramones took the stage before a small crowd (which consisted of, among others, the bartender, his dog, and Andy Warhol). They played a short set that electrified the crowd, and signaled the beginning of a new sound. Soon the CBGB bands became renowned: Television, Blondie, the Stooges with Iggy Pop, the Talking Heads, MC5, Patti Smith, the Velvet Underground, and the New York Dolls. With the nascent punk scene taking root in his venue for country and bluegrass, Kristal decided to change his mind and change his direction. He kept the name, however, and to this day still gets questions about what it means. Often, he says, people ask him, "What's a gormandizer?"

He says, "It's a voracious eater of, in this case, music."

Though **St. Mark's Place** between Second and Third Avenues is still clutching to its iconoclastic roots, it's getting harder and harder for the one-time heart of counterculture to take itself seriously – what with its string of cheesy t-shirt vendors, banks, and sandwich shop chains.

But the block certainly had its day. And as long ago as the 1960s, no spot had more relevance than the building at 23 St. Mark's. For decades the site was the Polish National Hall, but in the mid-1960s, when the floodgates of bohemian culture were opened in the East Village, the owner's son converted the basement into a bar called the Dom. The place took off, attracting all walks of artists, musicians, and poets in the area.

In 1966, the Dom fell into the hands of Albert Grossman, the hard-boiled rock manager whose clients included Bob Dylan and Peter, Paul and Mary. He changed the name to Balloon Farm, and started bringing in newer, cutting-edge acts.

Then, in 1967, another change of ownership converted the Polish National Hall into the Electric Circus, a psychedelic discotheque that not only featured up-and-coming bands, including the Velvet Underground and the Jimi Hendrix Experience, but also displayed Warhol's Exploding Plastic Inevitable and other optical art shows, and blared dance music until dawn. Legend has it this was the site where Jimi Hendrix and Janis Joplin bedded down on several occasions, and where more heroin was shot up than in the entire East and West Villages combined.

The party lasted about four years. In 1971, the Electric Circus's owner died and left the building to the club's coatchecker, Joyce Hartwell, who turned it into a community rehab center. The place went out with a bang, however. The last concert at the Circus featured John Lennon, Yoko Ono, and Frank Zappa.

Today, after several renovations over the years, the site of extreme 1960s exuberance is being turned into a large bank branch.

New York Comedy Film Festival

nycff.com

New York Horror Film Festival

In October.

nychorrorfest.com

New York International Independent Film and Video Festival

It claims to be the largest in the world, touring Las Vegas and L.A., and attracting a fair number of stars. Holds three events per year in spring, fall, and winter.

nyfilmvideo.com

The New York Film Festival

Over 40 years old, run by the Film Society of Lincoln Center in October.

filmlinc.com/nyff/nyff.htm

New York Underground Film Festival

Anything goes, for more than a decade, every March.

nyuff.com

Tribeca Film Festival

Started by Robert DeNiro after 9/11 as a way to revitalize downtown, it draws big stars and big pictures in May.

tribecafilmfestival.org

Small Places

These are the places that want to grow up to be CBGB — landmarks in rock (or punk, or alterna-rock, or folk, or...) — basement bars largely clustered in the Village and the Lower East Side, with a few scattered elsewhere.

Arlene Grocery

Up-and-coming acts. The Strokes started out here.
95 Stanton St., bet. Ludlow and Orchard Sts.; 212-358-1633

Bitter End

A Village landmark since 1931, it's seen a huge roster of famous names.
147 Bleecker St., bet. Thompson St. and LaGuardia Place; 212-673-7030

Brownie's

Great for new bands. Sugar Ray, Creed, and the Verve Pipe had early gigs here.
169 Ave. A, at 11th St.; 212-420-8392

A Bad Town for Blue

Comedy isn't pretty, but in the 1960s it was at least supposed to be clean, which is why undercover cops at a **Lenny Bruce** show at Greenwich Village's Cafe Au Go-Go in November 1964 took note of the more than 100 obscene words the pioneering comic used — and then had him arrested. Bruce was convicted on obscenity charges, screwed up his own appeal, and died of a drug overdose in 1966, before more permissive times made blue material an essential part of most comedians' acts. In December 2003, Governor George Pataki gave Bruce New York State's first-ever posthumous pardon — a little f*@#ing late, if you ask us.

Take That, Second City

It took a bunch of Chicagoans to teach New York the joys (and terrors) of improv comedy. The four founders of the Upright Citizens Brigade — Matts Besser and Walsh, Ian Roberts, and Amy Poehler — came here in 1995, had a three-year run as a sketch comedy show on Comedy Central, and in 1999 used the proceeds from that to open the **UCB Theater**, a showcase dedicated to the rigors and flopsweats of made-up-on-the-spot humor. They fill seven nights a week with teams of desperately inventive comedians, all students from the UCB's master classes in the arcane and surprisingly strict forms of improv. The comedy can be uneven, and the pauses long, but the shows are cheap (mostly around $5), and when it works, there's nothing better. Best bets: Sunday nights, which feature more polished shows, and the Tuesday night "Harold" gigs (a long-form, structured improv usually performed by the more experienced). Besides, with graduates turning up as performers and writers at places like *SNL*, *MadTV*, *The Daily Show*, and *Late Night with Conan O'Brien*, you never know when a famous face will stop by and end up on stage for a little free-form exercise.
307 W. 26th St., near Eighth Ave.; 212-366-9176; www.ucbtheater.com; for class info, contact classes@ucbt.net

Into the Pit

If you can't get into the UCB, walk a few blocks north and try the PIT, or **Peoples Improv Theater**, which has less of a pedigree but just as much dedication to the art of working without a script.
154 W. 29th St., bet. Sixth and Seventh Aves.; 212-563-7488

Como Se Dice 'Lesbian Dial-a-Date?'

Shock jock **Luis Jimenez** doesn't always want to be the Spanish-speaking Howard Stern – sometimes, Stern wants to be the English-speaking Luis Jimenez. That's because Jimenez's morning show, "El Vacilon de la Manana," has been neck and neck with Stern's in the New York ratings since he hit his stride on La Mega/97.9 FM in 1998. Born in Puerto Rico, Jimenez relies on the same kind of crude sexual humor, and livens things up with the occasional prank for his Nuyorican and Latino audience – though he doesn't always get recognized as one of New York's most popular radio personalities, precisely because his show is in Spanish.

To keep our city's last shred of dignity, we note that both shows are beaten in the prime morning slot by 1010 WINS, the AM all-news station.

Cafe Wha
Dylan and Hendrix played here early on; now the excellent house band covers everyone, and gives way a few nights a week to funk or Brazilian music.
115 Macdougal St., at Minetta Lane; 212-254-3706

Joe's Pub
This club in the Public Theater is too eclectic to categorize, but very hip.
425 Lafayette St., bet. 4th St. and Astor Pl., at the Public Theater; 212-539-8770

Luna Lounge
Lots of local acts.
171 Ludlow St., bet. Stanton and Houston Sts.; 212-260-2323

Maxwell's
Actually in Hoboken – but many a westward-heading band makes their last stop in the tri-state area here.
1039 Washington St., Hoboken, N.J.; 201-653-1703

Apollo's Creed

Most people can tell you that the **Apollo Theater** in Harlem not only launched the careers of some of the greatest performers of the last century, but also became the first venue in the country to feature mostly black performers for a mostly black audience. But what many don't know is that when the historic theater first opened its doors in 1914, it pursued a starkly different entertainment philosophy – and the black community wasn't part of it.

Originally called Hurtig and Seamon's New Burlesque Theater, the hall first offered striptease and vaudeville acts for exclusively white audiences. Blacks, who were moving into the neighborhood in droves, weren't even allowed inside. The shows were extremely racy for the time, and as the city cracked down on all things immoral it went out of business.

New owners renamed the 1,400-seat venue the Apollo Theater in 1928, and taking heed of the sea change in local demographics, they began to showcase black performers occasionally. Then, in 1932, a new era in music history was christened when Duke Ellington and his band rocked the house with "It Don't Mean a Thing If It Ain't Got That Swing." The Apollo instantly became the hottest musical venue in town.

Management changed again, and this time a new policy was instituted: the Apollo would feature a permanent variety show format featuring top black performers. At the height of the Depression, the venue distracted audiences from hard times by offering live entertainment seven days a week, all year round. For the next few decades, every major entertainer appeared on the Apollo's stage: among others, Ella Fitzgerald, Count Basie, Nat King Cole, Billie Holiday, Stevie Wonder, Diana Ross, Louis Armstrong, Bo Diddley, Aretha Franklin, and the Jackson Five.

Mercury Lounge

Small and lounge-y, but they book big names. Great sound. *217 East Houston St., bet. Ludlow and Essex Sts; 212-260-4700*

Northsix

An indie rock paradise in Brooklyn. *66 N. 6th St., bet. Kent and Wythe Aves., Brooklyn; 718-599-5103*

Sin-é

Named for a famed spot on St. Mark's Place that launched Jeff Buckley and David Gray. Always a packed lineup. *150 Attorney St., at Stanton St.; 212-388-0077*

Village Underground

A small rock room with good shows and a real Village feel. *130 W. 3rd St., bet. Macdougal St. and Sixth Ave.; 212-777-7745*

All that Jazz

Not long after the Apollo Theater opened in Harlem to become the first major venue for black performers in the country, another seminal night spot took anchor in Greenwich Village.

By all rights, the **Village Vanguard** is the Carnegie Hall of jazz clubs, where the granddaddies of jazz cut their teeth and cut a path for generations to follow. Opened in 1935 by Max Gordon, a musical bohemian with a penchant for sniffing out talent, the Vanguard overnight became a launching pad for some of the country's most influential poets and musicians.

Although not exclusively a jazz spot in the beginning (famous folkies Woody Guthrie and Pete Seeger both played there, as did Lenny Bruce), the Village Vanguard hit its stride in the late 1940s and early '50s, when a pantheon of jazz luminaries ruled the stage, including Leadbelly, Harry Belafonte, Charlie Parker, Dizzie Gillespie, Miles Davis, John Coltrane, and Thelonious Monk.

Today, the venue is virtually unchanged from its Depression-era days. The ceiling is still notoriously low, producing raw, energetic repercussions, and new talent is still being discovered nightly. After Max passed away, his wife Lorraine took the helm and vowed to keep the hotspot true to its roots. That's why when you step inside the doors at 178 Seventh Avenue South, you'll not only hear today's newest sounds, but also the echoes of some of the greatest musicians of the last century.

Mid-sized Places

Bigger than lounges, smaller than Madison Square Garden. All offer comfortable spaces that are great for seeing big-name acts.

Bowery Ballroom
Once a vaudeville hall.
6 Delancey St., bet. Bowery and Chrystie Sts.; 212-533-2111

Photo: Daniel Hood

Irving Plaza
17 Irving Place, at 15th St.; 212-777-6800

Roseland Ballroom
Once an ice-skating rink, across the street from the former Studio 54.
239 W. 52nd St., bet. Eighth Ave. and Broadway; 212-247-0200

Jazz Clubs

Once upon a time they called 52nd Street between Fifth and Seventh Avenues "Swing Street," but that was in the 1930s, '40s and '50s, when Billie Holliday was around and Charlie Parker had Birdland. Those two blocks of brownstone clubs were the very heart of the jazz world — until someone discovered that high-rise office buildings paid more. Now jazz is spread out all over the city, with concentrations in Harlem and the Village.

Of course, there's **Jazz at Lincoln Center**, headed by Wynton Marsalis — though by the time you read this, it won't be at Lincoln Center anymore, having moved to new digs in the Time Warner Center at Columbus Circle (*jazzatlincolncenter.org*; *212-258-9800*).

Arthur's Tavern
Opened in 1937, it's the city's longest continually running jazz club. *57 Grove St., at Seventh Ave.; 212-675-6879*

Grand Slam

Whether you want to nurture the Eminem in you, or just want to give your Wednesdays a jolt, stop by the **Nuyorican Poets Café** in the East Village and try your luck in a slam contest.

Long before *8 Mile*, this hip-hop hotspot was churning out some of the best spoken-word artists in the country. Founded in 1973 by art professor Miguel Algarin, the Nuyorican is a nonprofit devoted to giving poets, musicians, visual artists, and comedians a place to shine.

Algarin originally held Nuyorican performances in his living room, but as the forum's popularity spread, so did his budget. In 1975 he rented space weekly at an Irish bar, which was more than paid for by the throngs of early fans of spoken word poetry. By 1980, the organization purchased its current home at 236 East 3rd Street.

Today, the Wednesday open poetry slams are the most popular events hosted at the Café. Rappers, poets, and freestylers deliver their lines during a preset time — usually no more than a few minutes. The competition is judged by audience members selected at random. If you win on Wednesday, you get invited back for the Nuyorican's formal competition slam on Friday. If you go far enough, you get invited to represent the Café in a national event, which is no small honor: The Nuyorican usually mops up the competition.

The Café also offers a range of stand-up comedy events, visual art presentations, and non-competitive poetry readings. For hip-hop fans, there's an open-mic night, as well as group performances. Though newcomers are not exactly as enticed to perform as they would be at, say, a karaoke bar, it's fascinating just to be in the audience. The nightly talent at the Nuyorican can be incredible, and more than worth the $7 price of admission.

Photo: Brad Dunn

Photo: Daniel Hood

cabaret

The Carlyle Hotel
Two venues: the Cafe Carlyle, where Bobby Short has a longstanding gig and Woody Allen sometimes comes to play jazz, and Bemelman's Bar.
35 E. 76th St., at Madison Ave.; 212-744-1600

Danny's Skylight Room
"Classic" cabaret – crooners, pianists, a little stand-up.
346 W. 46th St., bet. Eighth and Ninth Aves.; 212-265-8133

Don't Tell Mama
Perhaps the best-known, it's more theater-oriented, with open mic.
343 W. 46th St., bet. Eighth and Ninth Aves., 212-757-0788.

The Duplex
A great big grab bag of up-and-coming acts.
61 Christopher St., at Seventh Ave.; 212-255-5438

Feinstein's at the Regency
Home base of Michael Feinstein, with other big names appearing regularly.
540 Park Ave., at 61st St., in the Regency Hotel; 212-339-4050

The Oak Room at the Algonquin
Some call it a "once in a lifetime" experience – though we're not sure if that's because of the great talent or the high prices.
59 W. 44th St., bet. Fifth and Sixth Aves.; 212-840-6800

Photo: Daniel Hood

Rose's Turn
Upstairs is one of the city's oldest cabaret spaces; even more fun is the cramped piano bar downstairs, where the waitstaff and bartenders take turns belting 'em out. Loud and friendly.
55 Grove St., bet. Seventh Ave. and Bleecker St.; 212-366-5438

Birdland
The original was on 52nd Street, but this one still puts on a rotation of regular acts and big names.
315 W. 44th St., bet. Eighth and Ninth Aves.; 212-581-3080

Blue Note
Big names, very popular.
131 W. 3rd St., bet. Sixth Ave. and Macdougal St.; 212-475-8592

C-Note
Not always jazz, but good when it is.
157 Ave. C, bet. 9th and 10th Sts.; 212-677-8142

Iridium
Upscale, with a roster of local and big talents.
1650 Broadway, at 51st St.; 212-582-2121

Jazz Standard
Built around restaurateur Danny Meyer's BBQ restaurant.
116 E. 27th St., bet. Park and Lexington Aves.; 212-576-2232

Knitting Factory
Lots of stages, lots of acts, lots of styles.
74 Leonard St., bet. Broadway and Church St.; 212-219-3006

The Lenox Lounge
Home of the Zebra Room.
288 Lenox Ave., bet. 124th and 125th Sts.; 212-427-0253

Re-Appearing Act

Vaudeville and the dozens of little theaters it supported are long faded from the New York scene, and with them went the need for acts to sandwich in between the singers, the strippers, and the comics. Since magicians often filled this bill, they're pretty thin on the ground here – which alone is reason enough to admire **Monday Night Magic**, the weekly showcase for an ever-changing roster of prestidigitators that's been going on since the early 1990s. The fact that they're generally really good is a serious plus. If you need more, you can get a discount at a number of nearby restaurants just for having a ticket for that night's performance.
The Soho Playhouse, 15 Vandam St., bet. Sixth Ave. and Varick St.; 212-615-6432; mondaynightmagic.com

Getting Off Track

Forget steady 401(k)s, long-term bonds, or conservative mutual funds. Betting on the ponies is a great way to jazz up your investment portfolio. The percentages might not be there, but you'll have a lot more fun than poring over stock charts all day.

New York's a great place to get involved in this risky venture, not only because it houses both the Belmont and Aqueduct race tracks, but also because you don't have to go to either of them to experience the thrills. The city boasts one of the few places you can sidle up to a bar, have a meal, and pick ponies all afternoon.

Most Off-Track Betting parlors in Manhattan are merely busy wagering halls. With slips of paper everywhere and mixed cries of joy and suffering, each resembles an extremely low-rent stock exchange. But the **Yankee Clipper** beats all that. Housed in an 1840 landmark off the South Street Seaport, the restaurant/pub offers outstanding seafood and views of the East River. Best of all, the Clipper has an official OTB wagering booth, as well as rows of TVs dedicated to horse races from across the country. The bar is usually lined with regulars and littered with racing forms and newspaper entries.

Bet the exacta, order a pint and a side of crab cakes, and sit back and watch your portfolio grow.

Parlor Entertainment
Saturdays and Sundays at 4, Marjorie Eliot opens up her apartment for a couple of jazz sets. No cover, but donations are accepted.
555 Edgecombe Ave., Apt. 3F, at 160th St.; 212-781-6595

Smalls
For serious enthusiasts – it's BYOB, with 10 to 12 hours of jazz a night, from 10 p.m. to 8 a.m.
183 W. 10th St., at Seventh Ave.; 212-929-7565

Smoke
Check for big names.
2751 Broadway, at 106th St.; 212-864-6662

Tonic
Avant-garde jazz, with a klezmer brunch on weekends.
107 Norfolk St., bet. Delancey and Rivington Sts.; 212-358-7501

Up Over Jazz Cafe
Great jazz in Brooklyn.
351 Flatbush Ave., at Sterling Pl, Park Slope, Brooklyn; 718-398-5413

Nightlife

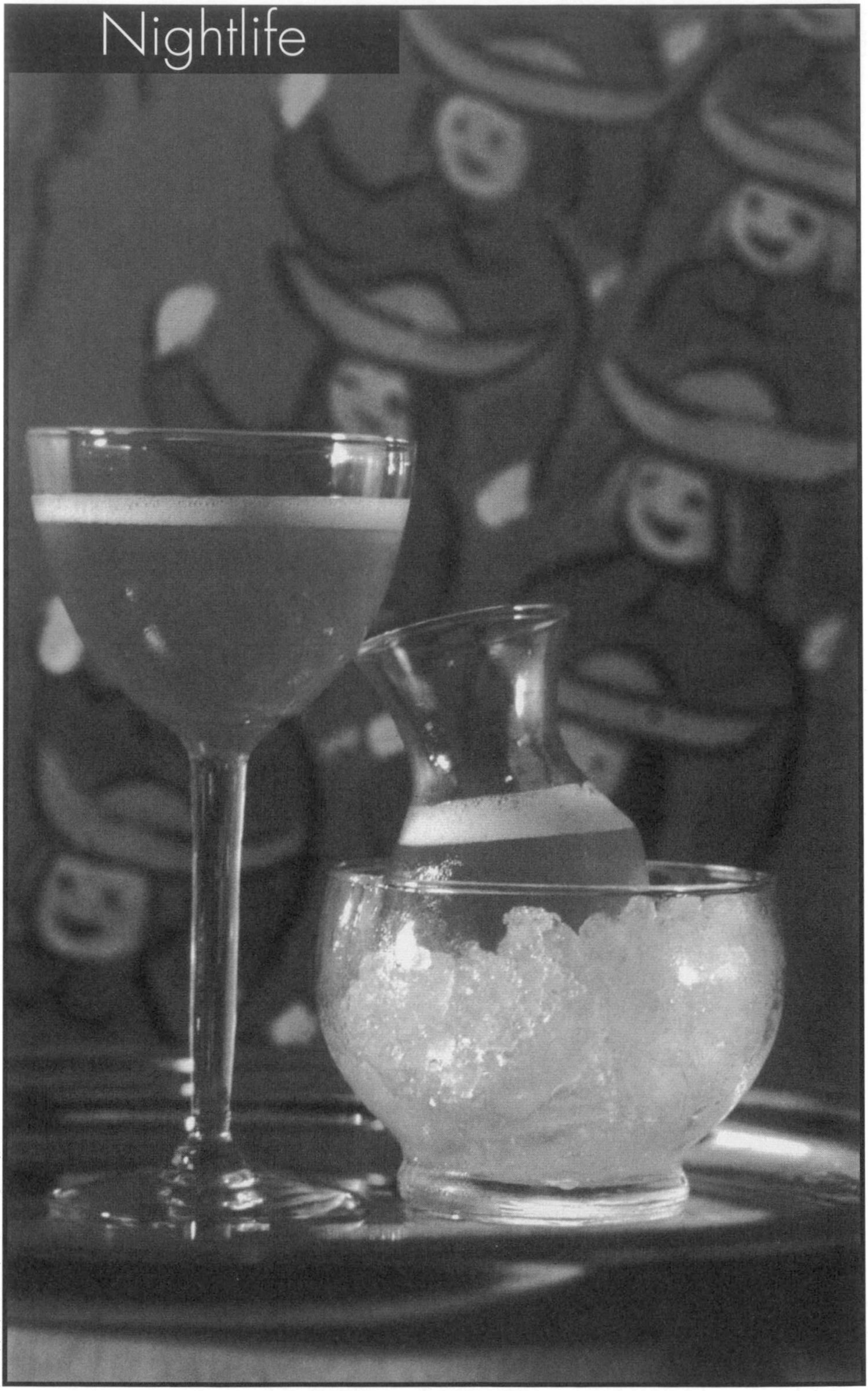

Photo: Courtesy Bemelman's Bar/Carlyle Hotel

After dark, some head for the velvet-rope spots to see and be seen, while others dive into nameless joints hoping never to be heard from again. New York caters to both, and all the broad spectrum in between, with a thousand spots designed to banish sleep in the city that never does.

Photo: Brad Dunn

A Classic Horseshoe

Few old bars in New York City have resisted the forces of gentrification as well as **Vazac's Horseshoe Bar** *(108 Ave. B, at E. 7th St.)* in the East Village. More commonly known as 7B, after its cross streets, this Manhattan classic has somehow retained its soul despite its constant popularity over four generations.

There's something about a spacious, corner tavern with tons of windows and a giant horseshoe bar that has attracted legions of drinkers over the years. The available liquors are many and cheap, the blaring jukebox is stuck in 1970s and '80s punk mode, and the patrons are an unusual mix of old and young, stylish and tasteless, mirthful and pensive.

It's no wonder that newcomers to 7B get a feeling of *déjà vu*: The bar's been in some memorable movie scenes: Frank Pentangeli gets dragged across the bar by his throat in *The Godfather Part II*, Paul Newman has his morning beer with an egg in *The Verdict*, and Crocodile Dundee delivers his "That's not a knife" routine outside the front door. *Angel Heart* filmed a scene there, and so did *Serpico, The Paper*, and *The Sopranos*.

Film crews aren't the only notable clients. Many a beat poet ruined his liver there; Allen Ginsberg lived around the corner. Rumor has it that a clique of Satanists hangs out every Sunday night.

What's charming about the bar is the photo-booth, the three vintage pinball machines, the bartenders who are invariably warm and receptive. What's less than charming are the bathrooms, which on a weekend night quickly morph into open cesspools. Written over the urinal in the men's room is a message to take your mind off the putrid surroundings: "Calm blue ocean, calm blue ocean."

forget Milwaukee

Watch enough TV and movies, and it's easy to imagine that our beverage list is divided between the smart cocktails of the *Sex and the City* set and the forties of malt liquor popular in the public housing milieu. But in between lies a vast middle ground dominated largely by **beer**, which only makes sense, given that North America's first beer was brewed right here in 1612, by Dutch explorer Adrian Block. (He had been stuck here when his ship burned, and later came back to colonize; he also named Block Island in Long Island Sound, as well as countless other places in the area.)

From then on, this was a serious brewtown, with almost 80 breweries by 1890, producing household names like Schaefer and Rheingold. Apart from a general warm glow, beer's greatest contribution to New York may be the Yankees: Col. Jacob Ruppert's brewing fortune allowed him not only to buy the team in 1915, but to stock it with top players like Babe Ruth and, eventually, to spend $23 million of his own money to build Yankee Stadium. Ruth may have built the House, but there's suds in the foundation.

Still, local brewing declined in the 20th century, hit hard by Prohibition and the aggressive national marketing of the big brewers in Milwaukee and St. Louis. By the 1980s, Schaefer and Rheingold had closed down their breweries, Miss Rheingold was no longer a local celebrity, and New Yorkers were drinking what everyone else was drinking.

That's all changed in the last two decades, thanks to the rise of microbreweries, and the dedication of local hopsheads. Nowadays, there's no excuse for drinking the same-old, same-old, and plenty of places to find a pint of something different. Try some of these:

Bars with History

Ear Inn

Who cares that it may be the oldest bar in the city, with a wealth of history buried in its basement? It's a great, grungy hang, with good eats. *326 Spring St., bet. Greenwich and Washington Sts.; 212-431-9750*

Photo: Daniel Hood

McSorley's

The one and only, celebrated in song and story. Well, story at least — *New Yorker* scribe Joseph Mitchell made this place a legend. Opened in 1854, they only admitted women in 1970, after a court case. *15 E. 7th St., bet. Second and Third Aves.; 212-473-9148*

Photo: Daniel Hood

Old Town

The best old-fashioned men's
room in town.
*45 E. 18th St., bet. Broadway and
Park Ave.; 212-529-6732*

Pete's Tavern

O. Henry's hangout.
*129 E. 18th St., at Irving Pl.;
212-473-7676*

Photo: Daniel Hood

P.J. Clarke's

Tin-ceiling setting for
The Lost Weekend, now with
an improved kitchen.
*915 Third Ave., at 55th St.;
212-317-1616*

The Blind Tiger
Ale House

Not a brewery itself, but famed for its vast selection
and for showcasing obscure microbrews from all over
the country, as well as the occasional free cheese.
Comfortable and slightly rough-hewn.
518 Hudson St., at W. 10th St.; 212-675-3848

Brooklyn Brewery

Photo: Daniel Hood

Their beers are
available in lots of bars
and delis, but you can
also go out to the source
on Friday nights, when
they open the actual
brewery and sell for a
couple of hours. It fills up
fast with Williamsburg
hipsters, and the wooden
tokens you buy at the
door to exchange for
beers at the bar are a
little odd, but where else can you lounge around on a
sack of hops while drinking the end result, in a brewery
where all the electricity comes from windpower? Plus,
they often have the brewer's ultra-popular seasonal
beers, like Monster, available when no else does. They
also do tours on Saturdays, and host tastings and art
events on other days of the week.
*Brewers Row, 79 N. 11th St., Brooklyn;
718-486-7440; www.brooklynbrewery.com*

Chelsea Brewing Company

Brewers of Checker Cab and a few others, with a great waterfront location.
Pier 59, Chelsea Piers, 18th St. and West Side Highway; 212-336-6440

d.b.a.

A little more upscale than the Blind Tiger, but with the same devotion to brilliant beers you've never heard of. BTW, d.b.a. is "doing business as...".
41 First Ave., bet. 2nd and 3rd Sts.; 212-475-5097

Heartland Brewery

You'll find lots of both suits and tourists at this rapidly expanding chain of brewpubs, so the prices are higher, but there's food and lots of locations, and their beers have won many awards. They'll also arrange private events.
127 W. 43rd St., at Times Square; 35 Union Sq. West; 1285 Sixth Ave., at 51st St.; 93 South St., at Fulton St.; 212-582-8244; heartlandbrewery.com

Some other places that take their beer very seriously:

Barrow Street Ale House

15 Barrow St., bet. W. 4th and Bleecker Sts.; 212-206-7302

Photo: Daniel Hood

Burp Castle

Self-proclaimed "House of Beer Worship," with a staff of "Brewist" monks. A little over the top... .
41 E. 7th St., bet. Second and Third Aves.; 212-982-4576

Irish Bars

Having no cuisine to speak of, the Irish gave us pubs, instead — and lots of them. This is a more or less random sampling of the millions and millions around Manhattan.

Abbey Tavern
354 Third Ave., at 26th St.; 212-532-1978

Dublin House
225 W. 79th St., bet. Broadway and Amsterdam Ave.; 212-874-9528

The Gaf
1715 First Ave., bet. 88th and 89th Sts.; 401 W. 48th St., bet. Ninth and Tenth Aves.; 212-262-2883

Kinsale Tavern
1672 Third Ave., bet. 93rd and 94th Sts.; 212-348-4370

O'Lunney's
A couple of generations of O'Lunneys make this place the friendliest joint near Times Square.
151 W. 46th St., bet. Sixth and Seventh Aves.; 212-840-6688

Paddy Reilly's Music Bar

All Guinness and only Guinness; music every night.
519 Second Ave., at 29th St.; 212-686-1210

Photo: Daniel Hood

Swift's Hibernian Lounge

That's Jonathan Swift: The bathrooms are wall-papered with *Gulliver's Travels*, and there's a mural of the man himself, plus Irish music in the back room some nights.
34 E. 4th St., bet. Lafayette St. and the Bowery; 212-260-3600

Tir Na Nog

Handy for a pint before a game or show at Madison Square Garden.
5 Penn Plaza, bet. 33rd and 34th Sts. on Eighth Ave.; 212-630-0249

Ulysses

A downtown watering hole from the owner of Swift's. With a raw bar, too.
58 Stone St., bet. Old Slip and Coenties Alley; 212-482-0400

The Ginger Man

A large selection, frequently mobbed by after-work suits; check out the tables way in back.
11 E. 36th St., bet. Fifth and Madison Aves.; 212-532-3740

Jake's Dilemma

430 Amsterdam Ave., bet. 80th and 81st Sts.; 212-580-0556

Mugs Ale House

Many, many beers. Home to the monthly meetings of the Malted Barley Appreciation Society.
125 Bedford Ave., at 10th St., Brooklyn; 718-384-08494

Peculiar Pub

A wildly wide-ranging selection of international beers, but kind of divey, and packed with NYU students.
145 Bleecker St., at LaGuardia Pl.; 212-353-1327

Ruby's Taphouse

Decent selection for the Upper East Side; frequently packed out with drunken young locals.
1495 Second Ave., bet. 91st and 92nd Sts.; 212-987-8179

Waterfront Ale House

540 Second Ave., at 30th St.; 212-696-4104; 136 Atlantic Ave., at Henry St., Brooklyn; 718-522-3794

Photo: Daniel Hood

What the Stork Brings

Running one of the city's greatest speakeasies and nightclubs, the **Stork Club** *(3 E. 53rd St. at Fifth Ave.)* wasn't always about keeping gossip columnist Walter Winchell well-oiled and making sure the monogrammed ashtrays on the celebrity tables were always facing the right way (that's toward the photographer); it also meant dealing with some of the most brutal criminals going – the bootleggers.

In fact, the Stork Club's founder, Sherman Billingsley, had done time for bootlegging himself in the Midwest before hitting the big time in NYC. But even a stretch in Leavenworth couldn't have prepared him for the cutthroat world of Jazz Age speakeasies. Almost as soon as he opened the place in 1929, Dutch Schultz tried to muscle in on the place, threatening union trouble if he didn't get a cut. Billingsley saw him off, as he did a threat from legendary gangster Legs Diamond – largely, the stories go, because he got protection from the greatest New York bootlegger of them all, Owney "the Killer" Madden, by making Madden a silent partner. Still, Billingsley wasn't entirely immune. At one point he was kidnapped by Vincent "Mad Dog" Coll, and beaten for three days for a $25,000 ransom.

All the while, the Stork Club was becoming the most famous nightclub in the country (and incidentally creating much of the culture of celebrity we now take for granted), and it thrived once the end of Prohibition brought calmer times. In the end, it wasn't gangsters that brought the Stork down; it was changes in the country. The club's racial discrimination was revealed when Josephine Baker and the NAACP staged a protest out front after Billingsley had refused to serve her, and by the late 1950s celebrities were finding other places to be rich and famous. In 1965, after bankrupting himself trying to keep the place open, Billingsley sold the building and died a year later. The site of the most famous nightclub in the world is now a pocket park outside the CBS Building.

Locals

There are hundreds of worthy locals scattered around the city; any selection is necessarily arbitrary.

Collins Bar
A good jukebox, and one looooong bar.
*735 Eighth Ave., at 46th St.;
212-541-4206*

Photo: Daniel Hood

Dive Bar
Dive as in scuba, not low-rent (though...). And a mean tuna melt.
732 Amsterdam Ave., bet. 95th and 96th Sts.; 212-749-4358

The International
Believe it or not, there's a little garden at the back of this comfortable cave.
*120 First Ave., bet. 7th and 8th Sts.;
212-777-9244*

McAleer's

A no-frills meetery.
425 Amsterdam Ave., at 81st St.;
212-874 8037

Peter McManus Cafe

An old-school drinkery, family-run
since the 1930s.
152 Seventh Ave., at 19th St.;
212-729-4602

The Raven

Always something interesting on the
TV, and great DJs most nights.
194 Ave. A, at E. 12th St.;
212-529-4712

Photo: Daniel Hood

Subway Inn

"Dive" as in "dive" — a nice, dingy
spot to begin your slide into
alcoholism. Right by Bloomingdale's.
143 E. 60th St., at Lexington Ave.;
212-223-8929

Bender is the Night

If you're a fan of Prohibition-era speakeasies or simply like to get drunk amid the ghosts of Fitzgerald and Hemingway, there's a bar in the Village with no sign — but it has your name written all over it. **Chumley's** is the dark party bar where the Lost Generation had its Lost Weekend.

In 1920s New York, you couldn't swing your arms without hitting a drunk poet or passed-out novelist. Many of them tanked up at Chumley's, which had to keep an extremely low profile to avoid getting raided by the booze patrols. Every night through an unmarked door at 86 Bedford Street poured all those initialed artists of the generation: e.e. cummings, T.S. Eliot, E.B. White, and those hip, young, free-thinking Ednas: Edna Ferber and Edna St. Vincent Millay.

And every night they got drunk and stumbled out the back door, which dumped them into a secret alley, hidden from the police. The gin mill hasn't changed much over the years. The front entrance is still harder to find than most, and the back door still dumps into an alley. The joint has made much of its literary past, and its walls, packed with photos of the old greats, pay permanent tribute to the vast sum of genius that got soused there. Though these days the place can feel more like a frat house than a writer's colony, Chumley's is still a great spot for a burger, a beer, and a whole lot of history. Best of all, the drinks are cheap.

The Right Priorities

To prove that New York's always had its priorities straight, we offer this: instead of building a city hall, the early Dutch authorities built a tavern instead — and used that for official business. Erected in 1642 at 71-73 Pearl Street, it operated as a tavern for 12 years, with the colony's government working upstairs, and only became the official City Hall in 1653.

If You're Wondering How We Knew

We can't prove this story, but we like it: in the mid-1800s, there was a local bar called the **Old Grapevine** at Sixth Avenue and West 11th Street that served as a clearinghouse for neighborhood gossip. During the Civil War, with the city in an uproar and news difficult to come by, its importance as a center for the inside story grew even stronger, and you could vouch for a story's authenticity by invoking the bar's name, thus giving birth to the phrase "I heard it through the grapevine." The bar is long gone, replaced by an apartment building in 1915, but its name lives on.

Getting Out of Control

It's easy to get confused – *Coyote Ugly*, the movie, was based on an article about a barmaid who used to work at **Coyote Ugly**, the rowdy bar – but the owners of **Hogs & Heifers**, another rowdy bar, claim that the filmmakers stole the layout and decor (including the dangling bras) at their place for *Coyote Ugly*, the movie.

Who cares? Both are very rowdy, and neither has Tyra Banks dancing on the bar. What they do have is plenty of redneck fun and the potential for grievous bodily harm, either from too much alcohol, the attentions of the bouncer, or the crowds, which have been swollen by tourists. And while Coyote Ugly (*153 First Ave., bet. 9th and 10th Sts.; 212-477-4431*) has a movie and the Lower East Side, Hogs & Heifers (*859 Washington St., at W. 13th St.; 212-929-0655; also 1843 First Ave., at 95th St.*) has bras belonging to Julia Roberts and Gwyneth Paltrow (they encourage women to leave them behind, and hang them up).

Or you can just head over to **Village Idiot** (*355 W. 14th St., bet. Eighth and Ninth Aves.; 212-989-7334*), which is a lot like the other two, without the tourist crowds.

When You're Feeling Flush

Photo: The Carlyle Hotel

Bemelmans Bar

Worth it for the mural by Ludwig Bemelmans, creator of the *Madeleine* books, who lived at the Carlyle.
35 E. 76th St., at Madison Ave., in the Carlyle Hotel; 212-744-1600

Bubble Lounge

350 different kinds of champagne.
228 West Broadway, at White St.;
212-431-3433

The Oak Room at the Plaza

A beautiful room with a great view of Central Park; great during snowstorms.
Northwest corner of the Plaza Hotel, Fifth Ave. and Central Park South;
212-759-3000

Photo: Brad Dunn

In the shadow of Port Authority lurks a pair of watering holes worth their weight in cheap draught beer. Both on Ninth Avenue between 39th and 40th Streets, and separated only by a sandwich shop, the **Bellevue Bar** and the **Holland Bar** were dive before dive was overdone.

The Bellevue is a dirty den for bikers, head-bangers, goths, and other usual seeds of seediness. The room is awash in blood-red lighting, and the owner, Jimmy Duff, drives a hearse to work. There's even an empty coffin in the back, which a few years ago was decorated with a "reserved for Bin Laden" plaque.

Perhaps most charming about the spot, besides the dingy Ms. Pac-Man game, the 50-year-old sofa, and the soft-core porn on TV, are the house-issued "Gone to Piss" cards that mark a taken bar stool. What place has more class than that?

Well, maybe two doors down. To call the Holland Bar a hole-in-the-wall is to overestimate its size. What square-footage there is goes to housing the tap, the shelf of cheap liquor, the bartender, and maybe a dozen bar stools. But it's the perfect place to knock back a mug on some sunny afternoon when you should be at work. The jukebox contains a legendary mix of greatest hits that, fortunately, do nothing to cheer up the delightfully glum atmosphere. Whether you've missed your bus or are riding out a storm, look for the faded orange awning and go in and pull up stool.

Temple Bar

Romantic and very, very dark.
332 Lafayette St., bet. Houston and Bleecker Sts.; 212-925-4242

The View at the Marriott Marquis

This somewhat touristy bar revolves, so time your $15 cocktail to last through one circuit of its panoramic midtown view. Then get out.
Marriott Marquis Time Square, 1535 Broadway bet. 45th and 46th Sts., 47th floor; 212-704-8900

Photo: Brad Dunn

Wined Up

Photo: Brad Dunn

Sometimes you want to skip dinner and go straight for the wine. Why not make a night of it? On every evening of the week, there's a free **wine tasting** happening in some wine shop somewhere in New York. You just have to know where to find it.

The best, and most regular, wine tastings are held at **Mister Wright Liquors** *(1593 Third Ave. bet. E. 89th and 90th Sts.)* This delightful shop hosts free tastings every Saturday starting at 4 p.m. Yes, free. Yes, every Saturday. Of course, the samples are usually poured from bottles costing less than $10, but who cares? There are a lot of hidden jewels at that price point, and you may have to roll up your sleeves and spend some time looking for them. Mister Wright imports bottles from Australia, Chile, and Hungary, as well as the stand-bys from California, France, and Italy. Best of all, there's no pressure to buy.

Another great spot is **Sherry-Lehmann** *(679 Madison Ave., bet. E. 61st and 62nd Sts)*. Though the free tastings do not run on a set calendar, they are usually on Fridays or Saturdays, and the samples are from all caliber of vineyards. The shop advertises in the *New York Times* every Friday to announce its weekly tastings. It's worth the 50 cents for the paper to find out when the wine starts pouring for free.

Of course, you can always make your love of vino-sampling into an official hobby by signing up with the Tasters Guild of New York. Dedicated to the pleasures of the palate, the guild calls itself "a unique society for wine and food lovers," and insists it is not just for the connoisseur, but for anyone looking to hone their tastes. Log on to *tastersguildny.com* to learn more about the New York chapter, as well as the club's 40 wine tastings every year.

Drinking Outdoors

Bohemian Beer Hall
A real old-fashioned beer garden.
29-19 24th Ave., bet. 29th and 31st Aves., Astoria, Queens; 718-274-4925.

Chelsea Commons
A nice pub with a back garden that's actually bigger than a postage stamp.
242 Tenth Ave., at 24th St.; 212-929-9424

Gowanus Yacht Club and Beer Garden
The yacht part is ironic. Actually, so's the garden part.
323 Smith St., at President St., Brooklyn; 718-246-1321

High Bar
Since you can't get into Gramercy Park itself, the Gramercy Park Hotel very kindly lets you use their tasty roof garden.
2 Lexington Ave., at 21st St.; 212-475-4320

The Iris and B. Gerald Cantor Roof Garden
From May to October, on Fridays and Saturdays, you can have afterwork cocktails on the roof of the Metropolitan Museum of Art.
Fifth Ave. and 82nd St.; 212-535-7710

City Cocktails

Two of the city's five boroughs have cocktails named after them. One is obvious, the other virtually forgotten.

By most accounts, the Manhattan was invented in 1876 by a bartender at the Manhattan Club in honor of New York Governor Samuel J. Tilden. The popular Democrat had smashed the Tweed Ring of Tammany Hall and was running for president against Rutherford B. Hayes. Democrats planned to toast Tilden's victory with this sweet new cocktail, but a heated Electoral College battle ultimately gave Hayes the keys to the White House. Tilden's political star set, but his drink lives on. It's a mixture of bourbon or blended whiskey, sweet vermouth, and bitters, served with crushed ice and usually garnished with a maraschino cherry. (Change it to Scotch whiskey, and you've got yourself a Rob Roy.)

The other borough-named cocktail, to which history has not been nearly as kind, is the Bronx. Legend has it that Johnnie Solon, a renowned bartender at the Waldorf-Astoria Hotel in the early 1900s, was challenged by a customer to make a new drink. He accepted.

Having just made a Duplex, which was equal parts sweet and dry vermouth with orange bitters, Solon decided to base his creation on this combo. He started with gin, added fresh-squeezed orange juice, and splashes of sweet and dry vermouth. The mixture was a smash, and Solon had to increase his order for oranges the next night. How it gained its name is a matter of speculation, but according to Albert Stevens Crockett's *The Old Waldorf Astoria Bar Book*, the bartender thought not of the borough itself, but of the Bronx Zoo.

Crockett claims that Solon said: "I had been at the Bronx Zoo a day or two before, and I saw, of course, a lot of beasts I had never known. Customers used to tell me of the strange animals they saw after a lot of mixed drinks." So, when the waiter asked him what his new cocktail was called, Solon replied, "Oh, you can tell him it's a Bronx."

Luna Park

Open only in the summer, and full of young and annoyingly beautiful people.
North end of Union Square Park, at 17th St.; 212-475-8464

Pier 63 Maritime

Calling it an old railway barge with a makeshift bar and burger stand, as well as a space for parties and salsa lessons, doesn't do it justice. The lightship *Frying Pan*, moored there, also serves as a dance club and performance space. If the slight swell gets too much, head south through Chelsea Piers to the **Chelsea Brewing Company**.
Pier 63, just north of Basketball City, 23rd St. and the river

Pen-Top Bar

The midtown view from the Peninsula Hotel is spectacular, as are the drink prices.
700 Fifth Ave., at 55th St., 212-956-2888

79th Street Boat Basin

Perennially crowded — go early and grab a table.
79th St., on the river; 212-496-5542

The King of the Cocktail

There's not much in the way of restoratives in the Restoration Hardware on Broadway between 22nd and 21st Streets, but there used to be — when the site housed a bar belonging to the fabled **"Professor" Jerry Thomas**, patron saint of the serious bartender and the founder of modern mixology.

Born upstate in 1830, Thomas came to New York in 1851 and opened a bar at Broadway and Ann Street, but he had a thirst for knowledge, and spent the next decade or so wandering the country, honing his craft, writing a cocktail bible called *How to Mix Drinks, or the Bon-Vivant's Companion*, and even touring Europe with a set of solid silver bar tools, before returning to the city in 1866 to stay.

He worked at the Metropolitan Hotel at Broadway and Prince before opening his 22nd Street bar, where he exhibited the work of cartoonist Thomas Nast and grew famous teaching the world to appreciate his punches, smashes, and cocktails. When he died of apoplexy at 55, he was widely missed.

Modern-day mixologists who have recreated his recipes say the drinks are almost unbearably sweet, but they still raise a glass in honor of the man who made slinging drinks both a science and an art.

Bars in Odd Places

Photo: Brad Dunn

Campbell Apartment

Tycoons used to have style. In the 1920s, John W. Campbell rented himself a giant space in a discreet corner of Grand Central Terminal, and paneled and decorated it like a Florentine palace. During the day, it was his office; at night, a lounge for his friends. He's gone now, but if you're properly dressed and willing to drop a little cash, you can drink away the time until your train with smart cocktails from the Jazz Age.
Southwest corner of Grand Central Station, 15 Vanderbilt Ave.; 212-953-0409

Photo: Daniel Hood

Guastavino's

The drink of choice under the 59th Street Bridge used to be ripple in a paper bag; since this swanky bar/restaurant opened in the under-bridge arcade, it's the "flirtini," a pink cocktail the bartender invented on the spot for Sarah Jessica Parker at a *Sex and the City* party. The place takes it name from Spanish architect Rafael Guastavino, who designed the signature arches. The soaring, unique space makes it a favorite for parties and events.

409 E. 59th St., bet. First and York Aves. (underneath the Queensboro Bridge); 212-980-2455

Pershing Square

The Guastavino's of the Park Avenue overpass — with more reasonable prices for the harried commuter than the Campbell Apartment. *90 E. 42nd St., under Park Ave.; 212-286-9600*

Corks A-Poppin'

With a wine list more than 200 entries long and a charming, old-world atmosphere, **Punch & Judy** *(26 Clinton St. , bet. Houston and Stanton Sts.; 212-982-1116)* is not only an oenophile's dream, but one of the best-kept drinking secrets on the Lower East Side.

The plush nightspot boasts a cellar full of vino from around the globe. Though the bar's bounty of red walls, red chairs, and red dishes may suggest a house preference for cabernets and merlots, the wine list has an equally comprehensive selection of delicious whites.

Owner Constantine Mouzakitis, who honed his wine-making skills in his family's business, has a knack for discovering unknown vineyards and importing unusual wines from the Mediterranean, Australia, South Africa, and some of the most rural areas of France.

While knocking back all those foreign imports, you can sample items from Punch & Judy's other menu. The chocolate fondue is the most popular, but the place also offers lobster club sandwiches, delicious fresh fruits, peanut-butter cookies, and cashew-covered bananas. With light Latin jazz flowing from the speakers and an extremely low-lit, tranquil setting, Punch & Judy is a great place to meet, drink, and unwind.

Photo: Brad Dunn

Beers and Burgers at Sunset

After the Boat Basin Café transformed from a quiet, outdoor beer hall to a standing-room-only, yuppie meat market, the owner came up a capital idea: He opened a second seasonal restaurant a little farther north.

The **Hudson Beach Café** *(917-370-3448)*, at 103rd Street in Riverside Park, recaptures everything its older sibling lost: peace, quiet, and quick beer refills. Overlooking the Hudson, the open-air restaurant serves delicious burgers, fries, and appetizers, and boasts a surprisingly complete bar. It's one of the hidden gems of the park — too far north to attract a pedestrian, post-work crowd, and too secluded to hook passersby.

Though it looks like someone's backyard tent party, the restaurant spans two levels in the park: the lower lies next to the sand volleyball courts and has restrooms, the upper is across from the dog run and offers the best river views at sunset. Live music is frequently provided by aspiring musicians working for tips, and the ambiance is typically unfettered by obnoxious frat-types. The café is open from late spring until early fall. Weather can be a deal-breaker, so if you think you need to bring a rain coat, you should probably tilt toward a different destination altogether.

Walls Have Ears

You can't belly up to a bar in New York without accidentally overhearing some nugget of wisdom, some failed pickup line, or some drunken, secret confession. After all, there are eight million stories in the naked city, and now thanks to a brilliant Web site, a bunch of them are online.

The Murph Guide, an Internet site devoted to New York's nightlife, posts an irresistible list of overheard conversations at bars across the city. The Bar Room Banter page, which is at *murphguide.com/overheard .htm*, claims that all lines printed there are actual quotes overheard by barhoppers and submitted online. Most of them are funny or sad, or both.

The site lists the bar, the address, and the date and time the conversation was heard, but not the names of the people who did the talking. It's a fascinating

Dance Clubs

APT

Once so secret they didn't even give out the address.

419 W. 13th St., at Tenth Ave.; 212-414-4245

Avalon

Lots of different rooms and styles, in the old church that was Limelight.

47 W. 20th St., at Sixth Ave.; 212-807-7780

Arc

6 Hubert St., at Hudson St., 212-343-1379

Cielo

So very, very exclusive that we know nothing about it; difficult to get in without knowing someone.

18 Little W. 12th St., bet. Ninth Ave. and Washington St.; 212-645-5700

Crobar

Giant dance club, part of a chain.

530 W. 28th St., bet. Tenth and Eleventh Aves.; 212-971-9595.

Copacabana

A giant place with exactly what you'd expect from the name.

560 W. 34th St., at Eleventh Ave.; 212-239-2672

collection, no doubt worth the attention of aspiring Ph.D. students in urban sociology.

Best of all, the site provides you an outlet to your own overheard tidbits. Log on and follow the instructions. Here's a sampling:

McFadden's Saloon (800 Second Ave., at 42nd St.)
Woman: I am a cool wife. I don't cramp your style, right?
Man: Yes, dear.

Tanda (331 Park Ave. South, bet. 24th and 25th Sts.)
Girl No. 1: I can't believe you are not going to say hi to him.
Girl No. 2: Say hi to who?
Girl No. 1: The guy sitting right next to you.
Girl No. 2: Why would I say hi to him?
Girl No. 1: Because you hooked up with him last week.
Girl No. 2: Oh... he looks different.

Moran's (501 Garden St., Hoboken, N.J.)
Man No. 1 (to Man No. 2): Wow, you're that much older than I am? So that means we masturbated to a whole different generation of girls growing up!

Banshee Pub (1373 First Ave., at 74th St.)
"I'd rather live here and die of anthrax than live in Canada and die of old age."

The Towerview (Roosevelt Ave., Woodside, Queens)
Woman No. 1: (talking about germs) I use a paper towel to open the ladies room door.
Woman No. 2: And I push the elevator button with my knuckle.
Woman No. 3: No way! I use my nose!

Windfall (23 W. 39th St.)
"If everybody in the world farts, how come it still stinks? Shouldn't we have adapted by now?"

Trinity (229 E.84th St.)
"If you can't move on the dance floor, you can't move in the bedroom."

Mad River Bar & Grille (1442 Third Ave., bet. 81st and 82nd Sts.)
"Can I have a pint of Chardonnay?"

Culture Club
All Eighties, all the time.
Check out the Pac-Man motif.
179 Varick St., bet. Charlton and
King Sts., 212-243-1999.

Five Spot
A soulfood supper club, with a mix of
soul, funk, hip-hop, and more.
459 Myrtle Ave., at Washington Ave.,
Brooklyn; 718-852-0202

Halcyon
The Williamsburg hotspot.
227 Smith St., bet. Butler and
Douglass Sts., Brooklyn;
718-260-9299

Lotus
Restaurant upstairs, club downstairs.
409 W. 14th St., bet. Ninth Ave. and
Gansevoort Sts.; 212-243-4420

Mission
Draws the chic celebri-crowd.
217 Bowery, at Rivington St.;
212-473-3113

Sapphire Lounge
Small, with less attitude
and more sweat.
249 Eldridge St., bet. Stanton and
Houston Sts.; 212-777-5153

Club Kid Killer

It's all in good fun until someone gets hurt – and by hurt we mean bludgeoned with a hammer, injected with drain cleaner, cut into pieces and dumped in the Hudson.

That's the short version of the story of **Michael Alig**, the king of New York's club scene in the 1990s. He came from South Bend, Indiana (where flamboyant and gay don't go down well) to Manhattan (where they do), in the late 1980s, and soon enough made himself a wildly successful club promoter, arranging raves and events that more often than not centered on Limelight, a dance club in a deconsecrated church at Sixth Avenue and 20th Street. His "Club Kids," dedicated to drugs, dancing, and wild fashion display (think Boy George with the commendable restraint), swept through the city on a hedonistic quest that made them famous as a group. This wasn't the exclusive 1970s party of Studio 54, but a movement for disaffected bridge-and-tunnelers, misfits, and outcasts who were willing to follow Alig's outrageous lead.

By 1996, though, the party was growing stale. Real gangsters had taken over the drug trade, Mayor Giuliani was cracking down on illegal parties, and Alig began arguing with an alleged drug dealer and Club Kid named Angel Melendez. On March 17, 1996, the argument turned physical. Alig's roommate Robert Riggs returned to their Greenwich Village apartment and found the two in a brawl – so he knocked Melendez out with a hammer. Then Alig choked him and brought out the drain cleaner. When Melendez was dead, they stored the body for almost a week in their bathroom, and then Alig, high on heroin, cut off the legs, put all the pieces in garbage bags, and dropped them in the Hudson. Riggs eventually confessed, and the police caught up with Alig, who's now serving 10 to 20 upstate, where the parties are more carefully supervised.

Already fading, the Club Kids fizzled out, and Limelight closed after the owner was convicted of tax evasion. Recently, though, the church was reopened as a club called Avalon, and Alig was portrayed on the big screen by Macaulay Culkin in *Party Monster*.

S.O.B.'s

That's "Sounds of Brazil," with lots of hot Latin and world music, and a feisty Brazilian menu and bar to prove it.
200 Varick St., bet. Houston and King Sts.; 212-243-4940

Spirit

A New Age-y dance club, with a spa and healthy restaurant attached.
530 W. 27th St., bet. Tenth and Eleventh Aves.; 212-268-9477

Suede

A mix of tunes.
161 W. 23rd St., bet. Sixth and Seventh Aves.; 212-807-6795

2i's

Known for hip-hop; also reggae and R&B, and lesbian and gay nights.
248 W. 14th St., bet. Seventh and Eighth Aves.; 212-807-1775

Gay Bars

Abbey

Young gay hipsters.
536 Driggs Ave., bet. N. 7th and N.
8th Sts., Williamsburg, Brooklyn;
718-599-4400

Code

Lounge-y.
255 W. 55th St., bet. Broadway and
Eighth Ave.; 212-333-3400

Eagle

Leather.
554 W. 28th St., bet. Tenth and
Eleventh Aves.; 646-473-1866

g

Chic cruising ground for the buff.
223 W. 19th St., bet. Seventh and
Eighth Aves.; 212-929-1085

Phoenix

A more relaxed alternative to the
nearby Cock.
447 E. 13th St., bet. Ave. A and First
Ave.; 212-477-9979

Get Down

Photo: Daniel Hood

With a nod toward Twilo, the bygone techno dance hotspot, **Filter 14** is a stripped-down, no-frills, adrenaline-pumping dance hall for those only interested in shaking it all night.

Actually, the place is bare-bones by accident – the owner apparently had to stop renovations because of a legal dispute. But the result is an unpolished, raw atmosphere that is not only refreshing, but also perfect for the type of mobs that pour in here. Weeknights are typically for the just-out-of-their-teens crowd, while weekends tend to be monopolized by a slightly older, but no less undulating, set.

Filter 14 earned its reputation, and frequent lines outside its door, through its rabidly electronica-fixated DJs, who manage to create a fresh, frenetic dance vibe every night. Though the hall was formerly the famous Mother Bar, the sound system is spectacular – even though it's on a smaller scale than the sounds at Twilo and its kind.

In the heart of the Meatpacking District, at 432 West 14th Street, Filter 14 has become one of the hottest underground dance scenes in Manhattan. Hopefully, by clutching onto its roughly hewn roots and innovative dance beats, it won't turn into just another pretentious club with long lines and stale rhythms.

Swing Set

Some would say the 20th century was blessed because swing dancing came in style not once, but twice; others that it was cursed for the same reason. Either way, judging by the number of zoot suits that show up at Lincoln Center in the summer, the dance trend might come full swing in the 21st century.

Long before that annoying Gap commercial, the **Midsummer Night's Swing** program at Lincoln Center has hosted thousands of swingsters, amateur and pro alike. The outdoor dances, which run throughout the summer months, were started in 1989 by Margaret Batiuchok, the president of the New York Swing Dance Society. For Batiuchok, it really doesn't mean a thing if it ain't got that swing: she wrote her 100-page master's thesis on the Lindy Hop.

Her efforts at Lincoln Center have paid off. Though swing's brief resurgence in the 1990s led to jam-packed Midsummer Night's Swing dances, the program has endured. Swing bands from across the country line up to play the venue. If you've never swing danced, don't worry: the program provides classes an hour before each event. Your $12 entrance fee will cover you for both parts.

Log on to *lincolncenter.org* to find out when the dances start.

Dance Den

If you prefer your nightlife packed with young, loud, ecstasy-riddled 20-somethings, set your compass for the **Sullivan Room** *(218 Sullivan St., bet. Bleecker and W. 3rd Sts.)* a basement dance hall in the Village where house music dominates and crowds of trend-setters and -followers bump and bounce all night.

Descend the stairs at the Sullivan and behold the scene: Persian rugs, velvet couches, and a blaring sound system that inspires fast dancing, shouting, and sweating all night long. Highly responsive bartenders pump out stiff drinks, while slumming semi-celebs head directly to their reserved, velvet-roped VIP rooms, which are furnished with Salvation Army assemblages of couches and tables.

Pyramid Club
For those who've seen
– and done – it all.
*101 Ave. A, bet. 6th and 7th Sts.;
212-473-7184*

Rawhide
Leather and chaps.
*212 Eighth Ave., at 21st St.;
212-242-9332*

SBNY Splash Bar New York
Exclusively gay dance club.
*50 W. 17th St., bet. Fifth and
Sixth Aves.; 212-691-0073*

Starlight Bar & Lounge
Good for just hanging out, with some
nights for lesbians.
*167 Ave. A, bet. 10th and 11th Sts.;
212-475-2172*

Though the front room is loaded with small tables, most are marked "Reserved." If no one is there, however, help yourself. If you're serious about dancing, don't bother showing up until after 1 a.m., which is when one of the resident techno DJs par excellence punches in. Pretty Caucasian during the week, the Sullivan Room gets a little more international – and little more soulful – on weekends.

Toybox
Dance club for all persuasions.
256 Grand St., bet. Driggs and Roebling Sts., Williamsburg, Brooklyn; 718-599-1000

Urge
Serious meeting and mingling.
33 Second Ave., bet. 1st and 2nd Sts.; 212-533-5757

Wonder Bar
Relaxed.
505 E. 5th St., at Ave. A; 212-777-9105

XL Bar & Lounge
A lounge that feels like a dance club.
357 W. 16th St., bet. Eighth and Ninth Aves.; 212-995-1400

Underground Sex and the City

The sex industry has many faces in New York. On one side are the raunchy pornographers and strip club operators; on the other are organizations like **OneLegUpNYC**.

This promoter of erotic liberation has a simple mission statement: To offer the most salacious soirees in New York geared toward those couples who want to free themselves from their remaining puritan values. How does this highly select, strictly underground organization do it? By delivering "quality, sensuality, and generous libidinous spicing."

According to Palagia, the mysterious, single-named nymph who created the carnal club, OneLegUpNYC has thrown a sensual-themed soiree every month for the last four years. She takes immense pride in selecting sexy couples to attend the debaucheries, where "men and women alike can explore themselves in an unbiased, sensually liberating environment."

The outfit offers three types of erotic soiree: Eat-In, Take-Out, and Sampler. For the Eat-Ins, OneLegUpNYC rents out one of the city's most sultry eateries for the night. You bring your own booze and they serve the edibles, though Palagia guarantees that neither booze nor food will be the main thing on your mind. The Take-Out parties are thrown at alluring bars reserved exclusively for the evening. Both of these sexy shindigs require all males to be escorted by a female, with gay couples more than welcome, too.

The Sampler soirees are held at bars, restaurants, hotel rooms, and even apartments. The organization recruits all types of underground artists, "from the burlesque to the exquisite," to perform at the sexual socials. Most of all, every party provides a clean, safe, sensual environment "with an abundance of eroticism and other delicacies."

OneLegUpNYC's chief goal is that patrons feel safe, sexy, and free. To that end, everyone must follow the rules or face banishment from the club. Absolutely no drugs are allowed. No recording devices. No prostitution. No one under 21. No ill treatment of anyone is allowed (S&M revelers look elsewhere). Lastly, Palagia says it's not a swinger's club. You must leave the parties with the person you came with. After that, well, that's your business.

You won't find this hedonistic haven in the phone book. So how do you get invited to the party? Log on to *OneLegUpNYC.com*, and follow the directions.

Cock-A-Doodle

If you're looking for a dirty, sleazy, unapologetically amoral night out on the town, **The Cock** *(188 Ave. A, near E. 12th St.)* is calling. At heart a one-night-stand pickup place for gay men, The Cock's unabashed seediness also draws a contingent of straight guys and gals who don't want to miss out on the depravity. The bar attracts a strange social hodgepodge that's equal parts curious stockbroker, ecstasy-addled art student, and East Village vamp.

Things get pretty blue every night of the week depending on the bar's theme: On "Cockstar" nights, which are hosted by luminary drag queen Mistress Formika, brave patrons compete at striptease karaoke; the combination of amateur singing and amateur stripping makes the always-crowded place go wild.

The music is as raucous as the crowd. Hardcore industrial sounds, and blaring grunge and goth rhythms scream out of a speaker system more suited to Madison Square Garden. An assault on your senses, an attack on your morals, and all the pleasurable repercussions of both are what you can expect at this East Village den of sin.

Lesbian Bars

There's a much smaller number of places for lesbians than for gay men, which leads many to comment that the scene can become uncomfortably incestuous — you're forever running into old girlfriends, or worse, competing with them.

Crazy Nannys
A mix of all flavors.
21 Seventh Ave. South, at Leroy St.;
212-366-6312

The Cubbyhole
Cozy.
281 W. 12th St., at 4th St.;
212-243-9041

Ginger's
Diverse and welcoming.
363 5th Ave., Park Slope, Brooklyn;
718-788-0924.

Henrietta Hudson
Very popular.
438 Hudson St., at Morton St.;
212-924-3347

Sexy Surveillance

Photo: Daniel Hood

When Big Brother wants to kick back, he goes to **Remote** *(327 Bowery, bet. 2nd and 3rd Sts.; 212-228-0228)*, an East Village club with a singular approach to the singles scene. From your retro-futuristic console (think Disney's World of the Future, circa 1959), you can scan the crowd through feeds from the more than 60 video cameras scattered around the lounge, and then use your handy phone to make long-distance contact. Be warned: pictures from the cameras also find their way onto Remote's Web site. When Big Bro's tired of watching, he heads to the lower level, which frequently features screenings of independent movies and other events.

Julie's

Quieter, and one of the few uptown.
204 E. 58th St., bet. Second and Third Aves.; 212-688-1294

Meow Mix

Live acts, DJs, and theme nights like Gloss Thursdays for the glamorous.
269 E. Houston St., at Suffolk St.; 212-254-0688

The Rising

Neighborhoody and laid-back.
186 5th Ave., at Sackett St., Park Slope, Brooklyn; 718-789-6340

Rubyfruit Bar & Grill

More grown-up, with a restaurant downstairs.
531 Hudson St., bet. 10th and 11th Sts.; 212-929-3343

Barracuda Bound

Despite its obvious location smack in the middle of Boys' Town (aka Chelsea), **Barracuda** *(275 W. 22nd St., bet. Seventh and Eighth Aves.)* has admirably resisted becoming just another predictable party boys' gay bar.

Owned by the same triumvirate that ran the legendary Crowbar in the East Village, where the city's most notorious drag queens held court in the early 1990s, the dimly lit club is a comfortably sleazy watering hole for pickup artists, out-of-towners, and after-work crowds alike. The place attracts not a few small-time celebs, who, like everyone else, come to drink, chat, spread out on one of the couches, or shoot pool in the back.

An average night sees a crowd evenly sprinkled with over-styled hipsters, suits, artistes, and youthful Abercrombie & Fitch types. The bar hosts heavily touted drag shows and other weekly entertainment, as well as a roster of talented DJs who keep the dance floor moving.

Another perk: the place is divided into two large rooms. The front is for those seeking an instant love connection, the back for the groups looking to lounge. Best of all, Barracuda pumps out plenty of happy hour bargains, like two-for-one drinks, and some of the best cocktails in the city.

A Drink and Some Civil Rights, Please

Photo: Daniel Hood

When the police raided the **Stonewall Inn** *(51-53 Christopher St., bet. Waverly Pl. and Seventh Ave.; 212-463-0950)* on June 27, 1969, they had no idea that they were making history. After all, the place was just another private club serving liquor without a license, and they suspected that is was Mob-controlled. That it was a gay bar didn't much matter, since the city's homosexual community was used to being shoved around. So when the cops started busting up the place and hauling out customers, the last thing they expected was a riot – but that's what they got.

Some say it was the heat, and some say it was the sight of struggling transvestites weeping as they were thrown into the paddywagon, and some say it was the fact that Judy Garland was buried that day. Most likely it was because they'd simply had enough oppression and decided it was time to fight back, which the crowd on Christopher Street did with cobblestones and bottles. As the riot grew to include upwards of a thousand people, the cops resorted to fire hoses, but that wasn't enough to stop the gay community from fighting the police again the next night, and the night after that.

While the *Daily News* got away with reporting the rebellion under the unbelievable headline, "Homo Nest Raided, Queen Bees Are Stinging Mad," the Stonewall Riots marked a turning point, the moment at which gays and lesbians took up a new, more militant stance, and from which they date their modern civil rights movement. The next year over 5,000 people marched in an anniversary demonstration, and there was no turning back.

There's a plaque on Sheridan Square marking the event, but the Stonewall itself is still there, much cleaned up but still a historic reminder.

Strip Search

Former mayor Rudy Giuliani may have stripped Times Square of its nudity and pushed most of what was the city's red light district into other boroughs (or into bankruptcy), but Manhattan still houses some of the most famous – and most sleazy – strip clubs in the country. You just have to know where to find them.

Baby Doll Lounge
24 White St.; 212-226-4870

Bare Elegance
216 W. 50th St.; 212-245-3494

Carousel Club
75 Clarkson St.; 212-627-9404

Executive Club
603 W. 45 St.; 212-245-0002

Lace
725 Seventh Ave.; 212-840-9139

Paradise Club
50 W. 33rd St.; 212-629-0060

When Booze is Bad

New York can be a tough town for alcoholics, and no one knew it better than Bill W., the co-founder of **Alcoholics Anonymous**. In the 1920s, he was a high-flying market analyst on Wall Street (one of the first), living in Brooklyn Heights, and an incurable drinker. By the 1930s he was in and out of Town's Hospital, a pioneering rehab center at 293 Central Park West, where had his "spiritual conversion" on Dec. 11, 1934, and began piecing together the 12 Steps that would help him – and millions of others – stay sober permanently.

AA dates its beginnings to a 1935 meeting between co-founders Bill W. and Dr. Bob in Akron, Ohio, but it was in New York that it was officially established, and Bill W. wrote the group's "Big Book," *Alcoholics Anonymous*, mostly at 182 Clinton Street in Brooklyn Heights. He and his wife lost that townhouse in 1938, and in 1940 moved into a house in the Westchester suburb of Katonah, about an hour north of the city. It's now a museum called Stepping Stones *(914-232-4822; steppingstones.org)*.

These days, you can find an AA meeting in any borough at almost any hour of the day or night; for info on meetings and help, call 212-647-1680 or visit *nyintergroup.org*.

NEW YORK STOCK EXCHANGE

Murder and crime rates are down to historic lows, and the city
is as safe as it's ever been — and yet we can't shake our bad rap
as a dangerous place. It's hard to overcome a past as checkered
as New York's, but when the skeletons in the closet are this
interesting, we're not sure we want to.

The Queen's Queen?

Centuries before the New York Dolls, ages before the waiters at Lucky Cheng's, and eons before trannies hit the West Side, a royal governor named **Lord Cornbury** caused a stir by exploring an alternative lifestyle — or so we thought.

Lord Cornbury (whose given name was Edward Hyde, as in Hyde Park, which was once part of his Hudson River estate) was appointed Governor of New York and New Jersey in 1701 by his cousin, Queen Anne. A standard New York pol, he was corrupt, profligate, and generally disliked, but what really made him infamous was the fact that he apparently had a habit of putting on his wife's ball gowns to stroll along Broadway, patroll the parapets of the harbor fortifications, and even, so the story goes, give his annual addresses.

Popular outcry got him recalled in 1708, leaving only the legend of New York's first (and only public) transvestite governor, backed up by a portrait in the New-York Historical Society *(2 W. 77th St., at Central Park West; 212-873-3400; nyhistory.org)* of a very mannish lady in a period dress. For a few hundred years, he's been a source of tittering or inspiration, depending on your point of view, for his courage in expressing his inner society woman.

Problem is, according to NYU historian and professional buzz-kill Patricia Bonomi, there's no evidence that he ever wore a dress at all. According to a book she wrote in 1998, the only sources for the Cornbury story are a few letters written long after the fact by his political enemies, and that portrait, which has no title or attribution, and may in fact be just a picture of a really ugly woman.

Allowing lack of historical proof to destroy a truly great scandal-myth, the New-York Historical Society has relabeled the portrait, but we say absence of evidence is not evidence of absence, and prefer to remember Cornbury as the first in a long line of New York men brave enough to indulge their softer sides.

Hail, Tri-Insula!

Staten Island occasionally threatens to secede from the city, and people often suggest that New York City should secede from New York State (an idea *Harper's Magazine* suggested as early as 1857). Only one person, though, has ever seriously proposed that the city should break completely from the United States. In January 1861, with secession in the air, corrupt mayor and noted nutcase Fernando Wood used his second inaugural address to outline a plan to create a new country, called Tri-Insula after Staten Island, Long Island, and Manhattan. City authorities enthusiastically agreed, and disseminated printed descriptions of the glorious new nation. The paper patriots quickly dropped the idea after the gunfire at Fort Sumter that spring.

Billy from the Block

New York has produced more than its share of unsavory characters over the centuries, but few would think that one of the Wild West's worst bandits called Manhattan his home town.

Henry McCarty was born on Nov. 23, 1859, at 70 Allen Street. He spent his first six years playing on the streets of the Lower East Side, which was then a haven for Irish immigrants, before moving out west with his mother and brother. They settled in Silver City, New Mexico, and it wasn't long before this young New Yorker started calling himself William H. Bonney, aka **Billy the Kid**.

With a notoriously short temper and blatant disregard of the law, Bonney shot and killed his first victim at age 18. The incident launched him into a whirlwind of

Photo: Daniel Hood

DEAD MAN'S CURVE

Doyers Street is a charming little road full of barbershops and grocery stands that branches off Mott Street on the south side of Chinatown. It bends sharply like a street in Europe, and if you didn't know any better you'd swear you were walking down one of the most peaceful, picturesque lanes ever laid in Manhattan. Unknown to most, however, this beautiful little bend is known as the "Bloody Angle," and bodies used to line the gutters here thanks to the violent ambushes exchanged by the most ruthless gangs in Chinatown history.

At the beginning of the 20th century, Chinese immigrants in New York discovered they had to join factions to survive. These secret organizations were known as the Tongs; some were harmless familial groups, others were ruthless criminal organizations. The worst of them were the Hip Sing and the On Leong, and they were bitter rivals for power in the fledgling Chinatown.

gunfighting and cattle-rustling that eventually made him a household name. Within just three years, he had killed 21 men, one for each year of his life.

Legend has it, and most scholars agree, that Billy the Kid was finally gunned down in the dark by his one-time friend Pat Garrett. He died in Fort Sumner, New Mexico, never having returned to the Lower East Side.

With its large bend and numerous hiding places, Doyers Street was a constant battleground beginning in the 1890s. Tong members would ambush their rivals with guns, knives, and hatchets, and leave their bodies in the street. The tabloids made much of the ongoing violence and gave the street its bloody nickname.

Intermittent periods of peace were achieved between the Tongs, but inevitably some minor offense would reignite the bloodshed. The war continued until the 1930s, when all of Chinatown allied itself to survive the Depression and to rally against an influx of Japanese immigrants.

Photo: Daniel Hood

Suicidal Tendencies

It's hard to keep a good customer base when your customers keep killing themselves — unless, of course, the suicides actually draw in more business.

Billed as "the roughest joint in town" in the late 1890s, **McGurk's Suicide Hall** at 295 Bowery earned its name from the distraught prostitutes and sailors who regularly killed themselves there in some grisly fashion. For every customer it lost to suicide, however, the saloon picked up dozens more, as a macabre kind of tourism sprang up around this worst of the worst Bowery dives.

One of the most notorious incidents involved a pair of down-on-their-luck prostitutes: Blonde Madge Davenport and Big Mame. On a depressing October night in 1899, the pair bought a bottle of carbolic acid and went to McGurk's to down the drink of death. Blonde Madge swallowed enough to do the job, but Big Mame pulled the bottle back at the last moment and accidentally poured the acid all over her face. She was horribly disfigured and later barred from the saloon.

In his historical book, *Low Life*, Luc Sante describes the saloon's attitude toward patrons looking to end it all: "Suicide attempts were so common that the waiters, upon getting an indication on the same, would form a flying wedge and hustle the party out before she (or occasionally he) succumbed."

Though the building that housed McGurk's still stands just south of CBGB's, the city has entertained the idea of tearing it down for a newer development. Leading the charge to make the famous saloon a landmark is famed feminist Kate Millet, who says its memory should be preserved.

Remember the General Slocum?

Photo: Daniel Hood

The destruction of 9/11 will reshape lower Manhattan in ways that can't be predicted, and that won't be clear for decades. The one thing that seems sure is that the dead of the World Trade Center will never be forgotten – but then, you would have thought the same of the victims of the city's second-worst disaster, and they're barely remembered at all.

On June 15, 1904, over 1,300 passengers embarked on the steamer *General Slocum*, most of them women and children from a Lutheran church group in Kleindeutschland, the largely German neighborhood around Tompkins Square Park. They were bound for their annual picnic out on Long Island, but somewhere around 125th Street in the East River, the steamer caught fire. While the captain desperately sought a place to land, crewmen fought the blaze with rotten fire hoses and sand buckets that turned out to be empty; the lifeboats were painted into their divots, so women and children dived into the water with life jackets that were so old and shoddy they immediately fell apart. Passing ships rescued those they could, and prisoners from nearby Riker's Island stole a rowboat and saved a number before being recaptured, but in the end 1,051 died, either by drowning, fire, or being crushed in the *Slocum*'s paddle wheel.

The entire city was outraged, the captain was jailed, and major overhauls were made to ensure the safety of the many

IN MEMORY OF
THOSE WHO LOST
THEIR LIVES
IN THE DISASTER TO
THE STEAMER
GENERAL SLOCVM
IVNE XV
MCMIV

Photo: Daniel Hood

REVOLUTION OVER BREAKFAST

In New York, it's not hard to find a bar where some famous author drank himself to unconsciousness, or a café where some famous poet wept herself to sleep. But how about a restaurant where expatriates met and plotted the largest Communist revolutions of the 20th century?

You can visit exactly such a place on the corner of East Broadway and Rutgers Street on the Lower East Side. Today the site is a Chinese restaurant called K. Wing Shoon, but before that it was the **Garden Cafeteria**, a 24-hour coffee shop and diner that has seen some heavy-hitting clientele over the decades. Russian expats Nikolai Bukharin and Leon Trotsky met here to plot Communism for their homeland, while American communists Emma Goldman, Alexander Berkhman, and John Reed gathered to plot it for theirs. Isaac Bashevis Singer came here a lot. Fidel Castro was practically a regular.

passenger ships that cruised the harbor (rules that, due to legal technicalities, do not apply to the Staten Island Ferry, which recently had a disaster of its own). Where the tragedy was most felt, though, was in Kleindeutschland, where nearly every household had lost a loved one. There were so many funerals that every hearse in the city was used, and soon enough the survivors could not face living in the old neighborhood, prompting a large-scale exodus. Within 10 years, the old German community was gone, moved uptown to the Yorkville area around 86th Street on the East Side. All that remains to mark the great disaster is a small fountain in Tompkins Square Park, though interest in the tragedy was sparked in 2003 with the release of a book on the subject – and the death of the last survivor.

Why the Garden Cafeteria? The food was good and cheap, the doors were always open, and the hustle and bustle afforded revolutionaries relatively private conversations.

In addition to his patronage of the Garden Cafeteria, Trotsky, for his part, had a memorable three months living in New York, after escaping from prison in Siberia and being exiled from France and deported from Spain, before finding himself below the Statue of Liberty in January 1917.

Along with Bukharin and Volodarsky, he edited the Russian-language socialist newspaper *New World*. Though he later wrote in his biography that, "My only profession in New York was that of a revolutionary socialist," historian Arthur Willert believes the technically savvy Trotsky also earned a lucrative salary as an electrician for Fox Film Studios. Whether he lived meagerly or stashed away dollars, he didn't stay long. When word arrived that the Bolshevik Revolution was underway, he rushed back to his country, where he was elected chairman of the Soviet Party in September 1917.

Topsy Meets Old Sparky

Coney Island has seen more than its share of bizarre things, but few more so than the execution by electrocution of a circus elephant for murder.

In late 1902, the builders of Luna Park maintained a herd of elephants both as attractions and to help in the construction of the amusement park. One of them, Topsy, grew "vicious" after serial abuse, and killed three men (one of whom had fed her a lit cigarette). The owners decided to put her down – and to charge admission to the execution.

Why electrocution? Because the carrots laced with arsenic had no effect, because hanging was deemed too cruel, but mostly because Thomas Edison offered. The Wizard of Menlo Park was in a battle with George Westinghouse over whose type of electric current would predominate, and Edison, who was a DC man, wanted to prove that Westinghouse's AC was too dangerous for household use. So on Jan. 4, 1903, Edison's men fitted Topsy out with wood-and-copper sandals and hit her with Westinghouse's AC for the edification of the crowd. Edison even filmed the event – a film that can be seen at the Coney Island Museum *(1208 Surf Ave., at W. 12th St., 718-372-5159; coneyislandusa.org)* as part of a memorial they've installed to the poor, abused pachyderm.

The Girl in the Red Velvet Swing

Photo: Daniel Hood

In 1906, you couldn't swing a dead cat without hitting a building designed by **Stanford White** or his firm, McKim, Mead & White. He was, figuratively and almost literally, a pillar of society – and so his murder that June, and the revelations that came out at the trial afterward, created quite a stir.

White, it turned out, had a thing for beautiful young chorus girls, whom he liked to entertain at the original Madison Square Garden, at 26th Street and Madison Avenue, which he'd designed and where he kept a private apartment with a red velvet swing for chorines to "romp" on. In 1901, his chorus girl of choice was a teenaged beauty named Evelyn Nesbit, who'd worked her way up from poverty on her looks. At the trial in 1906, she claimed that White drugged her champagne while she played on the red velvet swing and then raped her while she was unconscious, though the prosecution tried to portray her as a willing participant, a notion bolstered by the fact that for some time afterward she was the famed architect's mistress, accepting lavish gifts of money to support herself and her mother.

Whichever was the case, while she was his mistress the beauty was also pursued by other men, including actor John Barrymore and, more important, the unstable Pittsburgh millionaire Henry K. Thaw. Barrymore got her pregnant, but it was Thaw who eventually married her in 1905, after a stormy and frightening courtship. Though White and Evelyn had parted ways amicably by then, Thaw remained pathologically jealous of the architect – and in June of 1906 he traveled to New York, smuggled a gun into Madison Square Garden, and shot White three times in the face at a party in the roof garden he'd designed.

The trial that followed, in a courthouse on the site of the current Jefferson Market and Library at Sixth Avenue and 10th Street, was dubbed "The Trial of the Century" and quickly became a media circus, full of lascivious details and tearful testimony. Thaw lived comfortably at the Tombs, ordering in from Delmonico's, while the jury

A Chronology of Riots, Disasters, Plagues, Graft, and Other New York Low Points

Photo: Daniel Hood

1637

Governor Wouter van Twiller is dismissed by the Dutch West Indies Co. for, among other things, alcoholism, incompetence, and deeding himself vast amounts of company land in New York, including all of Governor's Island.

1641-1645

After putting a bounty on Indians, Governor Willem Kieft proceeds to massacre them wherever he can. Understandably upset, the Indians respond with massacres of their own. An uneasy peace is finally achieved after the colonists beg for Kieft's dismissal; he is sacked in 1645.

1702

Yellow fever kills over 500.

1712

Thirteen slaves are hanged, one starved to death, four burned to death, and one broken on a wheel as retribution for an attempted uprising that killed nine whites.

1741

Slaves account for between 15 and 20 percent of the city's population. John Hughson, a white innkeeper and fence, tries to start another slave uprising, but his conspiracy is discovered. Thirteen slaves are burned, 18 hanged, and 70 sold out of the city.

1776-1783

New York is occupied by the British. In two separate fires, nearly a quarter of the city burns to the ground. Over 5,000 American prisoners of war die in hellish conditions on British prison ships moored in Wallabout Bay in the East River — more than died in combat throughout the entire war.

1784

At the end of the Revolutionary War, vengeful patriots disenfranchise or banish most Loyalists, including large landholders like the De Lanceys, whose estates (all around the present Delancey Street), are confiscated.

April 13-14, 1788

Spurred by incidences of grave robbing, a mob attacks Doctors' Hospital of Columbia University, where dissections are taking place. In the end, the militia is called out and the mob is fired on. Five die.

deadlocked; a second trial found him not guilty by reason of insanity, and he was packed off to an insane asylum, from which he was released only a few years later.

Thaw divorced Nesbit, and lived a long life of madness insulated by money; Evelyn sank into addiction and second-rate roles, with the cold comfort of seeing a young Joan Collins play her in a movie version of the story. As for White — well, he was dead, and though he and his firm are considered giants in New York architectural history, by the time E.L. Doctorow got around to describing his murder in *Ragtime*, his masterpiece at Madison Square Garden had long since been torn down, and out of his countless designs, the only one of any significance still standing is the Memorial Arch in Washington Square Park.

The Socrates of Sex

In the 21st century, starring in a show called *Sex and the City* has made Sarah Jessica Parker a cultural icon. In the 1920s, starring in a show called *Sex* made **Mae West** a criminal inmate.

The Brooklyn-born vaudeville veteran wrote, produced, directed, and starred in her first Broadway play, about a well-traveled prostitute, and opened it to packed houses in 1926. Despite a storm of moralizing protest, free-and-easy Mayor Jimmy Walker let *Sex* run for almost a year, but when he went on vacation in 1927, the forces of prudery had it closed down and West brought up on charges of public obscenity and "corrupting the youth." The sexual Socrates was sentenced to ten days in the pen on Welfare (now Roosevelt) Island, which she did, by all accounts, standing on her head.

When she got out, she was an even bigger star than before, and moved right on to her next play, *The Drag* (about transvestites) — though it was staged in New Jersey. In all, West wrote six risqué plays, and their success, combined with her sexy image, led to a Hollywood contract and international fame.

Good Golly Miss Polly

Visit the Algonquin Hotel and everyone in the lobby will tell you about the famous Round Table gatherings that were held there in the 1920s – where all the wits of the age sat around being witty. But few know that the artistic elite of the Lost Generation also congregated regularly at another, less dignified, meeting place: a whorehouse run by a 24-year-old madam.

Polly Adler was New York's first lady of prostitution during both the Roaring Twenties and the Depressing Thirties. All the geniuses flocked to her famous bordellos: Dorothy Parker, George S. Kaufman, and Robert Benchley, to name a few. Her exotic, erotic brothels, with plush carpets and regal furniture, enticed not only those looking for degenerate debauchery, but also those artistic purveyors of the tacky and tawdry. Adler's ability to draw a crowd was second only to her thirst for action. "I am one of those people who just can't help getting a kick out of life – even when it's a kick in the teeth," she once said.

Born in Russia in 1900, Adler immigrated to the city as a teenager and worked in a corset factory in Brooklyn to make ends meet. At age 24, while pulling in extra cash working in a brothel, she had the opportunity to look after a gangster's apartment. She made a big impression, gathered her resources, and opened her own bordello. She learned how to grease the wheels of the law, how to serve plenty of alcohol during Prohibition, and most importantly, how to throw the most lavish, garish, and hedonistic parties in the city.

The most difficult challenge was relocating the whorehouses every time the heat was on from the vice squad. In her 1951 autobiography, *A House Is Not a Home*, she lists the general locations of her bordellos, but never actual addresses. They include rented apartments in buildings in the following areas: 50th Street and Seventh, 59th Street and Madison, 69th Street and Columbus, and 77th Street and Amsterdam.

1790
In the first federal census, New York State ranks fifth in slaveholdings, with 20,000; 2,000 of those are in the city.

1822
As a yellow fever epidemic grips lower Manhattan, city residents take refuge in a distant country town – Greenwich Village.

1832
Caroline Ann Trow immigrates to New York where, under the name "Madame Restell," she grows fabulously wealthy selling her Preventive Powders for abortions, and later builds The Palace, a $200,000 mansion at 52nd Street and Fifth Avenue. In 1878, hounded by reformers and do-gooders, she commits suicide.

1832
The first of many cholera outbreaks leaves almost 5,000 dead.

July 4-10, 1834
Poor whites riot against the notion of abolition, rampaging through Five Points, terrorizing blacks and destroying their homes and businesses.

By the 1930s, Adler had been arrested 13 times, but thanks to her paid-for political connections, had never been convicted. She retired from the bordello business around when the United States was preparing to enter World War II. You'd think a renowned madam with more than two decades of decadence on her hands would retire to some Playboy Mansion-type lifestyle, but not Polly Adler. Her thirst for action never abated, it just shifted forms: she moved to Los Angeles, and got a college degree at age 50.

Photo: Daniel Hood

June 21-22, 1835

Irish immigrants and native-born toughs square off in a series of running battles on the Lower East Side. Two are killed, and the original St. Patrick's Cathedral, on Mulberry Street, is menaced.

Dec. 16-17, 1835

A fire devastates the financial district, spurring expansion to the north.

1837

The Tombs, the city's most notorious prison, is built.

January 1842

Charles Dickens, a man who knows from slums, tours Five Points in lower Manhattan, and declares it as bad, if not worse, than anything he's seen in England. "All that is loathsome, drooping, and decayed is here," he says.

1845

A second fire in the financial district finishes what the first didn't.

Conceiving the Bomb

Photo: Daniel Hood

Sure, they called it the **Manhattan Project**, but everyone knows that was just a smokescreen, a cover for the fact that the real work was going on in Oak Ridge and Los Alamos, right? Wrong. The race to build the atomic bomb started right in New York City – at 90 Church Street, to be precise.

In the summer of 1942, the feds ordered Col. James Marshall of the Army Corps of Engineers to begin work on the bomb. Based in Syracuse at the time, Marshall immediately moved to Manhattan, to the Corps offices at 90 Church, to be close to the researchers and scientists at universities and labs in the city and on nearby Long Island. As was the custom in the Corps, he called his new division the Manhattan District, after the area where it was headquartered. When Gen. Leslie Groves took command a month or so later, he almost immediately moved the project out of the city – but the name stuck, and went down in history.

the five families

To put it simply, organized crime in New York City has a complicated past. Here's a rundown of the Five Families still making headlines today.

Photo: Daniel Hood

Gambino

No doubt the most famous of the Five Families, thanks to the tabloid appeal of former boss John Gotti, the Gambino crime family remains the largest Mafia organization in the United States. Crime authorities estimate the group has 30 separate capos, 300 made members, and more than 3,000 associates.

The family was hit with a major legal setback in the 1980s when former underboss Sammy "The Bull" Gravano defected and testified against John Gotti and his associates. The Teflon Don, whose nickname reflects his knack for getting acquittals, finally was convicted of murder and racketeering and shuttled off to prison in 1991. His son, John "Junior" Gotti, ran things for a while, but was replaced by his uncle, Peter Gotti, who was arrested in 2002.

Organized crime experts say the Gambinos are less sophisticated than the Genovese family, and less eager to expand their operations outside the New York area. With deeply entrenched operations in loan-sharking, illegal narcotics, pornography distribution, garbage collection, construction, Atlantic City casinos, and Garment District labor unions, the Gambino crime family is believed to gross more than $300 million a year.

Genovese

The courtroom turmoil that hit the Gambinos during the last 20 years benefited no organization more than the Genovese crime family. With 200 made members and 1,300 associates, the second-largest crime family in the country took advantage of the opportunity to expand their operations in New York and beyond.

The history of Genovese family is packed with colorful characters. Lucky Luciano ran the family in the 1930s. His successor, Frank Costello, was assassinated by Vincent "The Chin" Gigante, who was on orders from Vito Genovese — the new boss who renamed the family after himself. Anthony "Fat Tony" Salerno (in addition to

May 10, 1849

A minor feud between an Irish-American actor and an English one becomes a matter of local and class pride, leading to the Astor Place Opera House Riot and the calling out of the National Guard. Over 20 killed, over 150 wounded.

June 1857

The Metropolitan Police, set up by the state legislature, fight a battle with the Municipal Police, set up by the city, over an attempt to arrest then-Mayor Fernando Wood, who favored the corrupt Municipals. Over 50 cops on both sides are wounded. The resulting standoff — which criminals enjoy mightily — ensues until July, when the Municipals are finally disbanded by court order.

Sept. 12, 1857

The steamship *Central America*, bound for New York with close to $2 million in gold from California, sinks off South Carolina. Many New York banks, which needed the gold to answer a run on deposits, are forced to close, sparking a financial crisis and a depression that lasts until the Civil War.

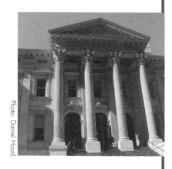

Photo: Daniel Hood

perhaps inspiring a "Simpsons" character) was an old-school gangster who ran the family in the 1980s, until the much-older Gigante took the helm.

Gigante became famous for wandering around Greenwich Village in his robe and slippers – hoping everyone would believe he was crazy. The ruse worked for a while, but "The Chin" was ultimately convicted and sent to prison. Currently, the feds believe Dominick "Quiet Dom" Cirillo is the street boss.

The Genoveses make most of their money from their stranglehold on the trucking industry, waste hauling, and control of the Fulton Fish Market. The New York Sate Organized Crime Task Force called the group, "the most stable, the best counseled, and the most diversified crime group in the country."

Lucchese

With 125 made members and 500 associates, the Lucchese crime family has been on a steady decline for decades. The third-largest crime family in New York suffered the brunt of numerous Mafia crackdowns and successful prosecutions in the late 1980s. Most of its leadership is still behind bars, running a family that is slowly losing its grip.

With expansive, coast-to-coast operations in the pornography industry, gambling, and labor union racketeering, the Luccheses have staged some of the most impressive, and creative, crimes in the history of American Mafia. The family realized money could be made in hijacking airport cargo – one of the leaders of these operations, Paul Vario, even inspired Martin Scorsese's 1990 movie *GoodFellas*.

Alphonso "Little Al" D'Arco ran the family for years until he made headlines by deciding to turn government informant against John Gotti Jr., and other Gambinos.

Bonanno

Founded during Prohibition, the Bonanno crime family has been plagued from the start by overly ambitious plans and internal warfare. Still, no other family had more impact on the current five-family structure of New York Mafia than the Bonannos.

Salvatore Maranzano, who was boss in the 1920s, declared himself "capo de tutti capi" – Boss of the Bosses. He called a meeting, or commission, of family leaders and became the principal architect of the five-family structure, in which the Mafia could best thrive in the city. After his assassination in 1931, his particular family was taken over by Joseph Bonanno.

Bonanno ran things smoothly for three decades until he dreamt up a crazy scheme to kill the top bosses of the rival families in New York and New Jersey. His plot failed before it started and he was forced to flee to Arizona, where he lives today.

The most notable incident in Bonanno history was when a young FBI agent named Joseph Pistone went undercover and penetrated the family's top leadership. He posed as a jewel thief named Donnie Brasco (played by Johnny Depp in the movie of the same name), and gained the trust of the family's top aide Dominick "Sonny Black" Napolitano (played by Al Pacino). His investigation led to the arrest of 17 made members of the Bonanno family – the largest Mafia takedown in history.

Colombo

In 1970, Joseph Colombo was not only given command of this Brooklyn-based family, but was allowed to rename it after himself. Bosses Thomas Lucchese and Carlo Gambino so honored him because he had informed them of Joseph Bonanno's plan to have them all assassinated. An internal civil war decimated the family in 1991, after John Gotti Jr. failed to broker a peace. Carmine "The Snake" Persico emerged victorious from the bloody "Colombo War," and attempted to rebuild this once greatly feared family.

Today the organization gets most of its cash flow from liquor distribution, funeral homes, auto dealerships, and catering. Though Persico is still thought to run the family, he is serving a 100-year sentence on racketeering charges.

"Clubber" Williams says, "I've had nothing but chuck steak for a long time, and now I'm going to get a little of the tenderloin." He thus gave the 29th Precinct (on the West Side below 42nd Street) its name, and himself a chance to accumulate a mansion in Connecticut and a yacht on a policeman's salary. It took Teddy Roosevelt to pry him out of the department.

Dec. 5, 1876
Close to 300 people die in a fire at the Brooklyn Theater, at Johnson and Washington Streets, leading to rules that exit doors must open out. There's a memorial to some of the victims in Green-Wood Cemetery.

1887
New York police officers get guns.

1890
Danish-born photographer Jacob Riis publishes *How the Other Half Lives*, a study of the appalling conditions in New York slums and tenements. Housing reform becomes an issue, and Five Points, the worst area of all, is eventually cleaned out.

February 1892
Social arbiter Ward McAllister publishes the list of "the 400" — those who are included on Mrs. Astor's guest list — in The *New York Times*. Everyone not on the list, including the Vanderbilts, is presumably unfit for society.

1901

Race riots in the West 20s and 30s force blacks to head uptown, eventually ending in Harlem.

Sept. 11, 1905

A Ninth Avenue El train jumps the tracks at 53rd Street. Twelve dead, over 40 hurt.

March 25, 1911

146 mostly female workers die in a fire at the Triangle Shirtwaist Factory, sparking a blaze of labor and safety regulations. The FDNY marks the anniversary with a small ceremony every year at the building *(23-29 Washington Pl., at Greene St.)*, which now houses classrooms, offices, and labs for nearby NYU.

1915

Mary Mallon is discovered working as a cook in the Sloane Hospital for Women. No big deal—except she had already been locked up once for spreading typhoid to families who employed her as a cook as early as 1906, so Mary was quarantined on North Brother Island in the East River, and died there in 1938. Only 33 typhoid cases and three deaths were officially connected to her; it was her obstinate refusal to accept that she was a carrier that led to her demonization as "Typhoid Mary."

How Lucky Luciano Won the War

1942: Wartime. New York, the country's most important port, is gripped with fear of German saboteurs. U-boats are spotted in nearby waters. Then, on Feb. 9, the *Normandie*, a luxury liner being converted into a troopship, mysteriously catches fire at her berth on the West Side. In a desperate scramble to protect the waterfront from enemy sabotage, naval intelligence contacts the longshoremen's union for help. The longshoremen direct the Navy to the mob, since nothing moves on the docks without the mob knowing about it.

Enter **"Lucky" Luciano**, who's been languishing in prison in far upstate Dannemora since his 1936 conviction for running a prostitution ring, and who still controls his syndicate. Ever the patriot, Lucky promises the Navy he'll keep the docks safe; he even offers to put the Allies in contact with his Mafia colleagues for the invasion of Sicily. He only asks one little thing in return: his freedom.

With the Arsenal of Democracy dependent on New York's shipping, the authorities agree, and Lucky proves true to his word: there isn't a single incident of sabotage for the rest of the war, and Sicilian mafiosi play a helpful role in the Allied invasion of Italy. Still, when the war was over, freeing Luciano outright doesn't sit so well with the authorities, particularly Governor Thomas Dewey, who'd put Lucky away in the first place. So they change the deal: Lucky can go free, but he can never set foot on U.S. soil again. In January of 1946, he's driven straight to the docks and put on a ship to Italy, never to return. He dies there in 1962, a bitter exile.

After his death, a "Last Testament" is released, in which Lucky claims that the whole thing was set up, and that one of his cronies, Albert Anastasia, burned the *Normandie* to force the Navy to make a deal. No proof is ever found to back up the claim, but remember, nothing moves on the docks without the mob knowing about it – including saboteurs, German or otherwise.

The Oddest Couple

Photo: Daniel Hood

Oscar should count himself lucky: he had Felix to keep him from being overwhelmed by his own mess. The real-life **Collyer Brothers** had no such safeguards, and the result was a bizarre tragedy that became a New York legend in 1947.

That March, responding to an anonymous tip, authorities tried to enter the brothers' run-down mansion at Fifth Avenue and 128th Street, but found all the doors and windows completely blocked by barricades of junk. By chucking garbage out the window, a rescue worker was able to slip into the room – where he found the corpse of an emaciated old man in a bathrobe. The body was identified as that of Homer Collyer, but the authorities knew Homer was blind and relied entirely on his younger brother, Langley. So where was he?

The house was crammed from cellar to ceilings with junk, including bundle after bundle of newspapers, stacked and piled to turn the house into an intricate maze, much of it booby-trapped. Day after day, tons of garbage were removed from the house: a Steinway grand piano. Assorted guns and ammunition. An X-ray machine. A baby carriage. Chandeliers. The jawbone of a horse. An entire Model T Ford. Human medical specimens. A kerosene stove. A collection of bank books containing about $3,000 (big money for 1947). And newspapers, newspapers, newspapers. The parade of junk ended up weighing 136 tons, and sometimes threatened to overshadow the mystery of Langley's disappearance, until the police finally dug deep enough and found his body crushed under a suitcase, three bread boxes, and a huge collection of newspapers. He had died not 10 feet from his brother, but it had taken 17 days to clear a path to him.

Sprung from one of New York's oldest families, the Collyers grew up in wealth and privilege, but after their parents' separation in 1909 their lives started going downhill: they shut themselves off from the world, disconnecting the gas, water, and power, fetching water from a nearby park, and relying on the kerosene stove for heat and light. As that section of Harlem declined over the next 30 years, the brothers grew paranoid about thieves and intruders, boarding up their windows and booby-trapping the house. In 1933, Homer went blind, and Langley devoted himself to his care, formulating a cure that included a steady diet of 100

Sept. 16, 1920

A wagonload of TNT explodes outside 37 Wall Street, the headquarters of J.P. Morgan and Co. (the scars are still visible). Over 30 people are killed, hundreds injured, and the NYSE closes for the day, though prices will rise the next day. Bolsheviks and anarchists are blamed, but no one ever claims responsibility or is arrested.

Nov. 13, 1921

For trying to talk about birth control, Planned Parenthood founder Margaret Sanger is dragged from the stage of the Town Hall Theater on West 43rd Street and arrested.

Aug. 6, 1927

Two bombs explode in the subway, in the 28th Street stations of the IRT and the BMT lines. Many are injured, one killed.

Nov. 6, 1928

Brilliant underworld boss Arnold Rothstein – alleged fixer of the 1919 World Series and mentor to Lucky Luciano, Legs Diamond, Dutch Schultz, and Frank Costello – dies two days after being shot outside the Park Central Hotel at Seventh Avenue and 56th Street by a gambler to whom he owes money.

Oct. 24, 1929

13 million shares of stock are sold on "Black Thursday," as investors panic and try to pull out of the market, starting the slide that continues through October 29, "Black Tuesday," when some say the market has bottomed out. They're wrong — prices continue to slide as the country plunges into the Great Depression.

Aug. 6, 1930

State Supreme Court Judge Joseph Crater leaves a chophouse on West 45th Street — and enters city legend, as "the missingest man in New York." He had cleaned out his files and cashed a couple of large checks earlier in the day, so some suspect he took it on the lam to avoid implication in a political scandal (he had bought his judgeship from Tammany Hall), while others suspect he was murdered by rival politicos, or perhaps in a blackmail scheme gone awry. But no one knows for sure: Crater is never seen again, and his body is never found.

Sept. 1, 1932

Mayor Jimmy "Beau James" Walker, who spent the past seven years chasing chorus girls, writing pop songs, changing his snazzy suits three times a day, looking the other way where Prohibition was

oranges a week. Local legends developed about the wealthy hermits of Harlem, who wished to be left completely alone.

And so they were, until that morning in 1947. The final irony is that the newspapers that crushed Langley were meant for Homer — his brother had saved every New York paper for years, on the assumption that once the orange cure restored Homer's sight, he would want to catch up on the news.

Rooming with Brando

About a decade before he starred in *On the Waterfront*, *A Streetcar Named Desire*, and other movies about moody, brooding tough guys, **Marlon Brando's** life was already anticipating his art.

In 1946, he was a young, starving artist devoted to mastering the craft of method acting. Not only was he forced to live in a tiny apartment on the northeast corner of Fifth Avenue and 11th Street in the Village, he had to share the space with an eccentric Russian violinist named Igor.

According to Brando biographer Charles Higham, the future Godfather got along famously with Igor at first — and made the most of their cramped existence. But soon enough he grew tired of the roommate and wanted to get rid of him. Apparently, a friendly chat wouldn't suffice. He chose to send the Russian his own kind of message. Brando cut open his violin and filled it with horse manure. Igor got the hint. He moved out as soon as possible.

Hitler's remark that people "will more easily fall victim to a big lie than to a small one" could have had no better illustration than the whopper told 20 years ago in a tiny apartment on East 23rd Street.

Today, few people remember the strange tale of **Dr. Josef Gregor** and his "Miracle Roach Hormone Cure," but at least one news agency and several TV anchors will never forget him. On May 22, 1981, Dr. Gregor invited members of the media to a special press conference at his eerie laboratory at 155 East 23rd Street.

Before a roomful of journalists, the self-described entomologist announced that he had not only created a strain of super-cockroaches immune to radiation and other toxins, but also that he had extracted a hormone which he himself had started taking. He called his discovery "Metamorphosis," and claimed that it cured just about everything – from the common cold and anemia to acne and menstrual cramps, and even provided immunity to nuclear radiation.

The reporters were allowed to wander through the laboratory, which was packed with roach specimens, artwork, renderings, and reams of scientific formulas and calculations. Then Dr. Gregor ended the press conference with the spectacular announcement that he was planning to make his miracle pills available to the public – completely free of charge.

The press delighted in the story, and a reporter from United Press International sent out a glowing article over the wire with the headline, "Roach Hormone Hailed as Miracle Drug." The story was published in newspapers across the country the next day, and soon Dr. Gregor's miracle was being discussed on radio and TV shows everywhere.

No one ever checked his credentials (he said he got his degree from the University of Bogota in Colombia); and no one was suspicious of the innumerable references to Franz Kafka's story "Metamorphosis," in which the narrator, Gregor Samsa, transforms into a giant insect. If they had, Dr. Gregor's real identity may have metamorphosized as quickly.

His real name was Joey Skaggs, a regular New Yorker with zero medical training, and he played the media like a fiddle. He appeared on WNBC's morning news program with live roaches in petri dishes and an

concerned, and, in his spare time, running the city, resigns in the midst of a probe that has revealed massive corruption.

Dec. 13, 1934

Albert Fish is arrested at 200 West 52nd Street for the 1928 kidnapping of a Manhattan girl – in large part because he wrote a letter to the girl's mother describing how he took the 10-year-old to Westchester, where he killed and ate her. Fish is later connected to the murders of children from Far Rockaway and Staten Island, and claims to have murdered, mutilated, and eaten hundreds more. He is executed in 1936.

Feb. 22, 1939

20,000 Nazis hold a rally in support of Germany at Madison Square Garden.

Nov. 16, 1940

An unexploded bomb is found at a Con Edison building on West 64th Street – the first of many scattered around Manhattan and Brooklyn by disgruntled former employee George Metesky. For 16 years, the "Mad Bomber" leaves explosives near Con Ed offices, in movie theaters and phone booths, and once in Grand Central. Though he injures many, none are killed before an early use of psychiatric profiling leads to his capture in 1956.

audio tape of "La Cucaracha," saying it was his organization's theme song. The press kept the spotlight on him for months — that is, until the brilliant doctor made another announcement that stunned the news world.

In September, Skaggs granted an exclusive interview to *People* magazine, in which he admitted that the whole affair was a hoax. He said his intention was to show just how gullible journalists can be, especially medical and health care reporters, and how easily someone can take advantage of news media's desire to dazzle readers with amazing stories — without doing the appropriate research.

After the hoax was revealed, neither UPI nor WNBC acknowledged any editorial irresponsibility — they even refused to retract their stories. As for Skaggs, he dismantled the fake laboratory in his apartment, freed his roaches, and began receiving as many requests for interviews about his elaborate stunt as Dr. Gregor had received for his miraculous hormone cure.

Skywalker

TO REACH THE CLOUDS
MY HIGH WIRE WALK BETWEEN THE TWIN TOWERS

PHILIPPE PETIT

In 1974, a French tightrope-walker attached a cable from the roof of one Twin Tower to the other, and then, a quarter-mile above an aghast crowd, walked the distance eight times. Many people remember the story, but few know the details of how he accomplished one of the most daring, artistic, and beautiful feats of the 20th century.

Philippe Petit was sitting in a Paris dentist's office in 1968, when he picked up a magazine and saw a sketch of the soon-to-be-built World Trade Center. An idea came to the apprentice tightrope-walker, and it became his obsession: He would walk between the tops of the towers.

As the buildings were erected over the next six years, Petit trained day and night for the stunt, and slowly plotted a way to carry it off. On August 6, 1974, he was ready. Using fake IDs, he and several friends snuck up both towers with 2,000 pounds of equipment on their backs. They had designed a complex web of cables and supporting wires that would be attached to various parts of the roofs with marlin-spikes, shackles, and pins. After groups on each tower assembled the support structure, they had to find a way of getting the heavy walk wire across the 140-foot gap separating the towers. The answer fit the romantic poetry of the entire stunt. An arrow attached to fishing line was shot from a bow from one building to the other, and they simply towed the cable across.

Despite his years of planning, Petit was resigned to the fate of physics: To be walked upon, the cable had to be stretched to a tension of 3.5 tons. But because the buildings were designed to sway with the wind, Petit knew that a bad breeze would cause his wire web to rip apart and send him to his death. He decided not to worry about what he couldn't control.

At a few minutes past 7 a.m., armed with his balancing pole, he walked across the wire to the amazement of the crowd below. He later recalled the exhilaration in his book *To Reach the Clouds: My High Wire Walk Between the Twin Towers*. "I could hear the horns of the cars below me," he wrote. "I could hear the applause, too. The rumeur [clamor] of the crowd rose up to me from 400 meters below." He called it a "crossing," describing it as "the pilgrimage of a mortal and a mortal pilgrimage. A mythical journey."

Whatever he called it, he did it not once or twice, but eight times. And not only walked, he danced, he strutted, he leapt so that both feet left the wire, and he even laid down on his back to watch a seagull flying above him. When he saw 40 police officers gathered on the roof, he knew his ecstasy was over. For his last crossing, he sprinted across the rope and fell into the arms of the cops.

His feat gave the harsh, as-yet-unloved towers a human face. His feat made news across the world, and though he broke 15 laws in the process, he received a slap on the wrist and was sentenced to give a free high-wire performance in Central Park for children.

When asked why he did it, the aerialist and expert juggler said: "When I see three oranges, I juggle; when I see two towers, I walk."

July 18, 1964
Protests over the police killing of a 15-year-old black boy turn to riots in Harlem and Bedford-Stuyvesant. Over the next five days, one person is killed and over 500 arrested.

Feb. 21, 1965
Malcolm X is assassinated by Muslim extremists at the Audubon Ballroom, at Broadway and 165th Street.

Nov. 9, 1965
A blackout hits the city (oh, and much of the Northeast and parts of Canada, too), stranding almost 800,000 people in the subway. New Yorkers handle it with aplomb — and nine months later experience a mini-Baby Boom.

April 23-30, 1968
Protesting Vietnam, Columbia students occupy university administration buildings; they are eventually violently driven out by the police, but not before they trash the university president's office — and kickstart a year of student protests nationwide.

March 16, 1970
At 18 W. 11th St. in Greenwich Village, a bomb factory run by the Weathermen, a domestic terrorist group, accidentally explodes, killing three.

April 10, 1972
Mob boss Joe Gallo is whacked at Umberto's Clam House, at Mulberry and Hester Streets.

Photo: Daniel Hood

No-So-Groovy Murders

If the Hippie dream was ever splashed in the face with cold water, it was when two peace-loving, drug-euphoric dropouts were found horribly bludgeoned to death in an East Village basement. The mysterious murders, which occurred just after the Summer of Love, sent shockwaves through the youth counterculture that was flourishing in the cafés, parks, and music halls from Washington Square to Tompkins Square.

James "Groovy" Hutchinson and his free-spirited companion, Linda Fitzpatrick, were last seen on Oct. 7, 1967. They were lying entwined on a sleeping bag on the sidewalk in front of the Psychedelicatessen at 164 Avenue A; they were hugging, happy, and high as kites. Hutchinson, who was probably the most-talked-about hippie in the Village, was known for letting all manner of strays, runaways, and drug-addled vagabonds crash at his pad. The drugs, the love-ins, the bohemian lifestyle were still relatively new to the general public, and local newspapers loved to write about him, going so far as to call him "his generation's young rebel," and "an urban Huck Finn." Fitzpatrick was the embodiment of a new kind of hippie herself: the product of a super-rich New England family, she dropped out, fell into the underground drug world, and went from marijuana to acid to speed in a matter of months.

On the morning of Oct. 8, however, they both became known as victims of gruesome murder, found bludgeoned in the boiler room of 169 Avenue B. Police theorized that they had been lured down there to buy LSD, and then had their heads beat in with bricks.

As friends and families mourned, and the bohemian community tried to make sense of the tragedy, the "groovy murders" quickly seemed to represent a harsh wake-up call for the peace-loving, psychedelic '60s. The local tragedy was followed soon after by national ones, including the assassinations of Martin Luther King Jr. and Robert F. Kennedy.

Though the initial police investigation turned up few leads, a major break came two years after Hutchinson and Fitzpatrick were slain. Two drifters — Thomas Dennis, 27, and Donald Ramsey, 28 — were arrested and confessed to the murder. Their motives were never revealed.

Coming and Going

Photo: Daniel Hood

Nowadays, 13 West 54th Street is the home of Aquavit, a sleek Scandinavian restaurant, and the only thing likely to give you heart failure is the size of the bill. In 1979, though, the townhouse between Fifth and Sixth Avenues was the home of **Nelson Rockefeller** – and the quickest way to heart failure may have been an attractive young employee named Megan Marshak.

On Jan. 26, Rockefeller, a former New York governor and U.S. vice president, died of a heart attack, reportedly in his office in Rockefeller Center. Within hours, though, the site was changed to his townhouse on 54th, and rumors quickly spread of a mysterious woman seen as the still-living multimillionaire was being loaded into an ambulance. That woman was Marshak, the 70-year-old Rockefeller's 27-year-old assistant, with whom he was supposedly working on a book that night.

The story that quickly took shape was that the old man's heart failed while he was having sex with his mistress, who (reasonably enough) freaked out and delayed calling for help until she could make him more presentable – a delay that may have cost him his life, since he died in the ambulance on the way to the hospital. However, Marshak immediately went into seclusion and Rockefeller's wife cremated him within two days (refusing all public ceremonies), so there's no proof. Make what you like of that fact that Nelson's will left Marshak a large chunk of money and the deed to a Manhattan property.

after a helicopter crash that kills four passengers and one pedestrian on the street below.

July 29, 1976-Aug. 10, 1977
David Berkowitz kills six and wounds seven in Brooklyn, the Bronx, and Queens. First called the Lover's Lane Killer and .44-Caliber Killer, he renames himself Son of Sam in letters to the police and newspapers.

July 13, 1977
Lightning strikes cause a citywide blackout – but the aplomb of 1965 is nowhere to be found. Fires and looting scar poor neighborhoods in Harlem, the South Bronx and Brooklyn. Two days later, police have made almost 3,800 arrests and the city has suffered almost $300 million in damages.

Dec. 8, 1980
John Lennon is shot outside the Dakota.

Oct. 29, 1984
67-year-old black grandmother Eleanor Bumpers is killed by police during eviction proceedings.

Dec. 16, 1985
Mafia boss Paul Castellano is murdered outside Sparks Steakhouse on East 46th Street, presumably on the orders of John Gotti.

Aug. 26, 1986
Robert Chambers murders Jennifer

Levin in Central Park. The "Preppy Murderer" claims the tiny Levin tried to force him to have sex with her, and eventually cops a plea. He was released in 2003.

Photo: Daniel Hood

Oct. 19, 1987

The NYSE sees a second "Black Tuesday," with the Dow dropping over 500 points. The drop is blamed in part on automated computerized stock trading programs.

March 29, 1989

Billionaire junk bond king Michael Milken turns himself in to face charges of racketeering and various types of fraud. He eventually pays $600 million in fines.

April 19, 1989

"Wilding" enters the vocabulary when the "Central Park Jogger," a young investment banker, is raped and beaten, and five black and Hispanic teenagers are convicted of the crime. Their sentences, though, are overturned in 2003, after a single man confesses to the attack.

March 25, 1990

Snubbed by a coat-check girl, a disgruntled patron sets fire to the

Minnesota Strip

Now packed with expensive restaurants and chic hotels, the stretch of Eighth Avenue from 42nd Street to 50th Street once was known, in its seedier days, as the **Minnesota Strip**.

In the 1970s, an unusually high number of teenage girls ran away from their homes in the Midwest and came to the big city to seek glamour and independence. Many of them stepped off the bus at Port Authority and, before they knew it, were lured into prostitution rings they could not escape. Pimps waited around the terminal, looking for starry-eyed runaways, and then offered to help them become rich and famous.

Because so many of these young women came from Minnesota, two vice squad officers from Minneapolis launched a relentless investigation. Detectives Al Palmquist and Gary McGaughey brought the issue to national attention when they uncovered a pipeline that funneled girls directly from their state to the New York sex industry.

The public outcry not only caused New York City police to step up prostitution patrols and crackdown on pimps and johns, but also inspired Hollywood to jump on board. The depressing 1980 TV drama *Off the Minnesota Strip*, starring Hal Holbrook, further magnified the nation's child sex trade.

Though the area around Times Square has been scoured clean during the last three decades, the Minnesota Strip is not completely a thing of the past. According to the Paul and Lisa Foundation, a nonprofit that fights child prostitution in New York, the problem persists. In addition, Kansas may have supplanted Minnesota with the dubious distinction of the most at-risk runaways. A 1996 study showed that 33 out of 262 children forced into prostitution were from Kansas.

Fortunately, Port Authority is more secure now than it has been in decades. Moreover, there are numerous establishments surrounding the bus terminal – including the Covenant House – whose mission is to find and help runaways.

Hell's Angel Hellion

Photo: Brad Dunn

You'd think it would be hard to find a bronze plaque honoring someone for murdering an innocent woman by throwing her off a roof. Not in the East Village.

Across from the Hell's Angels' New York headquarters at 77 East 3rd Street is a mural and plaque memorializing **Vincent "Big Vinny" Girolamo**. He earned his nefarious distinction on Sept. 21, 1977, when he allegedly tossed 32-year-old Mary Ann Campbell from the roof of the motorcycle gang's clubhouse. He reportedly performed the deed as his fellow bikers cheered him on.

His motive was never clear, but some believe the young woman had lodged several complaints against the rowdy gang, and this was her payback. Though Girolamo was never charged with murder, a different kind of justice prevailed in the end. Two years later he died from a ruptured spleen during a fight with a fellow Angel in Oakland, California.

The Manhattan chapter of the legendary gang has had other problems over the years. Since its establishment in December 1969, the East Coast hub has rivaled its West Coast counterparts in size and strength. Throughout the 1970s, members used the East Village clubhouse as a central station for their massive amphetamine trade.

The FBI got wise to the bikers' drug dealings and raided the clubhouse on May 2, 1985. They arrested dozens of Angels and sentenced the gang's leader to 16 years in prison.

A few years later, another neighborhood tragedy struck. According to police reports, two Angels tossed a handful of M-80 firecrackers into a burning metal trash can on Independence Day, 1990. The resulting explosion killed a 14-year-old boy. The bikers were charged with manslaughter and assault.

Photo: Brad Dunn

Happyland Social Club at 1959 Southern Boulevard in the Bronx. 87 people die.

Aug. 28, 1991

Drunken motorman Robert Ray falls asleep at the switch of a 4 train just north of Union Square; the train jumps the tracks, killing five and injuring hundreds. Ray escapes unharmed and heads upstairs to Union Square Park to drink some more while the bodies are brought out. He is sentenced to 15 years in prison.

Feb. 26, 1993

Islamic terrorists explode a bomb in the World Trade Center, killing six and injuring thousands.

1996

There are fewer than 1,000 murders in the city for the first time since 1968.

Aug. 9, 1997

Haitian immigrant Abner Louima is tortured and sodomized by police in a Flatbush Avenue precinct house. "It's Giuliani time," the cops allegedly say.

1998

There are only 629 murders in the city, the lowest number since 1964.

Feb. 4, 1999

Out of 41 bullets fired by four police officers, 19 hit Guinean immigrant Amadou Diallo, killing him outside his front door in the South Bronx as he reaches for his wallet. The cops are acquitted, and the upraised wallet becomes a symbol of the troubled relations between the NYPD and the city's minority communities.

March 16, 2000
Patrick Dorismond is shot by undercover police, sparking outrage in the Haitian and wider black communities.

June 11, 2000
Close to 30 women are assaulted and groped in Central Park during the Puerto Rican Day Parade while cops, under orders not to provoke parade-goers, stand by.

Aug. 14, 2003
Another blackout hits New York (and parts north and west, we hear). Locals waver between repeating 1965 or 1977; opt for 1965.

Oct. 15, 2003
The Staten Island Ferry crashes into its dock, killing 11 and injuring many more.

Jan. 10, 2004
Monologist, actor, and part-time Soho fixture Spalding Gray disappears. Friends and family fear he has thrown himself off the Staten Island Ferry – an idea the depressed Gray has mentioned before. His body was discovered in the East River in March.

Won't You Come Home, Bill Clinton?

"I feel at home." That's what former President Bill Clinton said of Harlem when he opened his first post-White House office at 55 West 125th Street, and it certainly seemed appropriate that the man many called "America's first black president" should have digs in America's most famous black community.

Thing is, home wasn't his original choice. When Clinton first began looking for office space in Manhattan, he settled on an 8,500-square-foot spread at Carnegie Hall Towers on 57th Street. That space, though, would have cost around $800,000 a year, and since ex-presidents' office space is paid for by the federal government, some taxpayers raised a stink. So Clinton retreated uptown, where the 8,300 square feet he finally chose will cost the country only $354,000 a year. It's still more than any other ex-president's office, but at least it's close to Sylvia's soul food, so no objections were raised – except by the New Black Panthers, who briefly protested the arrival of the "cracker." They needn't have worried much – locals say they almost never see Clinton.

Giant Rat Sightings

No, that giant rat isn't a result of radiation in the sewers – he's a sign of labor unrest, standing sentinel wherever unions are protesting unfair management practices. We used to think there was just one inflatable rat who offered his services to whichever union needed him, but because New York has a lot of unions, and they're frequently unhappy, there are actually a whole horde of rats, ranging in size from six to 30 feet tall, with 15 or 16 being average. They're most often called Scabby the Rat or the Rat King, but workers also like to name them after the most egregious member of the management negotiating team. One brave 30-footer was taken into custody in 1999 – for a parking violation – but was eventually released on First Amendment grounds.

Living

"Once you have lived in New York and it has become your home, no place else is good enough." – John Steinbeck

We couldn't put it better ourselves, so we didn't. Here are some tips for making the city homier.

The Lowdown on Brownstones

Photo: Daniel Hood

These days, any old townhouse or rowhouse is called a **brownstone**, even if it isn't actually made of brownstone, the chocolatey sandstone that was used to build thousands of single-family dwellings on the city's standard 20-foot-wide lots in the second half of the 19th century. Quarries in New Jersey supplied some of the stone, but the vast majority came from Connecticut, in particular from the Portland Quarry, which dug up some 10 million cubic yards of the soft, easily workable stone. In the 1890s, tastes changed and many of the quarries were closed.

Jump forward a hundred years to the 1980s, when gentrification reared its head and old brownstones were being snapped up all over the city. Many of the new owners discovered that brownstone's original virtues meant that it weathered particularly poorly, and that some of the hundred-year-old treasures were literally dissolving. The closing or playing out of the old quarries, though, made restoration difficult until 1993, when the Portland Quarry was reopened specifically to supply brownstone for repairs.

great addresses

Residential real estate is something of an obsession with New Yorkers. Instead of "What do you do?" we frequently ask "Where do you live?" as a conversation opener, often followed by "What's your rent?" or "How much did you pay for it?" We're told that people from other parts of the country are appalled by this, but here it isn't considered prying – we're all in the business of trying to live in this constricted space, and the details of your situation may provoke envy or pity, but never indifference. (Every week, for instance, *The Observer* devotes a page to the minutia of a number of apartment closings, starting with celebrity moves but always including those of a few average schmoes.)

With that in mind, here are a few addresses guaranteed to provoke envy and admiration (if you could ever get into them, that is):

Photo: Daniel Hood

The Dakota

Arguably the most famous apartment building in history, the story goes that when it was built in 1884, the Dakota was so far north and west of the city's established residential areas that people said it might as well have been in the Dakota Territory out west. Or so sloppy guidebook writers like us would have you believe; *New York Times* columnist and Secret Master of New York Architectural History Christopher Gray says that at the time, the Upper West Side was widely recognized as the next big thing, and no one thought it too far away. The name, he claims, comes from the Dakota's developer, Edward Clark, who liked the names of the Union's new Western territories so much that he proposed renaming Eighth through Twelfth Avenues after them – Montana Place, Wyoming Place, Arizona Place, and Idaho Place. Clark didn't get his way, but he did get to name his own building.

Either story works for us. It's still the site of John Lennon's murder (Yoko still lives there; fans and mourners still come by), the setting for *Rosemary's Baby*, and home, at different times, to Leonard Bernstein, Lauren Bacall, Rex

Gated Communities

These aren't California-style, mind you, but quiet treasures that have escaped the inexorable grinding of Manhattan's relentless grid. The gates here are unguarded, often unlocked – or sometimes opened for the politely inquisitive by those lucky enough to live within. The real secret of these secrets, though, is how cramped the houses and apartments inside can be, given how expensive they are.

Brooklyn Naval Yard

It's not really a community, per se, but the Naval Commandant's House, a great white mansion built in 1806, is a surprising sight behind the fences that block off the yard, which closed in 1966, after a century and a half that included building the *Maine*.
Little St., off Evans St. (off Hudson Ave.), Vinegar Hill, Brooklyn

Grove Court

Grove St., bet. Bedford St. and Sixth Ave.

Milligan Place

Off Sixth Ave., bet. 11th and 12th Sts

Patchin Place

The Village bywater where poet e.e. cummings lived (and died), in No. 4. (Marlon Brando lived here, too.) Oddly enough, according to The *New York*

Times, the alley's 10 houses contain the offices of no less than 15 psychotherapists.
Off W. 10th Street, bet. Greenwich and Sixth Aves.

Pomander Walk
One of the few outside of the Village, this row of quaint, tiny cottages was built in the 1921 and named after a popular play.
Block bet. 94th and 95th Sts., bet. Broadway and West End Ave

Photo: Daniel Hood

Sniffen Court
Another set of stables converted into expensive townhouses — and the site of the cover shot for the Doors' album *Strange Days*.
150-158 E. 36th St., bet. Third and Lexington Aves.

Washington Mews
Once a row of stables for the fashionable houses on Washington Square; some now belong to NYU.
Block bet. Fifth Ave. and University Pl., bet. Waverly Pl. and 8th St.

Reed, Judy Garland, Gilda Radner, Connie Chung and Maury Povich, Judy Holliday, and Boris Karloff.
1 W. 72nd St., at Central Park West

The Ansonia
Originally built in 1904 as a hotel (with a mini-farm on the roof for fresh eggs and produce), this apartment building has housed Babe Ruth, Flo Ziegfeld, Caruso, Rachmaninoff, Stravinsky, Toscanini, Mahler, Sarah Bernhardt, Tony Curtis, Paul Sorvino, Jack Dempsey, and Theodore Dreiser.
2109 Broadway, at 73rd St.

Perry Street Towers
Built in 2002, and despite some teething troubles, architect Richard Meier's glass towers have become two of the hottest addresses in the city, drawing Calvin Klein, Martha Stewart, star chef Jean-Georges Vongerichten, and Hugh Jackman (if only as a renter).
173/176 Perry St., at West St.

The San Remo
Since 1930, this co-op's two towers have been a landmark on Central Park; famous residents have included Marilyn Monroe, Dustin Hoffman, and Paul Simon.
145 Central Park West, bet. 74th and 75th Sts.

Photo: Daniel Hood

The Time Warner Center
Site of the most expensive condo in New York to date — an English financier's $45 million, 12,600-square-foot penthouse.
1 Central Park, at Columbus Circle

285 Lafayette
A downtown loft building that's been, or is, home to David Bowie and Iman, Patrick McEnroe, Ian Schrager, and Rupert Murdoch's son Lachlan.
285 Lafayette St., bet. Prince and Houston Sts.

950 Fifth Avenue
Where infamous businessman Dennis Kozlowski spent $18.6 million of Tyco's money for a duplex before being indicted for securities fraud. *Daily News* owner Mort Zuckerman has a place just upstairs.
950 Fifth Ave., at 76th St.

It's been called everything from the "Tower of Babel of creativity and bad behavior" to "one of the few civilized places in New York. And though the guest registry at the **Chelsea Hotel** is packed with the names of some of the most renowned artists of the last two centuries, the enormous inn boasts other things besides its clientele.

For one, the ornate, 12-story structure was the tallest building in New York north of Houston Street from its completion in 1884 until 1902, when it was eclipsed by the Flatiron Building. For another, it was the city's first co-operative apartment complex, a residential real estate arrangement that forever changed the face of home ownership in the city. Lastly, and what few people know, it was this seminal idea of a co-op structure that actually turned the Chelsea into a den for artists – not because it worked but because it failed.

For 20 years, the co-op system worked: owner-tenants shared the mutual maintenance costs of the building, a board was elected to oversee that maintenance, and everyone was, for the most part, happy. Then two financial panics struck in a row, in 1893 and 1903. Real estate prices in the city tumbled and the Chelsea went bankrupt. New owners swept in, the original tenants were kicked out, and the place was turned into a hotel – a hotel that quickly attracted all manner of unusual customers, from campaigning politicians to wandering artists.

The Chelsea earned a reputation for housing New York notables. By the 1920s, it was the first destination for writers, artists, poets, musicians, and philosophers, a characteristic that has stayed with it ever since.

Janis Joplin once said, "A lot of funky things happen in the Chelsea. Just like the California communes. Only it costs a bit more." Today, the rates for a single room run between $150 and $250 per night, doubles $175 to $300, and suites up to $350.

Here's a look at some of the people who have slept, or stayed up for days, at the Chelsea Hotel:

Mark Twain
O. Henry
Edgar Lee Masters
Sarah Bernhardt
Dylan Thomas
Thomas Wolfe (who wrote *Look Homeward Angel* there)

OUT OF THE CLOSET

Where else but Manhattan could a business devoted to organizing closets thrive? It makes perfect sense: on an island where closets are more valued than dining rooms, every apartment dweller could use a little help maximizing these minimal spaces.

Former fashion editor Melanie Charlton launched **Clos-ette** in 2002 to address the overwhelming, yet underserved, task of closet designing. Self-styled as "an architect, organizer, and stylist all in one," Charlton first performs an

Tennessee Williams
Leonard Cohen (who wrote "Chelsea Hotel
    No. 2" there)
Arthur Miller
William Burroughs (who wrote *Naked Lunch* there)
Claes Oldenburg
Willem de Kooning
Jackson Pollock
Donald Sutherland
Christo
Arthur C. Clarke (who wrote *2001: A Space
    Odyssey* there)
Patti Smith
Andy Warhol (who filmed *Chelsea Girls* there)
Jane Fonda
Bob Dylan (who wrote "Sad-Eyed Lady of the
    Lowlands" and had a child while living there)
Jim Carroll
Milos Forman (who directed *Hair* while living here)
Sid Vicious

analysis of your closet situation, then helps you delete the irrevocably out-of-style portions of your wardrobe, then designs and builds custom-made shelving and other storage devices in either hardwood or metal.

Her designs take into account obtrusive heat pipes, slanted floors, and all other manner of peculiar architecture found in Manhattan. What would you expect to pay for such a service? You might want to sit down: $250 for the initial consultation, $200 per hour after that, and 20 percent commission on supplies. For many New Yorkers, it must be worth it; Charlton's business is thriving. If you're ready for your own remodeling, call Clos-ette at 212-473-4162.

Wall Call

Murphy beds, fold-out couches, showers that convert into dishwashers: living in the sardine-sized apartments of Manhattan, New Yorkers have come up with tons of smart ways so save space over the years. But sometimes what you really need is a whole new room or closet. Instead of breaking code and building onto your fire escape, the best bet is to wall off that odd, unusable nook or corner.

The **Living Space Company** *(800-761-9947; living spaceinc.com)* builds and installs temporary walls in any space, for any purpose. Expecting a baby? The company will help you turn your small studio into an even smaller – but infinitely more usable – one-bedroom apartment.

Without using nails, nuts, bolts, or plaster – or anything else that will leave a mark on your beautiful wood floors – the company offers standard three-inch-thick sheetrock walls cut to any dimension. You actually don't buy the wall, you lease it. A typical 12-foot-long wall runs about $695 per year, but you can add French doors, frosted windows, and other frills for extra. When you want to revert to the old layout, the company comes and takes it away. No sign remains of a split-up apartment, and you never have to deal with the headache of installing and tearing down a real wall.

Mother Cabrini Shrine

Photo: Brad Dunn

Mother Cabrini High School and its chapel look like a lot of parochial schools around the city that were built in the 1960s – except most of them don't have pilgrims coming by and a saint's body in the altar. Born in 1850 in Italy, Mother Cabrini came to the U.S. in 1889 as founder of the Missionary Sisters of the Sacred Heart to minister to the Italian community in New York, and quickly got to work building schools and orphanages around the city and eventually across the country. She bought the Washington Heights spot where her shrine is before her death in 1917, and her body was enshrined there after her canonization in 1946 as the first American saint and the Patron Saint of Immigrants. And we mean her body, specifically; her head is kept in Rome, apparently, though the High School got to keep some other relics, including her glasses and a few cancelled checks.
701 Fort Washington Ave., at 190th St., by entrance to Fort Tryon Park; 212-923-3536

St. Elizabeth Ann Seton Shrine

Mother Cabrini, America's first saint, has the north end of Manhattan; Mother Seton, the first American-born saint (a subtle distinction, we know) has the south end. Born in 1774 into a well-to-do Protestant New York family, she converted to Catholicism after the death of her

Photo: Daniel Hood

A FRIENDLY WELCOME

Given New York's extraordinarily healthy self-esteem, the fear and trepidation with which some visitors approach it is a matter of puzzlement and concern. Enter the **Big Apple Greeters** *(212-669-8159; bigapplegreeter.org)*, a nonprofit group that pairs knowledgeable local volunteers with individual tourists or groups who are anxious or simply want an insider's viewpoint. If you're interested in a particular neighborhood, they can often provide you with a specialist, and they can handle a number of foreign languages, but all of the group's 400 or so guides can give a great introduction to the city. Since 1992, they've made New York a friendlier place for over 45,000 visitors, and significantly diminished the city's hard-earned reputation as a cold, cruel place – so the rest of us will just have to be that much ruder.

The Inside Scoop for Locals

Forgotten NY

Queens native Kevin Walsh maintains a remarkable Web site of architectural and infrastructural New-Yorkiana, and on an irregular basis organizes well-informed expeditions to some of the city's more obscure and fascinating nooks and crannies.
forgotten-ny.com

Jinx Magazine

An offbeat Web site dedicated to hard-core urban exploration — basically, they dress up in suits and break into abandoned buildings. They also hold monthly Athenaeums for discussions and debates on topics of interest or amusement to the urban adventure crowd.
jinxmagazine.com

New York Songlines

Author and editor Jim Naureckas has created a virtual street-by-street walking tour of Manhattan, with annotations for most every block.
nysonglines.com

husband in 1803, and was promptly shunned by family and friends. She became a nun, moved to Maryland to found the Sisters of Charity, and died in 1821. After a century and a half of campaigning, she was finally canonized in 1975. We should note that her official shrine is somewhere in the wilds of Maryland, though this local shrine stands next to a house she lived in before her conversion.
7-8 State St., bet. Water and Pearl Sts.; 212-269-6865

The Watchtower in the Heights

It's hard to believe that leafy, genteel Brooklyn Heights is home to the world's most mildly annoying religion. Then again, the clean-cut, clean-living Jehovah's Witnesses don't look all that out of place in the neighborhood — except when they're knocking on doors on Sunday morning to proselytize. Their founder, Charles Taze Russell, moved his Watchtower Bible and Tract Society from Pennsylvania to Brooklyn in 1909 to be closer to printing and shipping facilities, and the group has been based here ever since. It was only after World War II, though, that they began to buy up large chunks of the area. At present they own over 30 properties valued at over $200 million, including dormitories, eating halls, offices, and their headquarters at 25 Columbia Heights. Allegations of pedophilia and the fact that they don't celebrate any of the good holidays aside, they're controversial in Brooklyn because they don't participate in local life at all — they live and eat apart, shipping in all their food from society-owned farms upstate. And while their recent decision to sell a waterfront printing and distribution center at 360 Furman Avenue has real estate developers salivating over the possibility of river-view condos, their simultaneous move to build residence halls in nearby Dumbo has met with stiff resistance from the artsy crowd there, who like to sleep in on Sunday mornings.

Atomic Buddhism

Photo: Brad Dunn

The city as a whole has never suffered a nuclear attack, but one small part of it has: the statue of Shinran Shonin outside the New York Buddhist Church on the Upper West Side. It originally stood in Hiroshima, and miraculously survived the devastation of Aug. 6, 1945. It was brought here in 1955 as a symbol of hope for peace (provoking some unfounded fears of radioactivity), and is the focus of a yearly ceremony on Aug. 5. Shinran Shonin established "Pure Land" Buddhism in Japan in the 13th century; the church here was established in 1938. We suspect the real estate broker played down the origins of the house when they bought: It was built in 1902 by William Randolph Hearst for his mistress, Marion Davies.
331-2 Riverside Drive, bet. 105th and 106th Sts.; 212-678-0305

Signs of Islam

You'd hardly know there were over 300,000 Muslims in the city, if you went strictly by the architectural record. While most Christian denominations have more churches than they know what to do with, most Muslim

Photo: Daniel Hood

congregations meet in storefront mosques – except on the Upper East Side, where there's a beautiful modernist-inflected mosque designed by famed New York architects Skidmore Owings & Merrill. The gorgeous interior is open to all.
Third Ave. and 96th St.

Clay Creations

New York not only lays claim to the impressive American Craft Museum, which displays an amazing array of ancient and modern ceramics, the city also houses plenty of **pottery studios** in case you walk away inspired.

In fact, it's not hard at all to find a place that will fix you up with a chunk of clay, a spinning wheel, a helpful instructor, and a kiln where you can fire a whole new set of dishes for yourself. Most studios offer day rates as well as full classes. Here are three favorites; call ahead to find out hours and class availability:

Chambers Pottery
153 Chambers St., 212-619-7302

Mud, Sweat, and Tears
654 Tenth Ave., 212-974-9121

Our Name Is Mud
227 W. 29th St., 7th Floor,
212-904-1171

Dog Runs

Before 9 a.m., dogs can go offleash in all city parks — after that, though, the Park Enforcement Patrol is on the lookout, with ticket books handy. Enter dog runs, which have sprung up in large numbers over the past 10 to 15 years. A few are private, run by dues-paying members; most of them, though, are located in city parks and maintained by volunteers who take donations from users. This is just a sampling; for a complete list of city park dog runs, including many in the outer boroughs, visit *nycgovparks.org*.

Battery Park City

Two private runs, organized by Battery Park City Dogs *(bpcdogs.org)*. *W. Thames St., bet. Little West St. and Battery Place; River Terrace, at Murray St.*

Psychedelic Yoga

A lot of people said it was the LSD, but the man behind the psychedelic iconography of the 1960s, New York artist Peter Max, claims that his trippy paintings and designs had nothing to do with drugs, and a lot to do with yoga. In fact, Max was so impressed by the teachings of one guru, Swami Satchidananda, that he invited him to visit the city in 1966. Satchidananda, in turn, was so impressed with New York that he stayed in the U.S., eventually becoming a citizen, appearing at Woodstock, and opening several **Integral Yoga Centers**. Two are in Manhattan, and have been offering classes, programs, and enlightenment for over 30 years. The Village location also has handy health food and vitamin stores right next door.
227 W. 13th St., bet. Seventh and Greenwich Aves.; 212-929-0586; and 200 W. 72nd St., at Broadway; 212-721-4000; integralyogany.org

Super Buddha

Buddhism is probably the very last religion on the planet prone to one-upmanship or fighting for bragging rights, but in between Oms every Buddhist in New York must wonder: Who's got the biggest Buddha in town?

That honor goes to the **Mahayana Buddhist Temple** in Chinatown, with its two-story-tall, golden, magnificent Buddha. Look for the enormous faux pagoda front on the north side of Canal Street near the entrance to the Manhattan Bridge. The lobby is packed with paintings of bodhisattvas and decorated with candles and strips of paper with Chinese prayers. There's also a large urn where visitors burn incense in front of an image of Kwan Yin.

In the main hall, the enormous Buddha sits atop a lotus flower looking as content as always. An aura of blue neon light surrounds him and dozens of paintings hang around the hall depicting his life. One Chinese belief says Shakyamuni Buddha was 16 feet tall and had a golden body. If that's true, he has no better tribute than the statue at the Mahayana Temple.

Public services are held on weekends.

Dead Fish

Photo: Daniel Hood

One of Manhattan's oldest cemeteries has one of the city's strangest memorials: a vault honoring someone named "Preserved Fish." Is it a memorial to a real person, or an ancient inside joke?

Established in 1831, the **New York City Marble Cemetery** on East 2nd Street between First and Second Avenues was one of only two non-sectarian burial grounds in the city. Though it was open to the public, most of the plots were quickly sold off to New York's elite. Impressive vaults made of Tuckahoe marble went up seemingly overnight, bought by the richest families in the area. One of the first celebs interred at the Marble Cemetery was ex-President James Monroe, who was laid to rest within the vault owned by his son-in-law Samuel Gouverneur in 1831. Monroe's post-mortem residency in the East Village didn't last long, however. In 1857, the Virginia Legislature passed a resolution to bring their beloved commander-in-chief back to his homeland. Consequently, his remains were dug up, placed aboard a steamboat, and transported across the Mason-Dixon. The Marble Cemetery is filled with other names splattered across U.S. history books, as well as New York City street signs. There are the Varicks, the Hoyts, the Kips, the Lenoxes, and the Beekmans, to name a few.

So who, then, is "Preserved Fish"? Actually, he was a real person, and there's no joke behind his name. In the 19th century, "Preserved," pronounced with three syllables, was a venerable Quaker first name, meaning "Preserved in a state of grace." And the Fishes were a very rich and very well-known Quaker family who lived throughout New England. Of course, his parents must have had a sense of humor.

Either way, with a combination of names like that, it's fitting that Mr. Preserved Fish's name is preserved in marble for eternity.

Canine Court (Van Cortlandt Park)
A couple of huge runs, including a dog agility playground/obstacle course!
In from W. 252nd St. and Broadway, the Bronx

Carl Schurz Park
Two runs.
From E. 84th St. to E. 89th St., bet. East End Ave. and the river

DeWitt Clinton Park
Two runs.
W. 52nd St. and W. 54th Sts., bet. Tenth and Eleventh Aves.

Fish Bridge Park
Reclaimed for an old dump.
Dover St., bet. Pearl and Water Sts.

Photo: Spencer T Tucker/NYC Dept of Parks & Recreation

cemeteries

Though not exactly havens for sunbathing and Ultimate frisbee, the city's boneyards are little green gems in the asphalt jungle – and all those tombstones with famous names add an extra touch of morbid history.

African Burial Ground

In 1991, work on a federal office building downtown unearthed the bodies of colonial-era slaves, and started a heated debate over what to do with the remains. After years of protest, the government redrew its plans to create a burial ground, and in October 2003, the bodies of some 400 free and enslaved blacks were reburied on the site with appropriate ceremony, in hand-carved caskets.
Duane and Elk Sts.; interpretive center at 290 Broadway

Green-Wood Cemetery

When it was created in 1838, the city didn't have much in the way of parks, so fashionable Brooklynites used the beautiful landscape of Green-Wood for strolling and picnicking. The permanent crowd includes Albert Anastasia, Jean-Michel Basquiat, Leonard Bernstein, both Currier and Ives, Horace Greeley, Lola Montez, Samuel F.B. Morse, several Roosevelts, Margaret Sanger, F.A.O. Schwarz, Henry Steinway, Louis Comfort Tiffany, and Boss Tweed. Tours available.
500 25th St., Brooklyn; 718-788-7850; green-wood.org

New York Marble Cemetery

Monthly tours.
41 1/2 Second Ave., bet. E. 3rd and E. 2nd Sts.; marblecemetery.org

New York City Marble Cemetery

Visit by appointment, donation required.
52-74 E. 2nd St., bet. Second and First Aves.; nycmc.org

Hell's Kitchen/ Clinton Dog Run

Private, and difficult to find. Run by Hell's Kitchen Neighborhood Association *(212-957-3667)*. *Southeast corner of W. 39th St. and Tenth Ave.*

Madison Square Park

Somewhat undiscovered, and so cleaner and less crowded. *West side of Madison Square Park, near Fifth Ave.*

Mercer Houston Dog Run

Private; run by the Mercer Houston Dog Run Association *(Box 101, 51 MacDougal St.)*. *Northwest corner of Mercer and Houston Sts.*

Peter Detmold Park

A hidden gem behind Beekman Place. *E. 49th St., at FDR Drive*

Riverside Park

Three runs; very social. *Riverside Dr. at W. 72nd, W. 87th, and W. 105th Sts.*

Spanish and Portuguese Jewish Graveyards

Shearith Israel, now at 99 Central Park West, is New York's oldest Jewish congregation – it was founded in 1654 by Spanish and Portuguese Jews from the Caribbean. Not surprisingly, in the hundreds of years since they've had to bury some of their members, and so have left behind three little graveyards downtown: One in Chatham Square, from 1683, one on 11th Street, from 1805, and one on 21st Street, from 1829. The land is worth millions today, but Shearith Israel isn't looking to cash out, and every year around Memorial Day they hold a ceremony to honor their Revolutionary War veterans buried in Chatham Square.
55-57 St. James Place, at Chatham Sq.; 76 W. 11th, bet. Sixth and Seventh Aves.; 21st St., bet. Sixth and Seventh Aves.

Trinity Churchyard

This memento mori at the west end of Wall Street is most famous for the graves of Alexander Hamilton and steamboat pioneer Robert Fulton. Spare a glance for the gravestone of Charlotte Temple, though – the gravestone, not the grave, because there isn't one: She's a fictional character from a popular novel written in 1790, about an English girl who is seduced and abandoned by an army officer. In the novel, she starves to death in New York, and is buried by her father in Trinity Churchyard. (In the sequel, her daughter comes close to unwittingly marrying her half-brother.) *Charlotte: A Tale of Truth* went through some 200 printings, and was widely believed to be based on a true story, so much so that, in 1846, workers who were rebuilding Trinity Church put up a tombstone to the dead single mother.
74 Trinity Place, at Broadway and Wall St.

Trinity Church Cemetery & Mausoleum

After the city banned burials in lower Manhattan, Trinity was forced to look uptown for more room, so they bought part of John James Audubon's estate in Washington Heights in 1842 to create this large, green

Thomas Smith Park
Eleventh Ave., bet. W. 22nd and W. 23rd Sts.

Tompkins Square Park
The city's oldest; they also run a Halloween party for dogs.
First Ave. to Ave. B, from E. 7th to E. 10th Sts.

Tribeca Dog Run
Private; run by Dog Owners of Tribeca (71 Hudson St.).
Next to PS 234 on Warren St., bet. Greenwich and West Sts.

Washington Square Park
Often very crowded. But if your dog needs to score some weed, this run is very conveniently located.
South side of Washington Square Park, bet. Macdougal and Thompson Sts.

Cultural Festivals

The St. Patrick's Day Parade and the Feast of San Gennaro get all the hype, but they're just the tip of the iceberg (and a pretty drunken, touristy tip, too) when it comes to ethnic and cultural festivals. A sampling:

Chinese New Year

Ten days or so celebrating the lunar new year in Chinatown, including the Lion and Dragon Parade — but no fireworks.
January/February; throughout Chinatown

Easter Parade

The parade that gave birth to the song is still going, with plenty of fancy bonnets.
Easter Sunday; Fifth Ave. from 49th to 57th Sts.

Ukrainian Festival

Mid-May; E. 7th St., bet. Second and Third Aves.

The Feast of Mt. Carmel and St. Paulinus

An old-fashioned Italian saint's festival. Much more authentic than San Gennaro, with a procession carrying the *giglio*, a 50-foot tall

burying ground. Guests include Audubon himself, Clement Clarke Moore, and John Jacob Astor.
Amsterdam Ave., bet. W. 153rd and W. 155th Sts.; 212-368-1600

Woodlawn Cemetery

One of the largest in the city, Woodlawn hosts an unusual number of musicians, particularly jazzmen. Residents include Fatty Arbuckle, Irving Berlin, Nellie Bly, Ralph Bunche, George M. Cohan, Celia Cruz, Miles Davis, Duke Ellington, David Farragut, Jay Gould, Oscar Hammerstein Sr., W.C. Handy, Fiorello LaGuardia, Bat Masterson, Herman Melville, Robert Moses, Thomas Nast, Otto Preminger, Joseph Pulitzer, and Damon Runyon. Tours available.
Webster Ave. at 233rd St., the Bronx; 718-920-0500

Bless Ewe

For animal lovers who happen to be in town on the first Sunday in October: Consider yourself blessed. If you can make it to the **Cathedral of St. John the Divine** by 11 a.m., you'll not only behold one of the most majestic cathedrals in the world, you'll also witness the strangest parade of animals you'll ever see.

Each year about 5,000 people bring creatures from every phylum to celebrate St. Francis Day, in honor of the saint who stressed the importance of living in harmony with the natural world. With the help of their owners, the pets form a carnival-like procession — usually led by a special guest animal such as an eagle, camel, or elephant — and march to the altar to be blessed by the Episcopal clergy.

Since the tradition began in 1985, the clergy have blessed thousands of animals, including turkey vultures, skunks, tarantulas, horses, sheep, chickens, snakes, worms, algae, and a 3.5 billion-year-old Australian fossil. The event also has drawn top-level speakers, including former Vice President Al Gore and Dr. Carl Sagan.

Steam Dream

Sure, the East Village has plenty of places for getting hot and wet, but there's only one spot where you can get scrubbed with soapy, oak-leaf brooms afterward. The **Russian and Turkish Baths** at 268 East 10th Street are not exactly a secret to the thousands of hard-working regulars who drop by to drip, sweat, and unwind after their work is done. But most New Yorkers who have heard of the hot spa have never been there, and those new to town rarely stumble upon it, making the baths one of the unknown treasures of the city.

Built in 1892 by immigrant Jews who wanted a good shvitz, the Russian and Turkish Baths not only have stayed at the same site over the years, but also have retained the ambiance of the original – with the exception of a few cable TVs. Shvitz means "sweat" in Yiddish, and the moment you walk in the door, you get the idea. A wall of 200°F heat assaults every pore on your body. (It's like stepping into the Gobi Desert.)

As an ancient ritual, the shvitz is far more than just watching streams of sweat pour out of your body. After checking in, men are given a pair of unflattering baggy shorts, while women get a shapeless smock. Both are made of black nylon, which underscores the first rule of the shvitz: it doesn't matter what you look like. Everyone looks stupid, and no one cares.

What you do next is up to you. Most customers take a quick shower and head straight for the Russian room in the basement – a huge underground chamber heated by an oven that seems more suited to the engine room of a cruise ship. Forget those little hot-rock burners at your local health club sauna. This cooker stands 12 feet high and churns out more heat than the sun. Before long you'll be reaching for one of the dozens of plastic buckets that line the bath filled with tap water. Dump it on your head, and you're in heaven.

After you sweat all those toxins out of your system (and overhear a lot of gossip in the process), you're ready for the final part of the shvitz: the platza. Here you get scrubbed and pounded with a lathery broom

obelisk with a statue of St. Paulinus on top.

Late June; Shrine Church of Our Lady of Mt. Carmel, N. 8th and Havermeyer Sts., Brooklyn

Puerto Rican Day Parade

A chance for the Nuyorican community to celebrate – and the rest of the city to lay low.

Second weekend in June; Fifth Ave. from 44th to 86th Sts.

Gay Pride Day

Actually a weekend, with a giant slate of parades, dances, and other events.

Late June; Fifth Ave. from 52nd to Christopher Sts.

West Indian American Day Carnival/Parade

A huge celebration, with great food and music.

Labor Day Weekend; from Eastern Parkway and Utica Ave. to Washington Ave., Brooklyn

Brazilian American Festival

Labor Day Weekend; 46th St. bet. Park and Seventh Aves., and Sixth Ave. bet. 44th and 47th Sts.

German-American Steuben Parade

A little-known reminder of New York's once-enormous German population.

Late September; Fifth Ave. from 63rd to 86th Sts.

Want to shop like an immigrant? If you need an obscure spice or a too-hot-for-words chili pepper for that authentic dish, you can find it in New York.

Arthur Avenue
Food shops in this old Italian neighborhood draw back droves of Italian suburbanites for cheeses, meats, pastas, baked goods, and all other things *cucina*-related — as well as hand-rolled cigars. *Arthur Ave., south of E. Fordham Rd., the Bronx; arthuravenuebronx.com*

Asia Market Corp.
Pan-Asian groceries. *71 1/2 Mulberry St., at Bayard St.; 212-962-2020*

with oak leaves as bristles. Nature never felt so good.

The Baths are open seven days a week from 9 a.m. to 9:30 p.m. as follows: both sexes on Monday, Tuesday, Friday, and Saturday; men-only on Thursday and Sunday; and women-only on Wednesday. Call 212-674-9250 or 212-473-8806 for more information.

Ancient Chinese Secret Sculpture

Photo: Daniel Hood

Confucius says: "Respect death and recall forefathers, and the good in men will again grow sturdy." The Chinese philosopher is indeed respected, dead, and a forefather. But few people know that the good in him has again grown sturdy — in the form of a beautiful black and green marble sculpture in south Chinatown.

When the **Confucius Plaza** public housing development was completed in 1976 at the foot of the Manhattan Bridge, the Chinese Consolidated Benevolent Association commissioned a monument to the apartments' namesake. Sculptor Liu Shih got to work on the magnificent statue of the 5th century B.C. philosopher that now stands between Bowery and Division Streets. At the time, the 44-story housing complex marked a giant step in Chinatown's expansion into the Lower East Side. As the Asian community grew, so did the number of monuments celebrating famous Chinese and Chinese-American people. Today, as Confucius looks thoughtfully toward a dry cleaners, you can read his sage writings, which are carved in both English and Chinese on his marble base.

Once upon a time, city residents loved to vote as often as possible. Tammany Hall operatives in the 1800s made a specialty of sending bearded men to the polls early, shaving off their side whiskers so they wouldn't be recognized for their second vote, shaving them down to their mustaches for a third, and ending election day with a final, clean-shaven vote.

On the honest side, one New Yorker even went to jail because he wanted to vote – though it was complicated by the fact that he already lived in jail. In 1894, Michael Cady was a vagrant who regularly had himself committed to the Tombs in order to have a place to stay. Since he considered himself pretty much a full-time resident, he tried to register to vote with the Tombs as his address, and found himself on trial for illegal registration, since the state constitution says prisons cannot be considered places of residence. Either way, he ended up back in the Tombs.

That kind of fervor has sadly died away in New York: from highs astonishingly close to 100 percent in the 1950s, voter turnout has declined to regularly below 50 percent, and sometimes below 40 percent. In fact, as recently as 1999, the city had *fewer* registered voters than it did in 1952, though the overall population has soared. Some of this is due to a growth in the number of immigrants who choose not to become naturalized citizens, and some to white flight, but mostly it reflects a general apathy.

If you want to rouse someone from that apathy, you can get them a voter registration form from the city's Voter Assistance Commission (ci.nyc.ny.us./html/vac/home.html), or call the Board of Elections (212-VOTE-NYC). Registrations need to be received at least 25 days before an election.

Atlantic Avenue

A Mecca for Middle Eastern foods, led by **Sahadi's**, a large, swanky shop; **Oriental Pastry & Grocery** across the street is a smaller, quainter version. There's also **Damascus Bread & Pastry** for baked goods.
Damascus Bread & Pastry: 195 Atlantic Ave., bet. Court and Clinton Sts., Brooklyn; 718-625-7070
Sahadi's: 187-189 Atlantic Ave.; 718-624-4550
Oriental Pastry: 170 Atlantic Ave.; 718-875-7687

Kalustyan's Spices and Sweets

Foods, spices and sweets from around the world, particularly the Middle East and India, since 1944. Over 30 kinds of dried chilis!
123 Lexington Ave., bet. 28th and 29th Sts.; 212-685-3451; kalustyans.com

Kam Kuo Food Corp.

A giant Chinese supermarket.
7 Mott St., bet. Canal St. and Chatham Sq.; 212-349-3097

Communist Block

Photo: Daniel Hood

The Soviet Union may have crumbled in 1991, but the **Communist Party USA** is more than alive and kicking in the 21st century. And unless your political leanings are to the extreme left, you probably didn't know that the party's national headquarters has stood in the same unprepossessing building in Chelsea for the last three decades.

A few years ago, you could stroll past the storefront at 237 West 23rd Street between Seventh and Eighth Avenues and scan the tomes in the window of the Unity Book Center. The titles may have tipped you off — *Capitalism in Crisis* or *Another World Is Possible* — but few passersby realized that the shop was not only owned and operated by the Communist Party USA, but also that the nerve center of the entire organization is right upstairs.

The party purchased the former family court building in the 1970s, and opened the bookstore to give the organization a public face, where the comrades sold books on radicalism, black history, and labor movements, as well as posters and buttons.

Of course, the party's ranks have thinned some since its heyday in the Depression era. But with the death a few years ago of its notorious leader Gus Hall, the Communist Party is trying to adapt to new times. For one thing, the group is now online at *cpusa.org* with its slogan, "Workers of the World, Log In!" and where fledgling reds can read the party's literature and even sign up to become a member. They need as much new blood as they can get: From its peak membership of 66,000 members nationwide in 1939, the party's pool is now down to about 15,000 — most of whom live in New York City.

For the most part, the group's headquarters in Chelsea is run on the principles it preaches. The party's 15 full-time employees, including its national chairman, earn the same $350 weekly salary, which doesn't go far on an island where even studios rent for up to $2,000 a month. The staff, however, did have to resort to a little bit of capitalism to keep its headquarters in business. You won't see the Unity Book Center on the street level anymore (it's been moved to the third floor) because the party decided it could rent the highly valuable real estate to help fuel its expenses.

A Kinder, Gentler DMV

Photo: Daniel Hood

The much-ballyhooed drop in crime is great and all, but the single best improvement in urban living is the **License X-Press** office of the Department of Motor Vehicles *(300 W. 34th St., bet. Eighth and Ninth Aves.; 212-645-5550)*. It's just for license and registration renewals and plate surrenders, it's open late on Thursdays, and they zip you through an assembly line at high speed and with a cheerful attitude that threatens to undermine the DMV's long-held reputation for sloth and cruelty.

Ain't Easy Being Cheesy

Where else would you expect the oldest Italian cheese store in North America to be located? Still family-owned and operated, just like it was 112 years ago when it opened, the **Alleva Dairy** *(212-226-7990)* on the edge of Little Italy has served up the best homemade mozzarella and ricotta to five generations of cheese-lovers. The Alleva family opened the shop at 188 Grand Street, near Mulberry Street, in 1892 just as Italian immigrants started arriving in America by the boatload. Overnight, the shop became an essential stop for a cultural cuisine so dependent on the cheese food group. Besides its fresh and smoked mozzarella, which is still handmade daily, the store offers a delicious selection of nondairy staples, including excellent fresh tomato sauces, homemade pasta, and a wide range of smoked and cured meats. Which means you can make one stop in Little Italy and go home with all the ingredients for an outstanding Italian feast.

Green-markets

Photo: Daniel Hood

There are greenmarkets in over 30 locations in the five boroughs, many of them open year-round, open only to regional growers — which means lots of tired farmers getting up at 3 a.m. and braving traffic jams to bring fresh produce to an empty lot or park near you.

The **Union Square Greenmarket** *(17th St., bet. Park Ave. and Broadway, at the north end of the park)* is the largest, and is open four days a week year-round. Most of the others are only open once a week, and many are seasonal, but they're all worth a look as an alternative to the stunted dregs available in the average supermarket. Some of the year-rounders:

MANHATTAN

Bowling Green
Broadway and Battery Pl.; Tues./Thurs.

The Loving Cup

The Statue of Liberty. Yellow cabs. The Empire State Building. Subway tokens. New York has no shortage of emblems that are recognized the world over. But one of the city's most overlooked icons is a little paper cup that's as omnipresent as a Yankees logo and as familiar as the Brooklyn Bridge.

New Yorkers have been drinking their coffee and tea out these charming, blue-and-white numbers for almost 40 years. Yet even lifelong residents don't know that the New York cup has a name: the **Anthora**, which is a deliberate misspelling of amphora – an ancient storage jar.

More than 200 million Anthora cups are sold every year, more than 90 percent of them in New York City. Designed by the Sherri Cup Company and launched in 1967, the paper coffee cups became an instant bestseller.

Perhaps it was their convenient 8-ounce size – a perfect dose of morning caffeine. Perhaps it was their intricate blue-and-white design, bereft of gimmick or advertisement. Or perhaps it was because the cup's Greek-styled letters spelled out an upbeat message in a city known for its rough edges. The words, "We are happy to serve you," stand above three steaming cups of coffee and between two strong pillars.

Either way, they can always be found in stacks 50 high at diners, delis, and doughnut stands across the city. Though the competition has recently caught up with the Anthora – mostly because advertisement-emblazoned cups can be cheaper – the New York icon is still a great deal. At press time, a case of 1,000 cups was going for $25.95.

Of course, over the decades, the emblematic cup has seen its share of impostors. Currently, the Premier Paper Manufacturing Company sells a strikingly similar cup with a Greek statue throwing a discus. Meanwhile, the Imperial Pare Company offers a blue-and-white cup with *four* pillars and the message: "It's Our Pleasure to Serve You."

If you are handed one these mimics, enjoy your coffee, but don't be mistaken: there is only one original New York coffee cup, just like there was only one Babe Ruth.

The Original Black-and-White Cookie

Photo: Daniel Hood

You can find tasty black-and-white cookies at some of the many bakeries in the **Chelsea Market** at Ninth Avenue and 15th Street, but you'll be hard-pressed to find the most famous black-and-white cookie of all – the Oreo. Which is too bad, considering it was born there.

Back in 1912, after two decades of mergers between regional baking companies had produced the vast National Biscuit Company, the whole block of buildings between Ninth and Tenth Avenues and 15th and 16th Streets was the cookie capital of the country – and it was in those factories that Nabisco, as it came to be known, first invented the creme sandwich cookie we all know and love with milk. Like so many other ungrateful cookies, the Oreo (and its maker) abandoned the city for factory-bakeries elsewhere around mid-century, and by 1956 the whole complex was sinking into industrial decay.

The Market rescued the place in 1996, and now it houses a whole roster of small-scale bake shops, like **Amy's Bread**, the **Fat Witch Bakery**, **Eleni's Cookies**, and **SaraBeth's Bakery**, as well as a butcher, a dairy, a cheese shop, a flower shop, a fruit and produce store, a wine store, and several nice little restaurants. And if all that and a post-modern, faux-dilapidated chicness weren't enough, the whole place also offers free WiFi access *(chelseamarket.com)*.

BROOKLYN

Greenpoint-McCarren Park
Lorimer St. and Driggs Ave.; Sat.

Borough Hall
Court and Remsen Sts.; Tues./Sat., sometimes Thurs.

Grand Army Plaza
Northwest entrance to Prospect Park; Sat.

BRONX

Lincoln Hospital
148th St. and Morris Ave., south of hospital; Tues. or Fri., depending on season

For more greenmarkets, including seasonal ones, and operating hours, visit the Web site of the Council on the Environment in New York City, *cenyc.org*.

Good Stuff Indoors

Too cold for the greenmarket? Try these (generally upscale) indoor markets and gourmet food shops, which offer a lot more than just produce. Many deliver.

Citarella

Less in the way of produce, but lots of great, fresh seafood and meat, and gourmet foods. *2135 Broadway, at 75th St.; 1313 Third Ave., at 75th St.; 1250 Sixth Ave., at 49th St.; 424 Sixth Ave., at 9th St.; 461 W. 125th St., bet. Morningside and Amsterdam Aves.; 212-874-0383*

Eli's Vinegar Factory

Pretty much everything, from the man who brought you Zabar's. *431 E. 91st St., bet. First and York Aves.; 212-987-0885*

Fairway

A produce staple of the West Side. Check out the walk-in freezer at the warehouse-y 125th Street store. *2127 Broadway, at 74th St.; 212-595-1888; 2328 Twelfth Ave., at 125th St. and West Side Hwy.; 212-234-3883*

Cupcake Café

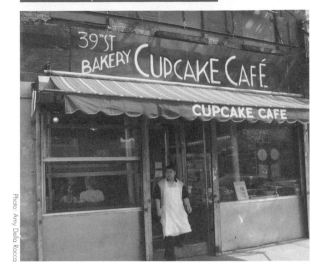

Photo: Amy Della Rocca

You would never guess by its exterior that a rundown, ramshackle bakery on the shady side of Ninth Avenue would produce cakes and confectionaries sought after by New York's rich and famous.

It's almost a given that if you hang around long enough at the **Cupcake Café** on the corner of Ninth Avenue and 39th Street, you'll see a celebrity of some kind step in and pick up an order. The shop's unbelievable wedding cakes, butter-cream frosting flowers, and delicious cupcakes are renowned throughout the city. The shop itself is so under-manicured, however, that visitors rarely even notice it.

Run by master bakers Ann and Michael Warren, the Cupcake Café offers a menu of beautiful, scrumptious cakes and desserts for any occasion. The shop is staffed by young artists, who somehow apply their various music, acting, or painting talents to the unique array of sweet dishes.

All the baking is done in the back, and the sugary aromas alone make it a worthy destination. If you don't want an entire cake, you can order a hot cinnamon roll or a creamy cupcake. The best thing about visiting the bakery is that the constant warmth of the place keeps the icing moist — it'll never flake off into your lap if you eat it here.

Log on to *cupcakecafe.com* to check out their list of cakes, and then call 212-465-1530 to place an order.

Give Us Your Huddled Reindeer

Like so many other foreign immigrants, **Santa Claus** entered the New World through New York – and had his name changed in the process, too. St. Nicholas had been popular in Europe for centuries, and the Dutch brought their version, Sinter Klaas, and his December 6 feast day to New Amsterdam with them, but the growing English population didn't really take much notice of it until 1804, when John Pintard, a founder of the New-York Historical Society, started pressing for a more family-oriented celebration as an alternative to the then-customary drunken revelry with which New Yorkers greeted Christmas. He made Sinter Klaas, Americanized to Santa Claus, a focal point of his kinder, gentler holiday. In 1809, Pintard's friend Washington Irving declared St. Nick the patron saint of the city in his *Knickerbocker's History of New York*.

But Santa was still pretty unformed – he could be anything from a gnome to a gaunt old man, in robes or breeches and a tricorner hat. Two other New Yorkers would fill in the details that make up our current idea of the jolly old elf. In 1822, Dr. Clement Clarke Moore, son of the episcopal bishop and owner of a farm that covered most of modern Chelsea, wrote "A Visit from Saint Nicholas," which introduced fatness, chimneys, and reindeer into the mix and became an instant hit. (Some have claimed that another New Yorker, Henry Livingston, actually wrote the poem, which was originally published anonymously, but the jury's still out on that.) And starting in 1862, Boss Tweed-baiting cartoonist Thomas Nast created the finishing touches in a series of drawings done for *Harper's Weekly* that located Santa's workshop at the North Pole, introduced Mrs. Claus and the elves, and settled the wardrobe of red trimmed with white fur.

Garden of Eden

Giant mountains of produce – and in Brooklyn, too.
162 W. 23rd St., bet. Sixth and Seventh Aves.; 866-222-0434; 310 Third Ave., bet. 23rd and 24th Sts.; 212-228-4681; 7 E. 14th St., at Fifth Ave.; 212-255-4200; 180 Montague St., bet. Court and Clinton Sts., Brooklyn Heights; 718-222-1515

Gourmet Garage

Originally meant to provide fresh produce and more to restaurants; now open to all.
301 E. 64th St., bet. First and Second Aves.; 212-535-5880; 453 Broome St., at Mercer St.; 212-941-5850; 2567 Broadway, at 96th St; 212-663-0656; 117 Seventh Ave., at 10th St.; 212-966-2887

Whole Foods Market

A huge selection of natural and organic foods; delivery to large part of Manhattan.
wholefoods.com; Time Warner Center at Columbus Circle, 212-823-9600; 250 Seventh Ave., at 24th St., 212-924-5969; more locations are planned

Life is Sweet

New Yorkers are fat. And when they're not fat, they're struggling to stay thin. Places like these are why.

Photo: Daniel Hood

The Donut Plant

Giant, gooey, often wildly flavored donuts. Go early.
379 Grand St., at Norfolk St.,
212-505-3700

Pre-Parade Magic

The **Macy's Thanksgiving Day Parade** has attracted millions of families over the decades who cram along side streets to watch the over-sized animal balloons drift down Broadway. The sight is indeed spectacular, but better than that, and more accessible, is what happens the night before.

Many New Yorkers know that the best time to see the balloons is the Wednesday night before Thanksgiving, when they are inflated and given life in Central Park. But it's a trick missed by many out-of-towners. All you have to do is steer your kids to 79th Street and Central Park West. Enter the park and follow the sound of helium pumps. Every year, parade organizers let families wander through the preparation area and witness the magic process that gives life to some of the oldest characters in pop culture: Charlie Brown, Kermit the Frog, and Snoopy, as well as more modern personalities like Barney and Jimmy Neutron.

The balloons are magnificent to behold as they slowly take shape and rise above the trees of Central Park. After that, you can sleep in on Thanksgiving, stay warm, and watch the parade on TV.

holiday heaven

Christmas may have been commercialized, but no place does commercialization better than New York. That said, December here isn't *completely* about creating consumer need, and even when it is, it's pretty spectacular.

Dueling Santas

Macy's invented the department store Santa in 1870, and their version's still going strong, but he's got serious competition from the South Street Seaport's Strolling Santa, who's rapidly becoming the alterna-Claus of choice.

Dueling trees

Rockefeller Center's tree lighting, which developed from a Christmas tree workers put up on the site while the center was being built, has inspired lots of copycats, so now you have your pick of tree-lighting extravaganzas, from the Winter Garden down at the World Financial Center all the way up to Harlem on 125th Street, and in between at Washington Square Park, Lincoln Center, and the Metropolitan Museum of Art.

The Christmas Revels

Since their debut in 1979, this group has been combining song, dance, and theater from a wide range of countries to celebrate the Winter Solstice at Symphony Space.

Photo: Daniel Hood

Economy Candy
If you like your candy in large quantities and at a discount, this Lower East Side stockpile is the place for you. They've also got toys, gumball machines, and an assortment of the biggest Pez dispensers we've ever seen. And it's been in the Cohen family since 1937.
108 Rivington St., bet. Essex and Ludlow Sts.; 800-352-4544

Hungarian Pastry Shop
Old World treats make this a fave of the Columbia kids, opposite St. John the Divine.
1030 Amsterdam Ave., bet. 110th and 111th Sts.; 212-866-4230

Magnolia Bakery
Cupcakes made famous in *Sex in the City*.
401 Bleecker St., at W. 11th St.; 212-462-2572

Christmas trains

Photo: Daniel Hood

The Fifth Avenue windows of various Swiss airlines and banks used to showcase intricate little train sets around the holidays; those are gone now, but the Transit Museum puts up a nice little display in its Grand Central Terminal store. For something considerably larger, the "Station at Citicorp Center" at 53rd Street and Lexington Avenue has four tracks on three levels, with settings representing the city, the suburbs, and upstate New York, and all four seasons. The best, though, has to be the Holiday Train Show at the New York Botanical Gardens in the Bronx. The trains are fine – what really makes it wild are all the New York landmarks the tracks run past, all of which are made out of various plants and have to be seen to be believed.

Eight days are better than one

If Hannukah is more your thing, the world's largest menorah is lit every night during the Festival of Lights at Grand Army Plaza, at 59th Street and Fifth Avenue.

Mondel's

This tiny shop has been selling handmade chocolates since the 1940s, and for much of that time, Katharine Hepburn had a standing monthly order. Unless you're her, don't bother the staff when they're busy.
2913 Broadway, at 114th St.; 212-864-2111

Out of the Kitchen

We'd put this bakery's cupcakes up against Magnolia's. And they make a nice black-and-white cookie, too.
456 Hudson St., bet. Morton and Commerce Sts.; 212-242-0399

Yura & Co.

A tasty bakery, with a restaurant down the block.
1645 Third Ave., at 93rd St.; 212-860-8060

little New Yorkers

Kids who grow up in the city tend to do it fast, in part because there are so many tempting adult-oriented opportunities staring them in the face all the time. There are, however, a lot of kid-friendly things to do out there.

Not that it needs mentioning, but the **American Museum of Natural History** is a perennial favorite, as are the **Bronx Zoo**, the **Central Park Zoo**, **FAO Schwartz** (which seems to continue on despite two bankruptcies), the **New York Aquarium**, and the **Bronx Botanical Garden**. Here are nine alternatives.

1. Connie Gretz's Secret Garden, at the **Staten Island Botanical Garden** *(1000 Richmond Terrace, Staten Island; 718-273-8200)*, is a hedge maze with a garden as the goal, designed after Frances Hodgson Burnett's *Secret Garden*, all overlooked by a three-story medieval castle complete with moat and drawbridge.

2. On one level, the **Urban Park Rangers** are just the City Parks Department's park rangers; on another, they're a great way to keep kids both entertained and outdoors. They run a huge range of programs, from the sort of flora-and-fauna-related tours and demonstrations you might expect to the Little Red Lighthouse Festival in the

Police Report

No local law-enforcement agency in the world gets more attention than the New York City Police Department. Its crime-control tactics, undercover operations, and counter-terrorism training are studied and mimicked in major cities around the world. Here's a look at some NYPD facts you may not have known:

• It was the star-shaped copper badges that the city's police officers wore in 1845 that led to the term "cops."

• The first female officers, called Police Matrons, were appointed in 1891.

• Officially established in 1898, the NYPD's first Police Commissioner was future president Teddy Roosevelt.

• With more than 40,000 police officers, the NYPD ranks as the sixth-largest standing army in the world.

Photo: Spencer T Tucker/NYC Dept of Parks & Recreation

• By comparison: the NYPD is larger than the FBI, the Chicago Police Department and the Los Angeles Police Department combined (they have about 15,000, 16,000, and 9,000 officers respectively).

• In New York, there is one police officer per 209 residents; in Los Angeles, that ratio is one to 409.

• The Police Commissioner is appointed by the mayor, and the current commissioner, Raymond W. Kelly, is the only person to have served two nonconsecutive terms, under Mayors Dinkins and Bloomberg.

• In 2003, overall crime in New York sank to its lowest level in 40 years.

• If you log on to nyc.gov/html/nypd/html/pct/cspdf. html, you can check weekly crime statistics for any precinct in the city.

fall (with rides, games, and more celebrating the famous lighthouse under the George Washington Bridge), to free skating lessons, storytelling events, hawk-and-horse exhibitions, and a million other things. For the more adventurous, they run orienteering and survival classes, so you can read a compass and build a fire when you're lost in Jamaica Bay. Visit *nycgovparks.org* and be prepared to poke around.

3. Five museums that are actually *for* kids, as opposed to tolerating them, are the world's oldest: the **Brooklyn Children's Museum** *(145 Brooklyn Ave., at St. Marks Ave., Crown Heights, Brooklyn; 718-735-4400; bchildmus.org)*, which was founded in 1899; the **Children's Museum of Manhattan** *(212 W. 83rd St., bet. Broadway and Amsterdam Ave.; 212-721-1234; cmom.org)*; the **Staten Island Children's Museum** *(1000 Richmond Terrace; 718-273-2060)*; the **Liberty Science Center** *(Liberty State Park, 251 Phillip St., Jersey City, N.J.; 201-200-1000; lsc.org; accessible by ferry or PATH train)*; and the **Children's Museum of the Arts** *(182 Lafayette St., bet. Broome and Grand Sts.; 212-941-9198; cmany.org)*. All have lots of hands-on activities and special programs.

4. It doesn't get much better than cops and firemen, so take the kids to the **New York City Police Museum** *(100 Old Slip, bet. Water and South Sts.; 212-480-3100)* and the **New York City Fire Museum** *(278 Spring St., bet. Hudson and Varick Sts.; 212-691-1303)*. The word is that the Fire Museum, which inhabits a grand old firehouse from 1904, also throws a great birthday party. Also very cool is the **FDNY FireZone** *(34 W. 51st St., bet. Fifth and Sixth Aves.;*

212-698-4520), a fire safety center that, among other things, simulates a live blaze to teach kids (and adults) how to handle themselves in a fire.

Photo: Daniel Hood

5. Before **South Street Seaport** *(Fulton and Water Sts; southstseaport.org)* was a mall and a drinking destination for Wall Streeters, it was just a little pier with some old ships kids could climb around on. So ignore all the new stuff and head right for the lightship *Ambrose* and the gorgeous four-masted *Peking*, which are still great to climb around on. There are plenty of planned arts and crafts events, and the galleries further inland offer historical and cultural exhibits, most with a nautical theme (that means lots of ship models, which are cool), or you can head offshore on one of their harbor cruises. Some of the ships are available for charter or for dockside parties, and the Seaport can throw a pirate-themed birthday party aboard the *Peking*.

6. Of all the city's colonial-era sites, the **Queens County Farm Museum** *(73-50 Little Neck Parkway, Floral Park, Queens; 718-347-3276; queensfarm.org)* may be the best for kids. It's a working farm dating back to 1697, with pettable animals, tours of the historic farmhouse, and pretty full schedule of programs, from arts and crafts to corn mazes, berry festivals, and hayrides.

7. Into every child's life, a little culture must fall; the trick is to make it painless. Best bet: the **Amato Opera Theater**'s "Opera in Brief" program *(319 Bowery, at Bleecker St.; 212-228-8200; amato.org).* One Saturday a month, they put on a full-costume, 90-minute version of a classic opera, with narration woven between the songs to explain the storyline. Tickets are cheap, and the shows start at 11:30 a.m., so you have all afternoon to make up for the educational experience.

Photo: Daniel Hood

- In New York City you need a permit to transport carbonated beverages.

- The penalty for jumping off a building is death.

- Women may go topless in public, providing it is not being used as a business.

- You may not smoke within 100 feet of the entrance to a public building.

- A person may not walk around on Sundays with an ice cream cone in his/her pocket.

- Slippers are not to be worn in public after 10 p.m.

- No deck of cards is allowed in any apartment located within a mile's radius of an armory.

- It is illegal to open an umbrella in front of a horse.

- In New York City, beanshooters are illegal weapons for children.

8. Two stores that mitigate the commercial experience really well are the **Scholastic Bookshop** *(557 Broadway, bet. Prince and Spring Sts., stroller entrance at 130 Mercer St.; 212-343-6166)* which offers all kinds of fun and educational events in its very cool space, and **American Girl Place** *(609 Fifth Ave., at 49th St.; 877-AG-PLACE)*, which has a café, a theater with live shows, a hair salon for their historically accurate dolls, and, naturally, tons and tons of dolls and accessories. (They'll also do birthday parties that get pretty extravagant, and you can even hire the place for late-night kids' parties.)

9. Once home to the most adult of entertainments, **Times Square** is now pretty much a paradise for kids. Between the three Disney perma-shows, the enormous **Toys R Us** *(Broadway at 44th St.)* with its indoor ferris wheel and amazing toy displays, the **MTV Studios and Store** *(Broadway at 44th St.)*, the arcade at the **ESPN Zone** *(Broadway at 42nd St.)*, the **Hershey Store** *(Broadway at 48th St.)*, and **Madame Tussaud's** *(234 42 St., bet. Seventh and Eighth Aves.)*, there's a way for every age group to spend tons of Mom and Dad's cash.

Photo: Daniel Hood

The True Cost of Education

So, what does it take to get your child into one of Manhattan's exclusive schools? How about a million dollars and your professional reputation? That's what it cost well-respected Citigroup telecoms analyst Jack Grubman in 2002. He wanted his twins to go to the exclusive $11,000-a-year 92nd Street Y Nursery School, so he asked his boss, Citi chairman Sandy Weill, for a little help. Happy to oblige, Weill made a call and donated $1 million to the 92nd Street Y – and all he asked in return was that Grubman say nice things about AT&T, on whose board Weill sat. An analyst only has his reputation, so when word got out, Grubman was finished on Wall Street – but that's OK, because if his kids hadn't gotten into one of the elite nursery schools, their lives would no doubt have been ruined. Ruined!

Or so feel many of those New Yorkers with too much money. If you want to see what all the fuss is about, wander by schools like **Spence** *(22 E. 91st St., bet. Fifth and Madison Aves.)*, **Chapin** *(100 East End Ave., at 84th St.)*, **Dalton** *(53 E. 91st St., bet. Madison and Park Aves.)*, the **Little Red School House** *(272 Sixth Ave., bet. Bleecker and Houston Sts.)*, or **Brearley** *(610 E. 83rd St., off East End Ave.)*. These are some of the private elementary and high schools that going to a good nursery school can get you into. We suggest wandering by, because getting in is pretty much out of the question: all cost over $20,000 for a single year's tuition.

• It is unlawful to eat soup with a fork, and to suck up spaghetti strand by strand.

• It's against the law to walk down the street while reading.

• It is illegal to shoot at a rabbit from a moving trolley.

• It's illegal to speak to a person while riding in an elevator and you must fold your hands while looking forward.

• You must purchase a license to hang clothes on a clothesline.

• The following means of making a living are illegal: skinning horses or cows, burning offal, growing ragweed, and burning bones.

• "It is disorderly conduct for one man to greet another on the street by placing the end of his thumb against the tip of his nose, at the same time extending and wiggling the fingers of his hand."

• The New York City Transit Authority has ruled that women can ride the city subways topless. New York law dictates that if a man can be somewhere without a shirt, a woman gets the same right. The decision came after arrests of women testing the ordinance on the subways.

• A fine of $25 can be levied for flirting. This old law specifically prohibits men from turning around on any city street and looking "at a woman in that way." A second conviction for a crime of this magnitude calls for the violating male to be forced to wear a "pair of horse-blinders" wherever and whenever he goes outside for a stroll.

• Before enactment of the 1978 law that made it mandatory for dog owners in New York City to clean up after their pets, approximately 40 million pounds of excrement were deposited on the streets every year.

• In 1999, Mayor Giuliani signed a bill declaring it illegal to play three-card monte on the streets of New York City.

• In 2003, New York City's administrative code still required that hitching posts be located in front of City Hall so that reporters can tie their horses.

Child's Play

Manhattan is not the easiest island to tour with kids; it's also one of the hardest on which to raise them. If only children could be like cars: it would be nice to drop them off at some secure location, go out for a night on the town, and pick them up exactly as you left them.

Fortunately, someone already thought of that, and went out and created the **Manhattan Treehouse** – the best thing to happen to New York parents since the Central Park Carousel. You drop off your kids at 148 West 83rd Street, go paint the town whatever color you like, and then pick them up just as they're zonked out and ready for bed. The Treehouse takes care of everything in between.

First, they've got the safety issue covered: the adult-to-child ratio is about as high as it gets. Three grown-ups look after a maximum of five children age 3 and under, and three more watch over a maximum of 10 children older than 4. This means two things: your child will always be monitored, and you should make reservations because the Treehouse never accepts more than 15 children at a time.

They also have the fun issue covered: your kids can participate in dancing games, theater productions, and music shows, or play alone with a huge range of toys. The instructors are young, energetic, and eager to entertain. If your little one gets tired, there are plenty of playpen beds to crash in.

Best of all, prices are in-line with going babysitter rates. Depending on how many hours you'll be out, the cost runs from $38 to $52 for your first child, $18 for every child after that. Get your Broadway tickets and dinner reservations squared away first, then call the Treehouse at 212-712-0113 to save a spot for your kid.

index

index

index

index

index

index

index

index

index

index

index

index

Brad Dunn has written for *The New York Times*, the *New York Daily News*, and *Popular Science*, and has worked as a speechwriter for the New York City Police Department. He currently works for Court TV.

Daniel Hood has worked as an editor for *The Wall Street Journal*, the *Daily News*, and a number of trade and business publications in New York. He has also run a freight elevator on 57th Street, and published five novels.

Both Brad and Dan live in New York.